CREATR

she who makes

LUCY H. PEARCE

WOMANCRAFT PUBLISHING

Other titles by Lucy H. Pearce

Medicine Woman

Burning Woman

Full Circle Health: integrated health charting for women

Full Circle Health: 3-month charting journal

The Rainbow Way: cultivating creativity in the midst of motherhood

Moon Time: harness the ever-changing energy of your menstrual cycle

Moods of Motherhood: the inner journey of mothering

Reaching for the Moon: a girl's guide to her cycles

For my creative tribes of blood and soul.

And the creative lights that have shone the way for me.

COPYRIGHT

Published by Womancraft Publishing, 2019
womancraftpublishing.com

ISBN 978-1-910559-49-9
Also available in ebook format: ISBN 978-1-910559-48-2

Cover and internal art by Lucy H. Pearce.
Cover design and diagrams by Lucent Word.

Parts of this book have been adapted from articles or chapters previously published in:

The Rainbow Way
dreamingaloud.net
Rebelle Society
Facebook posts
Naked Money
Juno magazine

Permissions

The author has sought, as far as possible, permission to reproduce quotations used in this book and has abided by fair use policy. All quotations and ideas have been referenced to the best of the author's ability. If you feel that your words or work have not been fairly acknowledged, do not hesitate to contact the publishers and this will be rectified in future editions.

PRAISE FOR *CREATRIX*

As a woman artist and writer my life is devoted to the practice and study of creativity and how it works. So I love seeing the way that Lucy has uplifted creation, with both mystical and practical tools for women to access the power of creation. Every bone in our body is a creative bone, but sometimes we can forget that. Her work celebrates the access to the prowess possible for us when we create!

Shiloh Sophia McCloud, artist and founder of Intentional Creativity®

Creatrix is soulful medicine that speaks empowering encouragement to women artists, writers, healers and energy workers of these specific times. Lucy weaves truth, inquiry and much needed practical guidance into the timeless and potent experience of saying YES to the creative Work that calls us…in all its mysterious, dynamic ways. I highly recommend it!

Hali Karla, contemplative artist, teacher and creativity coach

I was once more touched by Lucy's beautiful, inspiring, and sometimes uncanny ability to reach through the page directly into the very heart of things – sometimes things unvoiced, unspoken, unconscious, invisible, and then there they are…right in front of me suddenly, on the page, woven into form by this remarkably gifted woman.

Molly Remer, author of *Womanrunes, Goddess Devotional, Sunlight on Cedar*

Creatrix is a heartfelt and soul-stirring reminder that our creativity, intuition, and desire to help and heal are powerfully connected and so very needed in the world today. Every page felt like an invitation to remember who we really are as creative beings. I'm so glad this book exists!

Flora Bowley, Brave Intuitive Painting, Creative Revolution

CONTENTS

THRESHOLD

3

4

5

CENTRE

THRESHOLD

WELCOME

...to the Book

> Inside you there's an artist you don't know about...say yes quickly if you know, if you've known it from before the beginning of the Universe.
>
> Rumi

The first book I wrote changed my life.

I have since learned that books have a tendency to do that. You start writing them because you think you know enough about the subject, and quickly find yourself undergoing a drastic education in every aspect of yourself and the topic in order to bring forth the book.

My first book, *The Rainbow Way*, was written for myself as a new mother, struggling to find time to be creative as a way of preserving my own sanity. It was a cry in the dark: for answers, for methods of making creativity happen, and for a tribe of creative women. I felt utterly alone and deeply strange for my unstinting need to create. Until I became a mother I had taken my creative needs for granted. It was only when my time and energy to create were severely limited that I realised how central they were to me as a person.

I knew I was onto something when the idea for the book first hit me: there was nothing like it out there. I took Toni Morrison's sage advice: "If there's a book that you want to read, but it hasn't been written yet, then you must write it." And so I, who had consumed several thousand books as an avid reader, wrote my first book and then walked the well-worn path of desperate wannabe author looking for a publisher.

After several rejections I found a publisher and my first book won gushing endorsements from many creative heroines of mine. It hit number one in multiple Amazon categories in the UK and US. It seemed I was correct in my hunch: creative mothers were yearning for encouragement and support. They were longing to be seen and heard and helped. My book was doing good in the world. And it wasn't just mothers. Creative men were seeing the impact it was having on their female partners, and were reading it. Women without children, who were trying to find time to fit creativity into their lives, were buying it as a gift for sisters or best friends, but reading it first. I had thought that the market was saturated with books on creativity for a general audience. But it seemed there was still much of value that readers were getting from my book. I was intrigued, but too busy working on other projects to follow it up.

But the emails kept coming. Messages telling me of tears as they read it. Of manuscripts that had been put away that were now being dusted off having read my book. People coming back to painting after years. New blogs, poems, magazines, businesses…inspired by my book.

It was incredible. Humbling. Exciting.

Since then I have written lots more books and started a publishing company more aligned with my own vision: one that celebrates women's creativity, supports them emotionally as they launch their work, pays them fairly and promotes them sustainably. I have taught creative blogging, self-publishing with my *Be Your Own Publisher* e-course, creative writing via my *Your Authentic Voice* e-course. I have danced the line of creative expression with my *WORD+image* course, as well as mentoring many creative souls. Each day I have new conversations about creativity with women and men around the world. I have been interviewed multiple times for print magazines and podcasts on the topic of creativity. I have written many blog posts and a couple of anthology pieces on the subject. And read even more widely on it. In short, I have been amassing material on the topic, and am delighted to finally share it in one place. It is exciting to have the opportunity to incorporate the insight and experience I have had into my own creative practice and making a creative living, in the years since writing *The Rainbow Way*.

Though I still find it terrifying, I also find it immensely satisfying, starting conversations about the profound, overwhelming and transformational experiences of our human lives. So many of us are longing to partake in these raw, hard-to-articulate discussions about the experiences of creativity, spirituality, sexuality and birth-giving that shape every layer of our beings. We have so little opportunity within our culture to give voice to and share notes on them. Often we find we lack the courage, the words to express our feelings or a safe space to start that conversation. Many of us are looking for people like us: creative communities, collaborators and tribes, but don't know quite where to start, because even owning our creativity, "coming out" as a Writer or Artist can be so challenging. Putting our work out into the world even more so. Making a living from it can seem nothing shy of impossible.

Please know I understand how hard this is. I hope that this book, in combination with my others and their associated Facebook groups, will help to support you on each stage of that journey, with the insight and practical advice from many of us who walk The Creative Way alongside you.

....

As always, I had to live this book as I wrote it. Over the three years I was working on this book, I found my own life being transformed by The Work. There were no short cuts or glamour in the writing of it, just a strange and spiralling path into the darkness as my own and family's daily lives were totally rewritten by illness and incapacity. The five-day working weeks of 9.30-3pm that I had finally gotten, now all three of my children were at school, were suddenly decimated. I had no time or energy to create: everything I had was being used to cope moment by moment and support others. I had to put our publishing company and my own creative career on ice, and then gradually reclaim each part – but on a far more limited schedule. I had to reclaim what mattered and learn to leave the rest.

I discovered how vital small daily doses of creativity were to me. When I was unable to engage in anything creative all colour, purpose and reason for living drained from my life. I had to do creative things with my hands and mind. More than I had ever understood. For the first year I couldn't write or paint, I could read very little, so instead I watched a lot, took up knitting, listened to more music, started to draw again and made seasonal spirals. It was only on reflection that I realised that the urgency of claiming the time to create is much, much more than just making art: creativity has become my spiritual practice, my healing, my way of living in this world. I create to live.

On the outside it may not have looked that different, but on the inside the shift was profound. Instead of being too-often steered by the expectations and needs of others or the marketplace, I deepened my relationship with and understanding of the archetype of the Creatrix. I learned to embody her energies more fully – to work with her, rather than sacrifice myself at her altar. I learned to get out of the way and let her lead more than I ever had before, however messy, strange or uncomfortable the results. I learned that the creations made in this space were somehow leading me forwards, through the dark.

And so, I had to recreate the book that I had started. I was called, once again to dive deeper into what creativity means and how it works, into its energetics and archetypes, into the psychology of creativity and our souls. I had to follow my own passions: to stop writing what I thought I should, and dare to do it my own weird way. I had to get deeply uncomfortable. I am aware that this means that parts of the book will make you uncomfortable too, depending on what has been suppressed in your own life and expression. Maybe it will be my use of the word soul, or references to ritual or magic. Perhaps it will be my use of many analogies from the birthing process, that I and many other women who have given birth have found to be an extremely useful embodied metaphor for the creative process. But I know that for others who have not had babies, or have had traumatic pregnancies or birthing experiences these may be challenging. If this is true for you, I ask you to take a step back from your personal embodied experience and to imagine these birthing metaphors within the context of a nature documentary.

Or maybe it will be my predominant focus on women and my playful use of language that highlights this. So many books on creativity through the ages have been written by men, centring on the male experience of creativity and using exclusively male examples. This book unashamedly rebalances the scales. Whilst there is no exclusion of the male or masculine, you will find that the majority of the contributors, case studies and quotations are from women. And you will find the pronoun *she* is most commonly used.

This is not to say that a creatrix is *only* a woman. Nor are all women interested in creativity. And certainly not all women artists are creatrixes. What defines a creatrix is less the sex of the body that a person was born into, but rather that they live in contact with that in our culture which has been designated the Feminine – the fluid and flowing – and devote themselves to bringing these qualities to birth through their bodies. In the words of Justine Musk,

I see a creatrix as someone who uses his or her creativity to take the feminine wound and transform it. To take us from pain to power. To release the shame that keeps so many of us trapped and fearful. To give voice to authentic feminine experience – every bit as bold and loud and vibrant as it wants or needs to be.[i]

Like falling in love or giving birth, the experience of creative inspiration has been described by thousands of voices over the years. But it doesn't make it any easier to explain! Often myself and the featured creatrixes found ourselves wordless, trying to share experiences that transcend words. As one of the contributors, Eleanor Brown, says,

> "
>
> Creativity suffers under great scrutiny from ourselves or others.
>
> SARK, *Succulent Wild Woman*

Trying to talk or write about creativity is almost impossible – I'm not sure there is a way to describe a process that is a kind of alchemy. Putting it into words is like trying to contain the uncontainable.

As I progressed with the book, I realised that this is exactly as it should be: creativity is a form of magic, one that happens unseen in the dark, in the space between the known and the unknowable. To seek to shine the full light of conscious awareness on it is a very Western approach. We cannot, should not, seek to rationally understand the processes of mystery or try to break them down into nuts and bolts. And so, whilst this book attempts to give language to creative experience and maps the terrain, it also leaves space for revelation and mystery.

Creatrix seeks to achieve what I have never seen elsewhere, covering both The Work of soul and the worldly work of creativity. Many books focus on one aspect or the other – my intention is to integrate both strands, because, I believe they are part of the same process.

The book is divided into six Circuits, each representing one 'round' of The Creative Way, as well as this Threshold chapter and the Centre.

Circuit One explores what creativity is. It defines The Creative Way and introduces the archetype of Creatrix.

Circuit Two shares the necessities for creativity and the structure of the creative process.

Circuit Three dives into the soul of creativity and its spiritual dimensions.

Circuit Four explores the energy dynamics of creativity.

Circuit Five expands into some of the key human challenges that we must navigate in order to share our creativity.

Circuit Six brings the process out into the world and focuses on the practical considerations of earning a living from our creativity.

Centre brings us back to the central tenet of the book, placing our expanded understanding of creativity as both work and Work in a global and historical context once again.

Each Circuit ends with Creative Inquiry and Creative Practice to help you to engage more directly with the content of the book. Interspersed between the chapters are woven creative Experiences from myself and the contributing creatrixes.

After years of hearing how women love to underline and highlight passages in my books, this book has your creative interaction built into the heart of it, with space at the sides for comments and notes and the seeds and snail trails of patterns to encourage you to doodle as you read. In the past I have resisted drawing in books because I didn't want to mess them up, but in the last couple of years it was the books that I was invited to draw in that have stayed with me the most. Something about interacting with the content on the pages and adding my own mark helped the material to sink in deeper. So dive in, please don't hold back because you're worried you'll mess it up – follow the dotted lines, add to them, embellish them, add colour…make this book truly yours.

...to the Creatrixes

> Here she comes, running, out of prison and off the pedestal: chains off, crown off, halo off, just a live woman.
>
> Charlotte Perkins Gilman

This book was written by many women around the world. Each of us alone, reflecting on our own experiences. I then wove these disparate pieces together into my manuscript at the end. What fascinates me is the similarity of themes and motifs that run through each woman's experience. Most contributors simply had the basic topics of the book; we were writing blind of each other. I only had a conversation with a few of the women in person, which I then asked them to expand upon in writing. And yet our words are cohesive, which lets me know that the process we are describing is universal. However, I must caution that only their own words speak directly to their personal experience, and they may well not agree with everything that I have written. Just as you may not. And that is okay. One experience does not invalidate another, as women have so often been taught, but rather each adds richness and diversity.

To have these women's words and hard-won insights in the book is a privilege, because each of them is special to me. We have found ourselves drawn into each others' orbits because of our creativity, through odd synchronicities and the insistence of mutual acquaintances. I am so grateful that, thanks to the wonders of the internet, I am connected to them. We have passed the creative gift backwards and forwards through mutual inspiration, gratitude and support, through conversations and collaborations. Some of these women have literally saved my life during my darkest days. All of them have changed it. To call them soul sisters may sound trite, but it is my truth. My life is filled with their music, words, images, figurines and other creations. Their creativity, their being, their vulnerability, their beauty and strength inspire me daily. I am infinitely richer because of them. I know myself better through their creations. This is why I invited them here, to share their wisdom with you.

If you read my first book on creativity, *The Rainbow Way*, you will recognise some of them from there. Those women contributed to that book when they were still new mothers. Now we are several more years down the road of motherhood, our children older and our projects are now impacting the wider world around us. Many of us are now the main family breadwinners through our creative work, whilst others have poured this energy in a voluntary capacity towards national campaigns of political and social change and international collaboration.

The creatrixes featured range from their twenties to fifties and are scattered across Europe, the US and Australia. We certainly do not represent every woman, but a fair diversity: some of us are partnered, some single; some mothers, some not; some gay, some straight; and we hark from various economic and cultural backgrounds.

All of us have travelled through life-shifting experiences. Collectively we have known: chronic and terminal health diagnoses of ourselves and loved ones; miscarriages and unplanned pregnancies; partner separations; the sudden deaths of close family members; depression, anxiety and mental health breakdowns; losing homes...not to mention the political, emotional and environmental disruptions that are the backgrounds of all our lives in these turbulent times. And all of us have used our creativity to help us navigate through these challenges. We have dedicated ourselves to creating beauty and healing from the chaos of our inner and outer worlds. I am reminded of the quote from Michelle Rosenthal,

Trauma creates change you don't choose,
Healing is about creating change you do choose.

Note the key word in both sentences: create.

We don't make art because we have perfect lives or immense privilege. We create in order to live through the lives that have revealed themselves through us, because of, in spite of, the chaos, the confusion, the grief, the anger, the overwhelm, the terror, the trauma, the tragedy, the feeling of powerlessness. We cannot control much of what happens to us in our lives, but if creativity is our default processing response, our ability to heal and transform is enabled.

One of the creatrixes, Erin, who recently lost her mother, puts it so well,

"Tell me about the artist's struggle, what is something you struggle with daily?" she asks.
"grief"
it tumbled from my mouth. instantly. grief is the daily struggle.
it isn't my artistic struggle. it is my life now.

it was given to me without asking.
and life is my artistic... being.

We use our creativity to find and weave the beautiful and the meaningful through and from these experiences, in order to reach an understanding of ourselves and an acceptance of unacceptable situations. We create in order to both transcend and immerse ourselves more fully into the feelings that are otherwise too hard, too big or too overwhelming to feel. In a world where there is neither the time nor the space to experience the depth and mystery of our lives, we create both. We make our lives our art, creating our own unique and original body of work within and from our own bodies.

I recognise that each of these women walk The Creative Way, each has dedicated her life to it. Each has found a way to weave herself into the world, and the world through her heart by using her creative skills. Each has made impacts on the world around her through the harnessing of her creative energies. Each has become attuned to her own creativity, its ebbs and flows, and honours it as the centre-point of her life. Each is a beautiful and very human example of the Creatrix archetype embodied.

Let me introduce them to you.

Clare is an artist based in Liverpool, UK, who creates creative community with a radical and irreverent approach. She sells a range of stunning clothes made from her artwork. My mum first met her at an art retreat that I gifted to her, and insisted that I make contact as she was my sort of woman. How right she was.

Dawn is a poet and mother based in the UK who writes about and for healing passionately and authentically. A student on my *Your Authentic Voice* course, she has blossomed as she has reclaimed her connection to her voice.

Eleanor is a songwriter and music-maker who connects deeply with the natural world and the changing times, creating from both the descent and the rising. She lives in the UK. I share the story of our creative collaboration later in the book.

Eli is an artist and writer who has a talent for building creative communities that support and nourish. Originally from the UK, she lives in Denmark. I have contributed to several of her powerful online community projects.

Erin is a US-born mother, painter, photographer and writer of motherhood and womanhood. She is a celebrated creatrix of political movements that have shaped her heartland of Ireland, and gained her an Irish passport in recognition of her work. We have been online friends for many years.

Jen is a mother based in Ireland, who is reclaiming her creativity through painting and teaching classes in nature connection. We became good friends from meeting at a local women's group.

Laura is a mother and writer, creatrix of rich spaces for togetherness. She is a doll-maker specialising in healing dolls, and creatrix of the Babóg project that brings women together to create dolls for each of the babies lost in Ireland's Mother and Baby Homes. Originally from Scotland, she is based in West Cork, Ireland and is a soul friend.

Lewis is a singer-songwriter, performer and co-founder of Embodied Artists. She is passionate about archetypal work, and is based in Brockley, UK. We were brought together through my book, *Burning Woman.*

Lucy is a mother, writer, visual artist and creatrix of ceramic goddess and female figurines based in Australia. We were fortuitously thrown together by people misspelling our names when they referenced our work on the internet. We have never met but I call her my name sister.

Marsia is a US-based photographer, artist, singer-song writer and storyteller of deep soul. I first found her work through the soundtrack to the movie *Things We Don't Talk About: Women's Stories from The Red Tent* and we later camped next to each other at the Daughters of the Earth gathering, sharing morning exchanges about the movements of a bear in the woods!

Mirin is a yoga teacher, artist, poet, writer, clothing designer and cook who lives a nomadic lifestyle traveling the globe. She is also my only real blood sister in the world.

Molly is a mother, home-educator, writer, priestess and entrepreneur. She is a well-known creatrix of goddess and female figurines designed to empower and heal women through every phase of their lives, which we sell on our Womancraft webshop. She lives in the US.

Rachael is a mother, writer, entrepreneur, a creatrix of ritual and products for women's and girl's menstrual journeys. She is based in the wilds of Wales. We have been online friends for many years.

“

The people who are crazy enough to think they can change the world are the ones that do.

Steve Jobs

Tracy is a writer, performer, mother and embodied movement practitioner exploring the liminal spaces of what it means to be human. My best friend and deeply beloved creative collaborator, she also lives in Wales.

Zoé is an emerging artist in many forms – painting, sewing, ceramics, writing – and the French translator of my book *Reaching for the Moon*. A mother, she lives in Switzerland.

You can find out more about them and links to their work at the back of the book.

...to Me

If we haven't met before, let me introduce myself a little more.

I am a multi-passionate creative who loves words, pattern and colour. Though best-known for my books – both as publisher and author – I have worked as an artist in paints, pens, buttons, clay, sand, stones, leaves, drama and dance. I have collaborated in various media, led groups and run arts festivals. I have spent twenty years teaching creativity from improvisation to blogging, via creative writing and image making to adults and children. I'm also a mother of three and was recently diagnosed with Aspergers.

My intellectual background is in the History of Ideas – philosophical and other ideas in a historical context. I love this approach, but it is a field dominated by male voices and the rational. My soul's passion is in the transformation of consciousness and the empowerment of women. And so my Work is dedicated to exploring and embodying this knowledge, adding in lost Feminine perspectives, in what I call Living Philosophy. I try to do so in language that makes these ideas accessible to those of us outside of academia, in the hope that it can contribute to personal and cultural transformation.

If I could tell my nine-year-old self or even my eighteen-year-old self what I do, she would pee herself in delight, barely able to believe that she would one day earn her living doing what she most loved in the world.

But I remember when this was just a dream.

For the whole of my life, before I finally got up the courage to write and then self-publish a book, I was always asking: *what is the way…how do I do it?* I would go to writers' talks at conferences and festivals, write them letters, read their blogs. I wanted to know the magic formula.

Nowadays I'm on the receiving end of that. From others just starting out on their creative path, wanting to know: *how do you do it?*

I know it might be just a dream for you. And that getting from your private vision to integrated physical reality probably seems nigh on impossible. Often when we are in that situation we expend a lot of energy, looking everywhere for the bridge that will take us from here to there.

Most of my work, I realise, is being that bridge for others: shining a light on the realities of The Creative Way. The Way that is right there before you, hidden in plain sight, covered in the weeds of shame, the need for approval, the fear of failure, the desire to be perfect or to keep yourself safe.

I'm here to help share what I know of the creative process with you. But let me tell you here and now, up front: there's no seven-step magical formula to instant fame and fortune. There are no shortcuts to making creative work that matters. And anyone who tells you that there are, is simply after your money. The Creative Way necessarily incorporates failure as well as success. The richness of the creative path is that we must each make it in our own image for it to nourish our souls. It must be this or it is nothing.

I've made my living entirely from my creativity for many years now. Whether this is your intention or not, creativity makes all of us who engage with it a life worth living. A life more challenging and rewarding than one without it. A life where we are more fully engaged.

Let this book be a mirror to help you to see yourself more clearly, your brightness and your shadow, to help you understand your own unique creative self. Let it open your eyes to the tribe of creatives around you and help connect you with them. Let it guide you to create the life you want for yourself.

The world needs as many of us as possible on The Creative Way.

I'm so glad you're here.

...and Finally, to You

> "A writer only begins a book. A reader finishes it.
>
> Samuel Johnson

Creative Inquiry

Only half of this book currently exists. The half I have written. The other half comes from what you bring to it, what emerges from your bodymind and soul as you read it. I must warn you now if you're new to my work: reading my books is not a passive process! They require that you open yourself to the energy that is transmitted through them and find ways to let it into your own life.

All creativity starts with curiosity. With inquiry. With questions: *I wonder what if…? Why does…? How about…?* As Day Schildkret so beautifully puts it in his book, *Morning Altars*,

> *If wondering is a dance, then questions are its choreography. Good questions move you. They connect you to that which you're wondering about. And the purpose of asking questions is not so you can finish dancing but so you can get more into the dance.*

Questions hold power. But often we back away from them. Either because we are scared of the answers…or because we are scared that we don't have the answers.

I get it, it's easier and safer not to ask questions, so you'd rather not, thanks very much all the same. It's why many of us leave therapy well alone until we're pretty far along the road of life and all out of other options. But inquiry is where it's at if you want things to start shifting in your inner world – and inner shifts tend to precede outer shifts. And both help to loosen your creative flow. Naming our truth unleashes magic.

So, here's the deal: at the end of each Circuit, I'm going to ask you some questions. And your job is to consider them. Don't force a quick, off-pat, clever or rational answer. Brood on them. Let them gestate within. Sleep with them. Take a walk with them. Journal them. Come and join us on our Creatrix Facebook group or bring them to your book group or women's circle or art group and discuss them with others. Whatever works for you. But, please, give yourself the opportunity to live creatively into these inquiries. Even the simple, stupid-seeming ones. Especially them. Allow the possibility that they might be doorways into the dark for you.

Let's start from now. Right here. Take a moment and get a sense of where you are in your life, in your creativity.

Your Creative Self

- What brings you to this book? What are you wanting from it? What are you feeling nervous or sceptical about?

- What are your initial feelings about meeting myself and the other creatrixes?

- Do you currently consider yourself creative? Why or why not?

- When did you first feel that you were creative?

- How do you most enjoy expressing your creativity?

- In which areas of your life are you expressing your creativity at the moment: your work, your hobbies, your home, your relationships with partner, children or friends...?

- What is the creative dream that is currently tugging your heart strings? And what is standing in your way?

If you've read though these questions and allowed yourself to inquire, even if you haven't written anything down, the work has begun!

The insight will continue to unfold. You will notice that these questions will keep unravelling themselves in your life. You may find them niggling you. You might notice things in articles that you read, little clues leading you further along The Creative Way. You will begin to look more closely at where and how you are expressing your creativity…and looking for areas to do so more often. You will have to admit where you're shutting it down or running away from it.

You will begin living the questions out in your daily life. Until one day, a few weeks or months down the line, you'll realise that your answers to them are quite different to those you gave initially. You will realise that your creativity is a rich, vital, integral part of your life, and your understanding of The Creative Way is always evolving. As are you, dear one. And that is as it should be.

“

Doing is a quantum leap from imagining.

Barbara Sher

Creative Practice

My hope is that the questions above have initiated fruitful creative inquiry for you. But creativity is not just in the mind. It requires action and expression. And so each Circuit will conclude with Creative Practice: activities to help you to integrate what you are learning into your body. Of course you can ignore them. Or just do them in your head. Or bookmark them to come back to later.

Or you could accept the invitation and get creative with them!

A PORTRAIT OF THE ARTIST

Whether or not you consider yourself a visual artist, I invite you to take some images of you creating. Use a tripod, or the selfie setting on your phone, or ask someone you feel safe with to take them…

See how you feel about showing your face in the picture, does it feel good or too vulnerable? Try a photograph of your hands or body working, a picture of you ‘in process’. Take another of you with the tools you use to create.

And another of you with a finished piece of your work that you love.

Do you like them as they are, do you want to put them through a filter to make you look prettier or more acceptable? How about continuing the creative process digitally or manually through editing, collage, making one into a mixed media piece?

Print a copy out and place it on your desk, altar space or mantelpiece. Take some time to really witness it: do you notice anything that you weren't aware of before? Consider sharing it with others on social media or in real life. How does it feel to have your creative self witnessed? What can we see…and what can't we see in this image about what creativity means to you?

1

I am Creatrix,

Constantly becoming

Endlessly flowing

Without limits.

CREATIVITY

The Road Less Travelled

> Two roads diverged in a wood, and I –
> I took the one less travelled by,
> And that has made all the difference.
>
> Robert Frost

To live creatively is to take the road less travelled: this is The Creative Way. The path walked by we who have dedicated ourselves to embodying the archetype of Creatrix.

This book is a companion to support the life that unfolds when you say yes to The Creative Way. In it I hope to articulate a little of what lies unseen, to deepen your understanding of yourself, the role of creativity in your life, the joys and challenges of inhabiting the world as a creatrix.

It is not my job here to persuade you *why* you should create, nor teach you *how* you should create. I believe that long ago you made a deal with your creativity. Though sometimes you question it. Perhaps most days. You may try to cover it up. Tone it down. Hide from its demands. Censor its strangeness.

I'm guessing you probably question your sanity from time to time. As do many around you. Sometimes you long to throw it all in. To choose again. To have a normal life. To be normal.

But still this big energy keeps urging to be birthed out through you.

This book asks you to (re)consider the gift that you have been given and the courage that lies within you to commit more and more fully to embodying your creativity in every aspect of your life. And why this matters.

Because, believe me, it does.

You see, I don't believe that it's a one-way street. I think that this creative energy has intelligence and purpose. The Creative Way is a real thing, a living thing. And it's longing for you as much as you're longing for it.

You, dear one, are one of its chosen points of expression. It's time to honour that gift more fully.

What is Creativity?

> Creativity is not a talent, it's a way of operating.
>
> John Cleese

When people hear that I am passionate about creativity, one of the first questions that they ask is: *what exactly do you mean by creativity?*

Most people confuse "creative" with "artistic" and associate creativity with its end product – an accomplished painting or beautifully iced cake. But creative does not (necessarily) equal artistic. Creativity is the basic quality inherent in nature that is responsible for making energy come into form. Creativity is all around us, all the time. Plants produce flowers and fruits. Birds and insects lay eggs. Spiders weave webs. Creativity's basic biological purpose is to reproduce and sustain life. But it seems to do so in the most dynamic, beautiful, bizarre, extravagant and elegant of ways. Think of the exquisite markings on animal fur, the iridescent plumage of birds, the elegant design of a seashell, the lustrous sheen on a ripe berry, the intricate pattern of a braided river, the vivid colours of leaves in autumn, the seams of precious stones in caves… None of these beautiful forms are strictly necessary. And yet, this is how creative energy expresses itself as it reproduces and transforms the constituent parts of the natural world from one state to another. This creative energy is just as diverse and wondrous, as it expresses itself in music through humans from Bowie to bhangra, in visual arts from expressionism to Pride marches, from ballet to baking, from the extravagant clothes and scents of Chanel to the austere restraint of Zen monks writing haiku.

But creativity is not just about an end result. Creativity is the process itself: a way of thinking and problem-solving 'outside the box', finding innovative solutions. It is the application of the thought, *I wonder what would happen if…*onto the material world. At its heart creativity requires and engenders changing perspectives. I love renowned land artist Andy Goldsworthy's take on this, "You can walk on the path or walk through the hedge, there's two different ways of looking and I think that's the beauty of art, that it makes you step aside and discover a whole new way of looking." [ii]

Creative thinking – sometimes known as divergent thinking – has got us where we are now: a noisy man-made world of planes, mobile phones, computer games, smoked salmon foams and graffiti on the side of sky scrapers. It is at the root of all advances in science. Each advance in technology has boosted our ability to transform more natural resources into evermore complex and diverse products. It is no surprise, therefore, that creative thinking is the buzz word of educationalists and business leaders who want to make greater profits.

Over the past few hundred years human creativity has been harnessed for ego and greed on ever-grander scales, with little consideration of the repercussions of all this blue-sky creative thinking on the original creation we inhabit: the Earth and the lifeforms we share her with.

We have unleashed the creative minds of a few...but kept the creative souls of the majority suppressed, harnessing their energy to do the mechanical tasks that our machines cannot yet do.

But the brain is only half of the creative equation. And creating merely from the head produces soulless objects and disconnection. The soul, the body and feeling – the innate, energetic flow of creativity, traditionally associated with the Feminine – have been sidelined as insignificant or less important within the patriarchal model.

And so here we are.

To fully integrate our creative potential as a species, for it to be life-affirming rather than destructive to our planet and our health, it needs to incorporate mind and body, thinking and feeling. It needs to work with the Earth's creative processes, rather than ignore them.

> "Creativity is intelligence having fun.
>
> Joey Reiman

Conscious Creativity

As we have seen, all of nature is in a constant state of creativity. But *conscious* creativity is an ability that we as humans are unique in possessing. Our symbolic abilities, what Jeremy Johnson describes as, "the indecipherable gap between what makes us art-making human beings or pre-art making hominid ancestors," allow us to conceive of ideas and visions far beyond our basic instinctual or survival behaviours, and bring them into physical reality.

Conscious creativity at its best is deep communion: with ourselves, with our audience, with the world of forms and ideas, and with the divine or transcendent. Where consciousness meets matter, the imaginal realm meets the material realm and something new is made, on purpose.

Creating consciously allows us to reclaim the curiosity and wonder of earlier stages of development, before we, as individuals or species, 'knew' everything. It reminds us to look again to the clear blue sky and listen to the storming wind for the poetry that we have long forgotten. It insists that we reconnect to the mystery beyond words that holds us all the days of our lives. The promise of this state of being draws us back time and again despite the frustrations and the mistakes, the blocks and the disappointments.

As I said in *The Rainbow Way*, there is a juiciness to creativity where body and mind are both fully engaged, a sensuality which both produces and is nourished by the act and product of creation. Creativity is pleasing to us on a deep level: the feel of clay slipping through our hands, colours that make us feel more vividly alive as we paint, the energising feel of movement as we dance and the experience of music moving through our bodies. When we create, we tend to feel more fully alive and fully aligned with the natural flow of the Universe than at any other time in our lives. It is what we were made for, what we are here to do.

> In the end art may not be our invention at all...Picasso got it wrong: the early humans didn't invent art. Art invented humanity.
>
> J.F. Martel, *Reclaiming Art*

Creatrix Speaks

Essentially, I create to build a container, to contain the uncontainable, which has always felt necessary and urgent. First to collate fragments and then to transform them into a whole, a permanence. A formed song, and especially a recorded version of it, has given my self a place of holding, voice and expression. There is a certain alchemy to this. Of magic and medicine. It is a process of gathering the bones and then breathing life into them.

Songwriting has allowed me to access wisdom that bypasses my over-zealous brain and somehow transmutes the soul. I dive into the depths and create the medicine I need, often before I really understand it or truly embody it. It's an elixir of hope and healing. Birthing it into song form means I can continue to walk into it, to keep becoming, the medicine works deeper and deeper in a spiralling way, with new perspectives and resonance layering over time.

This lifetime of deep desire to form wholeness out of fragments is on one hand an endless gift of inspiration and energy. On the other it can also feel like endless pressure and panic. To try and capture every experience or moment and transmute it into a piece of art is overwhelming. To feel the need to say everything, all at the same time and in the most erudite way. To see a thousand tangles within and around me and a thousand stories waiting to be told. To see all the things that evoke emotion, inspire me, challenge me, all the things I want to desperately connect together. To try and weave all this, through the multiple dimensions I experience it in, into the two dimensions of words and then out again through the viscerality of music that transmutes it back into multiple dimensions and senses...it can take its toll. It can create an implosion, a freeze, a sense of never being complete and there being no end to it or no point to it.

The thousand fragments of writing and songs all build up, and there is the feeling that if I don't grab onto it in that urgent now, then something will be lost. And that's just the writing of the piece, before any physical recording process happens – which is a whole other story. I'm always working three projects ahead in my mind and not knowing where the resources will come from to be able to achieve that.

Quite frankly, this sort of sensory overwhelm and pressure creates burnout and madness. This compulsion to weave fragments into wholeness, and to keep producing and sharing work – it's been therapeutic, it's been a way to manage myself and the way I experience the world, and it's also been detrimental, urgent and all-consuming. It hasn't always felt like a choice, rather that I might die if I don't do this, which is actually a totally unsustainable, unrealistic and unhealthy story to carry.

Eleanor

The Highly Creative Person

Creativity is in our DNA. Wired into our brains, our hormones, our bodies. The creative process is innate to us as humans, and one which almost all of us engage with, usually unconsciously, on a daily basis.

But whilst we are all endowed with creative potential, not all of us might have raw artistic talent, well-developed skills of expression or the drive to develop our creativity consciously. Just as the majority of us are physically active to some degree every day of our lives, not all of us are naturally athletic nor do we have the discipline and drive to devote ourselves to being athletes. In both instances, the gift of raw talent is part of the equation. The rest comes down to a mixture of nature – our genes, neurology, character and drive...and nurture – encouragement, opportunities, training from good teachers and mentors to get the best from us to develop this potential. And then there is of course our own sizable contribution: commitment, regular practice, learned technical skills, supportive habits and lifestyle, and most importantly of all, building the confidence in ourselves and the courage to share our abilities publicly.

Just as there are some who need to run daily to be fully alive, for some of us the desire to create, the need to dream and imagine and make things is as necessary as breathing. We are those who Scott Barry Kaufman and Carolyn Gregoire refer to in their book, *Wired to Create*, as Highly Creative People.

We have a natural aptitude for creativity. We are passionate, curious, playful, intuitive and sensitive, with an ability to think outside the box. You can usually spot us from a distance. We're the ones with pink hair. Or walking barefoot out of choice. We're the ones in the eye-catching outfit, who are taking photographs of the trees or curled up immersed in a book. We're the ones whose brains are buzzing and who can't sit still, the ones tapping our fingers to an invisible beat and staring into space. We're the ones who shut ourselves away from the world to work on our next project. We're the ones that fill your bookshelves and playlists, whose work you choose to spend your spare time and money on in movie theatres and galleries. We're the ones who can speak direct to your soul.

We've known, for almost as long as we've been alive, that we're different to most of the rest of the world. We just didn't quite fit in. We were always

> The truly creative mind in any field is no more than this: a human creature born abnormally, inhumanly sensitive... Add to this cruelly delicate organism the overpowering necessity to create, create, create – so that without the creating of music or poetry or books or buildings or something of meaning, his very breath is cut off from him. He must pour out creation. By some strange, unknown, inward urgency he is not really alive unless he is creating.
>
> Pearl S. Buck

> We are all makers. The unceasing hunger to work with one's hands stems from the basic human drive for peace, security and freedom from fear. To transform the ugly and broken into something of meaning and beauty, to transcend the present like birds in flight: this is humanity's common thread.
>
> Valarie Lee James

too full of questions. Too detached. Too energetic. Too unwilling to be forced into the grey box called Real Life. We kept demanding to be heard. We loved to dress up or show off. We insisted on making up stories. And singing when it was time to be quiet. Or being quiet when it was time to speak. We kept wondering *how?* and *why?* And most of all, we kept making stuff. Making stuff happen. Making stuff up. Weird stuff. Cool stuff. Useful stuff. Incredible stuff. Making a mess. Making a fuss. Making, making, making…to the amazement, delight or annoyance of those around us. And what gave us the most joy was sharing that stuff we made with others who would share this enjoyment with us.

Maybe you are only just owning this part of yourself. Or realising how central it is to your health, happiness and wellbeing after a period or entire lifetime of denial and suppression. Perhaps all you knew previously that was when you made stuff you were happy and when you didn't, you felt dead inside. That trying to make things in real life – whether from dough or Lego, in drawing or writing – held such power for you. It mattered in a way that nothing else ever really had. For the moments you were doing it, it felt as if you were existing in some magical realm. You felt calm. Happy. At home in a world which otherwise you always felt a little at odds with. Even when creating was challenging – terrifying – somehow it was still worth it. And when people saw the things you made, they responded. And suddenly you found you too had been seen, really seen, perhaps for the first time. Suddenly you had a way to connect with other people. With the world. With yourself. As you are. Whilst at the same time making yourself up and being seen as you wanted to be.

For the Highly Creative Person this drive to create, to bring imagination to form and share the experience, is partly like a drug, and partly like oxygen. We need it to live.

Experience

Creativity is my best way to clarity and sanity, my literal, multi-coloured lifeline. My creations enable me to hold onto the fleeting inspiration which comes to me out of the blue – visions of hope, of joy, of colour. The creative process helps me to dive more deeply into ideas, to work through these insights in a physical way, learning more about them, and myself, as I do. It gives voice to the deepest part of myself which has no other means of expression. It helps me to be who I am supposed to be in the world, and contribute what I can.

For me creativity is an act of devotion, a path of extreme vulnerability, which has immense gifts both for me and for the world. It's a kind of apprenticeship or discipleship to an unknown mistress, and it's one that I feel very, very lucky to have.

As I find the courage to go deeper, to explore that which I have left hidden in this lifetime or others, as I dare to paint and write the selves which have been repressed and suppressed, I become more fully alive, more fully myself, and more deeply connected with others and the world.

And so my passion is in living my life so that I can become more and more immersed in creative flow, allowing it to infiltrate every aspect of my life: my mothering, my friendships, my work, how I earn my money, my leisure, my pleasure – my creativity once dammed now infiltrates everything.

”

When your soul awakens, your destiny becomes urgent with creativity.

John O'Donohue, *Anam Cara*

Create or Die

For many of us creativity is birthed from necessity. We need to make a living, so we turn our skills and imagination to what we have available – we do what we can, with what we have, where we are.

As Kiwi chef, Ben Shewry says,

> *There is a romantic story that people are just creative because that's what they like to do. And they just go round all the time creating. But that's just ridiculous in a way. Sometimes people just have to create out of pure necessity. If I didn't create stuff that was inspiring to people, that people liked, we were going to go broke.*[iii]

This has been my experience of creativity too. Creativity is often fuelled by a lack – of resources, opportunities, options, money or time. It is not necessarily art. Or even beautiful. Often we create to serve a need. We put our brains and energy to the service of what needs to be done.

There is nothing like an urgent deadline or a material need to set the creative wheels in motion. Creating at these times isn't a nice hobby. It is a life or death act: make money, feed the family, solve the problem or else...

This is how and why my first four books were written so intensively – I needed to make a more sustained living from my writing than magazines or blogging provided, so my husband could step back from a job that was stressing him out. Each of my books is still driven as much by the external need to provide financially for my family and create something that is needed by someone I love, as it is by the internal need to bring a particular creative seed to fruition.

> [Making art] is the only thing that makes me feel 100% free, 100% me, 100% like I'm living life fully.
>
> Kristina, *Lost in Living*

It is the reason why a lot of creatives become entrepreneurs – we are good at spotting needs and creating solutions. And it is why this book explores this aspect of creativity too, because the internal creative process and the external demands of earning a living creatively are often discussed separately. As though artists don't need to eat or pay bills. As though talking about money and the practical and emotional struggles in the same breath takes away the magic and mystique of making art.

I beg to differ – I think the two are intimately intertwined within our human selves. The perennial issue of how to live is one that haunts most artists their entire lives. At first it is how to earn enough to eat and house ourselves...whilst allowing the time and space needed to answer to our incessant creative drive. But as we become more successful one set of challenges seem to be replaced by another: where once we didn't have time to create what we longed to, because we were having to earn a living, now we don't have time because everyone wants a piece of us. Where we previously had to fight to get attention for our work, now we have to fight for our privacy to make it.

Whilst economic necessity is a driving force, the urgent need to create is certainly not *just* the need to earn a living. As Harriet Martineau, credited as the first female sociologist, remarked in the mid-nineteenth century,

> *I have been scolded in one form or another for working too hard [...] I have not done it for amusement, or for money, or for fame,*

or for any reason but that I could not help it. Things were pressing to be said; and there was more or less evidence that I was the person to say them.[iv]

Most creatives who have reached a comfortable income tend to be just as driven. Writers like Harry Potter creator, J.K. Rowling, who has a net worth of $1 billion, still creates at a gruelling pace. She says, "The truth is that I can't really separate a 'writing life' from 'life.' It's more of a need than a love." [v] Jacqueline Wilson, my eldest daughter's favourite author, is in her early seventies. One of the most celebrated writers in modern children's literature, with well over a hundred books to her name, she still produces two books a year. Best-selling author Danielle Steele still works twenty hours a day, releasing a mind-blowing *seven* new titles each year…she has written 179 books over the course of her career.[vi] Agatha Christie is the best-selling novelist of all time, with over a billion books sold in English and another billion in translation, yet still she kept writing all her life.[vii] It is not just money. These are the leaders in their fields. Yet still they are driven to create as if their lives depend on it. In the words of author Siri Hustvedt, "I feel so much urgency […] I'm working for my life. I am working like a maniac to get it in before I die." [viii]

This incessant, pulsating creative energy that passes through us is an exhilarating superpower. But at times it can feel more like a curse, which controls our attention and dictates our lives. Being driven too hard by our creativity, having to self-medicate to survive the extremities or the stresses of sharing and performing, the strain of being constantly on show, the high expectations of critics and fans, the fear of releasing this energy publicly all take their toll on the vulnerable humans who channel it through. The amount of drug abuse, alcoholism, depression and suicide amongst the creative community is a testament to the realities of what it means to carry this big energy.

I am struck by the fact that the majority of people look forward to retirement, so they can finally do nothing. But not Highly Creative People. The thought of years of rest and no plans are anathema to us. If anything, creative people increase in productivity as they age. Freed from family commitments, they dive deeper into their body of work and explore new creative disciplines. Angela Lansbury, a dear family friend, is still acting in multiple films a year. Children's illustrator Judith Kerr worked full time illustrating books until her death during the writing of this book. Even though both women were well into their nineties and had enjoyed long and successful careers.

Whilst some self-employed creatives cannot retire because of the lack of a pension, most creatives do not retire, even when they are financially comfortable. It is only death, not sickness, that stops them: David Bowie was recording music right through his decline with cancer, his death occurring two days after the release of his album, *Black Star*. Picasso and Monet painted until their deaths, continuing to follow their passions and evolve their styles. Frida Kahlo and Henri Matisse had special desks constructed for their sickbeds when bed-bound in their last years.

There is something in the Highly Creative Person's need to create that is existential – far beyond the worldly needs of earning a living or gaining fame: we live to create, and create to live.

“

The object of art is not to make saleable pictures. It is to save yourself...to make yourself alive. The point of being an artist is that you may live.

Sherwood Anderson

Experience

From the outside people marvel at my prolificity. But my ability to see creative projects through feels exasperatingly slow to me. Whilst I love to create, much of the time it is not particularly pleasurable or enjoyable. In fact, it is deeply stressful. I am constantly frustrated with myself, with the process and with its results. I am all too aware of my own flaws and limitations. My terror of releasing my work makes me ill. But still I create, because to do so is slightly less stressful than not creating. I am very proud of the creative babes I have birthed into the world and their impact on others.

I live under the constant urgency to birth not only this current project, but knowing that the next five are backing up behind it. Each big book takes two years – so that is ten years' worth of books going around my head most of the time before I've worked through the backlog of other ideas that I currently have gestating within me. And more ideas are joining up behind all the time. I have more ideas than I know what to do with. And less energy than I need to live my life.

After every book I say 'never again'...and everyone laughs at me. Within the week I'm working like a crazy woman on the next big project...or three. My mother-in-law often asks in a bewildered way why I work so hard. It is because I have to. I am compelled to. Creating is how I can stay alive.

Creative Superpower

Creativity is our superpower. But one that most of us have not been taught how to use. The ability to turn an idea into a painting, an event, a song, a concert, a costume...to articulate the unseen into form, to make the invisible visible, to make our thoughts heard, our feelings felt by thousands of people around the world, to divide our souls into a million pieces, and remain more whole: these are the gifts of the Highly Creative Person.

But just like the superheroes we came to know and love through the stories of childhood, these gifts might at first seem to be curses, when we don't understand them or don't know how to harness their energies.

Many of us have felt misunderstood, frustrated or even scared by our deep-rooted drive to create. Often we feel at odds with a world that is not so fascinated by the movement of light on the water, finding the perfect colour green, staying up past midnight or jumping out of bed at 6am with a song or a poem or a chapter that simply has to be written. A world that doesn't understand this incessant urge to create, which subsumes everything else. Especially the things that they tell us that we should value – like money, neat clothes, a tidy home, or a good job.

We may have spent half a lifetime being told off for day-dreaming, being anti-social, being a bit too...different. We might have been branded an attention-seeker, unrealistic, weird, a slacker... Creatrixes tend to habitually live against the grain, indulging in aesthetics, personal expression, questioning and subverting cultural norms.

Owning our creative powers takes us from passive passengers or victims, to active change-makers and powerful contributors to our shared culture.

It is time to accept our gifts.

"

A creative life is an amplified life. It's a bigger life, a happier life, an expanded life, and a hell of a lot more interesting life. Living in this manner – continually and stubbornly bringing forth the jewels that are hidden within you – is a fine art, in and of itself.

Elizabeth Gilbert, *Big Magic*

Creatrix Speaks

I've fallen in and out of love with creativity over and over again throughout the years. It's funny, because deep down I know it's a need, almost as if it keeps me sane, and when the absolute free flowing, spontaneous, non-judgemental, purposeless creativity is present all is well. When it's not, there's some part of me that is restless, deeply unsatisfied, slightly lost, something is definitely missing.

Mirin

ARTIST

Am I Really Creative?

Are you feeling like you might be in the wrong book – with all this talk of superpowers and Highly Creative People? As for gifted...*pah!*

If you're anything like the majority of creative people I have spoken with, you may have a hard time calling yourself an Artist, Writer, Actor, or any other capitalised creative type. Despite the fact that you love creating in whatever media you work in, you know just how scared and unsure you are, how far from perfect your skills and finished works are. Sure, your mother, your partner, your best friend would identify you as creative. Even your bank manager would...if you had one. But they're just being nice, aren't they? You're not selling out arenas yet. Heck, you're not even meeting the rent with what you earn from your creative work. So obviously this book is not for you.

I beg to differ. Far from being the odd one out, your feelings are typical of most creatives. There seems to be an innate nervousness to calling ourselves creative, to owning who we are and what we do.

I was gobsmacked that most of the women I spoke to when writing my first book, *The Rainbow Way*, really struggled with defining themselves as creative, let alone 'Artists'. And yet they painted pictures, wrote books, presented radio shows, sang or sculpted, or sometimes all those things and more! To the outside world it was what defined them...but still most of them could not own this label themselves. One woman who had made her living from writing for twenty-five years, wasn't sure if the term really applied to her! Another who went to art college forty years ago and has sewed and painted almost every day since shirked the label.

As one of our featured creatrixes, Eli Trier, so wisely points out,

> If you find yourself asking yourself "Am I really a writer? Am I really an artist?" The chances are you are. The counterfeit innovator is wildly self-confident. The real one is scared to death.
>
> Steven Pressfield, *The War of Art*

> *You wouldn't see a plumber, when asked what they do, bow their head, shuffle their feet and say 'Oh, I'm a plumber, but I'm not, you know, a Real Plumber.' [...] But you see artists doing it all the time.*

Why is this?

At first, I thought this feeling of inferiority was unique to women and the way we are socialised within patriarchy to be self-effacing. But as I spoke with male friends and professional creatives during the research for this book, I began to uncover the same reticence and deep-rooted uncertainty in most of them too. This bashfulness at owning our creativity, it seems, goes beyond gender. It is endemic in our culture. Because of what 'Artist' is perceived as meaning.

We tend to think of Art as grand and fancy, and ourselves as being rather small and insignificant. We know what is considered great – we have been well indoctrinated in that: the Old Masters of painting, literary giants and classical composers who are deified in schools and universities around the world, or the modern masters who earn hundreds of millions of dollars in movies and art auctions today. Our culture teaches us about Art as a commodity, and celebrity as something that goes along with it. It has little to teach about creativity, the lived process, the reality...

We see these Proper Artists, and know we aren't them. We learn early on that we don't really belong in this grand field called Art with our funny drawings and strange poems, our small performances and shaking hands. We know all our flaws, all our struggles, all our failures. We know we're not *that*...but then who are we, what are we? We don't know where we fit.

Creatrix Speaks

When I first began to scrawl out my thank you pictures for The Gratitude Project, it hadn't occurred to me to call myself an 'artist'.

In fact, despite the fact that I had created a huge amount of art, in a wide variety of media, over the course of my entire life, it had never occurred to me to call myself that.

However, I was compelled to create. Every week, I had to make a brand new painting for the project, and gradually, I began to paint more and more pictures (unrelated to gratitude) just for the joy of it.

I learned that the simple act of making art every day made me an artist.

I began to put making art first on my to-do list.

I made it a non-negotiable, because it made me so happy.

I discovered that whilst I love to draw cats and pots and cups of tea, drawing people just doesn't interest me at all.

I discovered that I love to draw in pen and ink and paint in watercolour. I discovered that the smell and the mess of oil paints puts me off.

I learned what sort of artist I was.

I kept producing work, and I kept publishing it. Some of it was awesome, some of it sucked. And then, a funny thing happened – people started getting interested. All of a sudden strangers were telling me that they loved my work and asking where they could buy it.

Someone got in touch and asked if they could sell my work for me.

I learned that I could make money from making art.

And a few years later, I learned that I didn't have to. That I could keep my art as a special sacred thing just for myself. To nourish and inspire me in both dark times and light.

My creativity is my greatest source of joy and connection.

All of this was born from a desperate attempt to claw myself back from a pit of despair. All of this came from the tiny seed of a thought – that the only way out was to say thank you.

Being grateful forced me to be authentic, and when I approached my life from a place of authenticity and gratitude, everything changed for me. I saved myself.

These days I create when I feel like it. I make whatever I want to make and I don't give two hoots about creating a 'cohesive body of work' or being a 'professional' artist. Making art is my expression of my truest self, and it's a precious jewel just for me.

Eli

My Family and Other Creatives

> Everyone is born creative; everyone is given a box of crayons in kindergarten. Then when you hit puberty they take the crayons away and replace them with dry, uninspiring books on algebra [and] history. Being suddenly hit years later with the 'creative bug' is just a wee voice telling you, 'I'd like my crayons back, please.'
>
> Hugh MacLeod, *Ignore Everybody: and 39 Other Keys to Creativity*

Early developmental experiences have a massive impact on all creatures, but as Highly Sensitive, Highly Creative People this increases tenfold. An understanding family that accepts and encourages us, teachers that nurture our talents, supportive and inspiring mentors and friends along the way…the abundance or lack of these directly impact how intact we make it through to adulthood, or how much recovery is required of us before we can fully claim our creative lives.

I am very lucky (though I haven't always felt this way!) to have come from an unusual family. Pretty much every member, for the last three generations, probably more, on both sides has been creatively self-employed. We number painters, fabric artists, potters, glass-blowers, wood-turners, authors, actors, musicians, publishers and architects amongst us.

I was fortunate to have been brought up creative, in a bohemian middle-class family, amongst many beautiful homes, with passionate people who are well-known in their fields. I was immersed in the creativity of others, and encouraged in my own expression. Creativity was normal in our bubble. And whilst in many ways it was really cool to have a creative family, in many others I really envied my normal friends with their normal families and regular incomes: the naval officers and doctors, the office administrators and shop workers.

You see, growing up in a creative family isn't always glamorous. I've learned firsthand how unpredictable the income of the self-employed creative can be, and how changeable the market for one's work. I've seen how important a good contract is, and how the lack of one can mean the loss of a livelihood. I've felt how hard creative failures are for the family and the individual and how mental health issues can scar the terrain of the Highly Creative bodymind.

And so, despite my creative background, it took me many years to fully accept and embrace my own creativity, and the baggage that comes with it.

For most of my life I have tried really hard to be normal. And that entailed shutting down my creative expression. But nurture – and nature – it seems are inescapable.

What I didn't realise as a young adult trying (and failing) to be normal, was that we are genetically super creative as well! There is a strong dash of neurodiversity in the mix in my family. Whilst I was aware of the Down Syndrome and dyslexia since I was young, I was less aware of the depression and anxiety of most shades that run strongly through the generations. And had no idea that autism ran through our female side. Until three generations of us were diagnosed.

Reflecting on my creative lineage got me to thinking about the creative capital that I have inherited, through my genes and my upbringing that made a creative career – a creative life – not only acceptable, but in many ways the only viable possibility for me and my family. And how so very many people don't get this as standard. They find themselves in this life with a Highly Creative soul, but little or no knowledge of the terrain, and little creative capital to inherit from their family or community.

One of my intentions behind this book is to share what I have been fortunate enough to inherit as well as my hard-won experience from along the way, in the hopes that it might take away some of the mystery which can make creativity seem so daunting.

Please know that I get what it feels like from the inside. Because even though I had all that in my background, I had (and still have) a loud voice in my head that says, *Wow! Look how talented all my family are. But me...I'm not creative. I'm just a weird mess.* You see, manual craftsmanship and visuo-spatial creativity run through my family. Whereas I have shaky hands and struggle to visualise anything in three-dimensions. My superpower is in researching and weaving ideas, in editing and shaping, in the intuitive use of words and symbolic images to express energy and emotion. My biggest passion is books – writing, reading, editing, publishing, collecting, curating, selling and recommending them – whereas several of my family are highly dyslexic and unable to read what I write.

And it's not just me. I know that most of my Highly Creative relatives at one time or another have felt out of their depths, unsure of what they really wanted to do and just plain scared about how to share their work with the world...or how to make a living from doing what calls their souls.

I don't know your story. You may have been born into a Highly Creative family...or you may be the first (that you know of) in your lineage. Whatever your family and educational history, whatever your background, all of us are born into a world that has little understanding of The Creative Way and that does everything in its power to keep us from it.

Creatrix Speaks

I am a little girl trapped in a suburban street in a house of swallowed pain and unsaid truth. I hide in my bedroom and walk about with my hand over my mouth in case something of the whirlwind of creativity, anger, freedom and colour spills out of me. It is not welcome here. I try to be as nice and good as possible to be enough to meet impossible standards. I stay in my bedroom so I can't be noticed.

It is a twisting dance I have heard repeated into adulthood by many women of not feeling they are being enough but also being too much. This is a place and a pattern I will repeat over and over in abusive relationships...recreating that house of cards by entangling myself in traps I couldn't see coming. It will bring me to my knees eventually.

From my bedroom I draw, scribble poetry, play, paint, write, invent dreams, make stories and magic worlds... Thank the stars that a creative force has also been with me since I was a little girl...a bright rainbow muse who has no care for the economic viability of ideas or how realistic they are. She has an insatiable need to create, to see what I vision come into being, to weave threads of magic that others say cannot be done and she has never left my side. It saves me over and over. I know I would not still be in the world without it.

Clare

What Do You Want to Be When you Grow Up?

When we are in junior school and asked the question: *What do you want to be when you grow up?* the response *artist* is as acceptable as *astronaut.*

But give it a few years and say to the well-meaning Careers Advisor that you want to be an artist or actor and chances are she gives you a tight smile and tries to steer you into a safe, known career: teacher or arts therapist. Something conservative. Careful. With a reliable pension.

Overtly choosing to be a professional artist from the outset is quite rare. Few of us actively choose The Creative Way as our Plan A. Because we are actively discouraged from it by a culture that neither believes in its value, nor understands how it works. We are slotted early on into boxes that our culture approves of: pursuing degrees or going straight into dull jobs. Or we zigzag aimlessly not knowing quite what we want to do or how to make it happen. Or we have kids sooner than expected and our lives are overturned by their needs. However our particular story unfolds, we leave our vibrant creativity behind us, our creative passions put on the backburner behind our adult responsibilities.

This was certainly true for me. Despite my family background, and multiple creative talents, I was academic and so was pushed hard by my school down the academic route. I fought back, choosing Art over History of Art for my A Levels, and Drama School over high-brow universities. But then anxiety overtook me and I didn't know how to handle it. Nor did anyone else. I didn't even know that's what it was – I was in my thirties before I learned to put that word to that feeling. So I turned my back on my creativity as it seemed to make it worse, by putting me into situations I couldn't handle. I switched courses and went to university. I won awards in History of Ideas and got published in an academic journal. But I stopped painting and acting and directing and singing and dancing. I folded up my creative dreams and tucked them into my desk drawer. Sharing my own expression felt too dangerous. It required being in the spotlight, people criticising me, being different. It put me in the firing line of the judgement of others. And I, after a lifetime of being different because of my undiagnosed autism, just wanted to be normal, to fit in.

"

The arts are not a way to make a living. They are a very human way of making life more bearable. Practicing an art, no matter how well or badly, is a way to make your soul grow.

Kurt Vonnegut, *A Man Without a Country*

Besides, I wasn't all cool and chilled out and funky like I thought Artists *should* be. I was socially awkward and trying hard to exist behind a mask of normality. And, I reasoned, the world had quite enough Writers and Artists. It certainly didn't need me. What did I have to offer? I would change the world through teaching instead, I decided. It would be safer. And the income would be more reliable. And so I went to Cambridge for my post-graduate degree, training to be a teacher of English and Drama. Because whilst my own creativity scared me, I knew subconsciously that I still had to be around the magic somehow.

And so I carried on along this path. Choosing safety. Choosing normal. I tried to make myself feel numb inside, because numb was easier than anxious.

Does my path sound familiar to you? Perhaps you have a story like mine too.

Or perhaps you were more like my siblings who – with enough space, time and financial and emotional support and a bit less anxiety – were able to dedicate themselves to their creativity straight out of school, walking The Creative Way through their late teens and early twenties. But time and again they too have stumbled and wondered if it was such a good idea after all, as they have struggled to earn a living, tried and failed and tried again to break into industries that are already overcrowded with thousands of other creative wannabes all looking for their big break.

Every single one of us starts from a different place in terms of family support, privilege, health and material needs. Each of us has our own level of challenge based on our age, gender, race, health, class and sexuality. Each of us has our own truth to tell that scares us.

We are each faced with a lot of unanswerable questions that only we can answer based on our circumstances at a given time… How much to invest in ourselves, in our creative education and materials? Which risks to take? When to compromise? When to push on? How long to wait for a breakthrough? When to specialise…and when to keep our options open? We have to decide which creative dreams to invest our time, money and energy into and which to let go. And regardless of circumstances, we all have to face the ultimate question: *Does the world want what I have to offer? Am I really good enough to offer it? And am I willing to do what it takes to walk The Creative Way?*

In a world that demands we work – and work hard – in a visible way, how can we defend what we do, especially in the early days, which to the rest of the world just looks like good fun? When *it* is spending days by ourselves playing with paints, learning lines, making up stories, day-dreaming, jamming with our friends… How can we justify being continually broke because we refuse to get a 'proper job'? How can we hold out hope for a creative dream we hope might come true? And how can we tell the people we meet what it is we do, when we can barely articulate or conceptualise it ourselves?

Creatrix Speaks

As a child I used to create all the time: paint, glitter, mud, flour, sticks, stones, pasta…in so many shapes and forms.

Then I started growing up, and gradually that wild and free-spirited creativity began to fade…slowly, slowly, until it was a distant memory. I wanted to fit in and be just like everybody else, to be cool, and that didn't mean being different. At school we were no longer creating just for the sake of it, for expression, for the sheer delight in it, but rather we were trying to achieve something, to tick certain boxes.

This was no longer the exciting experimental creativity of my childhood, it required technique and structure, and I struggled to tick the boxes. Thus, I came to the conclusion that I simply wasn't creative.

Yet some part of my soul was aching, longing for more than the rational, beyond the structures of this physical reality. Something was missing, yet I couldn't quite place my finger on what it was.

Sometime in my late teens or early twenties I began exploring festival culture, and somehow found myself drawing on people's bodies: it was fun and others really enjoyed it too, and so my confidence began to return. I was doodling, and my sister nudged me forward recommending an intuitive painting course. I tried it out and it was revelatory, I was a child again, no longer creating for some final goal, but for the sheer joy and delight of it. The spark was reignited, and I began to play with visual creations once again.

My creativity has taken many shapes and forms since then: painting, drawing, clothing making, jewellery making, pottery, cooking, calligraphy, idea development, poetry, movement, dance, spoken word, workshops, singing, the list goes on and on.

For me that is key to my creative process, to have permission to create without any objective, but rather just for the journey, allowing my art to reveal itself to both myself and others.

Mirin

"

All of us have to learn how to invent our lives, make them up, imagine them. We need to be taught these skills; we need guides to show us how. Without them, our lives get made up for us by other people.

Ursula le Guin

The Severed Self

As we have begun to see, few of us were optimally initiated into our creative potential. Each of us has our own personal stories of shaming, lack of support or being made wrong when we expressed ourselves. They are far from uncommon.

But I believe that the disconnect goes far deeper than these individual experiences. We need to dig deep beyond our own stories into our collective past to get a fuller understanding of why we struggle to own our creativity. Because it's a cultural issue.

Creativity is what defines us as humans. It has been a central part of daily life in every human culture until the modern era. Anything a society needed would have had to be found, adapted or made by hand. Crafts(wo)manship was central to human existence. Creativity equalled first survival, then thriving. And it would have been achieved with the combination of many talents of the whole community. Cooking and healing were art and science and spirit combined. As were hunting and weaving, the making of jewellery, clothing and vessels. The objects of daily life were imbued with stories and skills accumulated over generations, and used to forge communal identities through local variations of colour and symbol. We can still see this way of being in tribal cultures across the globe, as well as in the reliquaries of our museums from our own lineage. A pot, a hat, a wheel, a sword was not just a disposable, utilitarian object, but something made by hand and decorated with care and meaning.

For most of human history making was our core power. The proto-Indo-European word *magh*[ix] is at the root of many words: might (strength and power), may (to be able), make and magic... It is believed to come from Old Persian *maguš*, a member of a priestly caste ('mighty one').[x]

Ironically the same word is also the root of to the things that are taking over creation – machines (instruments of making) – under the dominance of industrial capitalism. The mechanisation of daily life is an obvious conclusion to patriarchy's centuries long drive to sever the connection between people, community, magic, meaning and making. First dividing women from men, then the arts and spirituality from each other, and later using science and technology to divide us from what we have always done.

And so here we are, in the twenty-first century, in a culture full of technology and entertainment, where meaning and beauty have been stripped from daily life. We have lost any sense of connection or value to the things we share our lives with, they have become status symbols, or disposable objects. Science and economics have been promoted as the only real way of valuing the world. And the creative and spiritual aspects of life have become specialised professions, little valued and open only to a few.

To worry about this is nothing new. During the Arts and Crafts movement at the end of the nineteenth century, artists such as William Morris and John Ruskin were dedicated to reclaiming beauty, craftsmanship and soul in the objects of daily life, as the Victorian world became ever-more mechanised. They recognised that how things are designed and made directly impacts the people that use them. Morris, the leader of the movement, argued that "without dignified, creative human occupation people became disconnected from life".[xi] In the words of Walter Crane in a book of essays by members of the Arts and Crafts movement,

> *It is a protest against the turning of men into machines, against artificial distinctions in art, and against making the immediate market value, or possibility of profit, the chief test of artistic merit.*[xii]

"

There is a vitality, a life force, an energy, a quickening that is translated through you into action, and because there is only one of you in all time, this expression is unique. And if you block it, it will never exist through any other medium and will be lost.

— Martha Graham

As an idealistic young adult, I knew I needed to find a way to recombine the arts, sciences and spirituality for myself. But I could find no single discipline, no university course to teach me how to do this. The older I have gotten and the more intense our cultural crisis has become, I find myself ever more strongly driven to reclaim this unsevered way of being, which places The Creative Way at the heart of life. I have a feeling you do too, which is why we're here together right now.

CREATRIX

Highly Creative Women

> Consciously or unconsciously we know that to be a creative woman entails huge risk. And this is what we have to overcome.
>
> Lucy H. Pearce (in Sharon Blackie's *If Women Rose Rooted*)

What does it mean to be a Highly Creative *Woman*, rather than just a Highly Creative *Person*? Why, in fact, do we need to differentiate at all?

Many women do not want to be defined as *female* artists – to them their sex or gender are simply beside the point. Their focus is on their creative work: what they need to make and want to share, which may or may not have anything to do with womanhood.

But this, sadly, is not where our culture's focus is. Still we are women first in the world's eyes. Our biological sex tends to define how our work is perceived and valued. It defines the roles we are offered, the tone of the reviews and the money we earn.

As we have begun to explore, to inhabit this world as an artist is challenging, but to do it in the body of a woman, using the voice and imagery of the Feminine, requires great courage. The Highly Creative Woman is considered twice strange: odd as non-conforming artist, and odd as woman. And she tends to be doubly devalued, as artist and woman.

Women's creative work, despite the fact that women make up half the world's population, is still considered niche. Books, movies, clothes are all highly gendered – with the understanding that those created by women will only be, should only be, of interest to women. Whereas male artists and writers are considered able to express the universal human experience.

We are – whether we want to see it or not – creating within a cultural context where, for most of his-story, women and the feminine have been the *subject* of art and the *object* of our collective gaze. It is said that it is easier for a woman to appear in the Met Museum naked, than it is as an artist.[xiii] As I shared in *Burning Woman*,

The nude female is at the centre of the Western world. Erotic, exposed, perfect, whatever that means at that precise moment in his-story: her body is carved into the form of fashion. From galleries to online pornography [...] The white masculine view has been the only and correct gaze, perspective and vocabulary.

"

As has been long observed, men are people, but women are women.

Cordelia Fine, *Delusions of Gender*

It is not until *very* recently, that women have been *allowed* their own creative expression. Whilst many craft disciplines such as needlework or baking were encouraged in women, albeit within the confines of the domestic sphere, others like sculpture or acting were entirely off-limits.

This is not ancient history. Women's creative expression is still silenced in so many different ways in the modern era. Male scriptwriters, producers and directors dominate film and TV writing, shaping the stories we tell.[xiv] As a consequence of this male speaking parts *still* predominate in films, TV and theatre.[xv] Male actors are paid multiple times what female leads receive – the most shocking recent example being Mark Wahlberg receiving $1,500,000 for reshoots of the movie (ironically titled) *All the Money in the World* where his female co-star Michelle Williams received less than $1000.[xvi] No, I didn't just leave some zeroes off.

Things *are* changing, but *slowly.*

Here's a quick test, for those of you who are in any doubt of the position of women in the arts. Name a male pre-twentieth century playwright, sculptor or visual artist. Now name another. Easy enough? Now repeat this same exercise but with women. Not one, but two. I'm guessing you're struggling a little more. If that was easy for you, then I envy your education. Try that exercise again with women of colour and see how well you do this time.

This is the legacy that creative women – even in the twenty-first century – have inherited. This is the education – conscious and unconscious – that we received: not seeing people like us creating things that speak to *our* souls in ways that reflect *our* experiences, *our* feelings, *our* bodies. Knowing that what we yearn to do, in many times and places, was considered criminal, insane or at the very least socially dangerous. This still impacts the art that we feel safe to make and share today.

And it's not just holding us as individuals back. We have barely begun to understand or harness our creative superpowers as a species, because we have focused on the vision and interests of only one small portion of one gender. Imagine what can happen when we release the stored potential energy of all of our creative expression.

Why Women Don't Make Great Art (and other lies)

In the Western mind, creativity has for centuries been broken into two spheres – Great Art – for that read white, male artists with wealthy and powerful patrons who have been able to dedicate themselves to the sphere of creating in rarefied studios, without dirtying their hands in the world. And craft – anything associated with women, queer, working-class or indigenous creative acts, which was considered of less skill or cultural importance, somehow less accomplished or valuable. These crafts were sullied somehow by the 'less than fully human' identities of their makers, as well as their utility. Great Art, you see, is a pure thing, only accessible by the genius of the white male.

> Remember this: the world loves powerful men and hates powerful women. Believe me, I know. The world will punish you, but you must hold fast.
>
> Siri Hustvedt, *Memories of the Future*

As a result, men's creative voicing of their struggles with sexuality, philosophy, identity, love, ambition, creativity and spirit have become glorified masterpieces in the canon of our culture. Whereas women's and queer works on the same themes were considered niche, strange, dull, discomforting or otherwise inappropriate subjects for Great Art. Even when women managed to be tutored by the greats and follow the rules of the establishment, their achievements tended to be systematically ignored, overlooked, or worse still, attributed to the men around them. As Siri Hustvedt writes in the Guardian,

> *Why is it hard for people to accept the intellectual and creative authority of artists and writers who are women? [...] Why was Simone de Beauvoir's original thought attributed to Jean-Paul Sartre? Why did it take centuries for art historians to recognise the canvases of the Italian baroque painter Artemisia Gentileschi as hers, not her father's, even those that were signed by her? [...] The evidence was there. They couldn't see it. Why?*

Paintings, novels and philosophy made by men feel more elevated somehow, more serious, while works by women feel flimsier and more emotional. Masculinity has a purifying effect, femininity a polluting one. The chain of associations that infect our thought dates back to the Greeks in the west. They are often subliminal, and they are emotionally charged.[xvii]

"

I would venture to guess that anon, who wrote so many poems without signing them, was often a woman.

Virginia Woolf, *A Room of One's Own*

In 2015 (*not* 1715) Georg Baselitz shared his informed opinion as to why Great Art included so few women: "Women don't paint very well".

And whilst this misogyny could easily be written off as merely an attention-grab by a publicity-hungry artist – which it is – it is also sadly representative of our culture's unspoken belief that what women made – and are capable of making – is not Great Art.

In her popular article on women and art, Camille Gajewski of Tate Exchange writes,

For centuries, women were systematically excluded from the records of art history. [...] Women have been and continue to be integral to the institution of art, but despite being engaged with the art world in every way, many women artists have found opposition in the traditional narrative of art history. They have faced challenges due to gender biases, from finding difficulty in training to selling their work and gaining recognition.[xviii]

Let us be very clear, it is not that women have not *made* art throughout his-story, it is that this art was often incorrectly attributed, unvalued and not woven into the narrative of our cultural history.

Abby Butcher of Ditchling Museum of Art and Craft in East Sussex, UK, said in a recent article in the Guardian that "craftswomen are 'undoubtedly' at risk of being forgotten and suffer from gender bias that sees male artists [...] dominate discussions of crafts history." [xix]

She believes the situation is exacerbated in the Internet Age, by the fact that less than 10% of Wikipedia editors are women. In order to counteract this, the Art+Feminism group has conducted more than 5,000 'Edit-a-thons', training volunteers on how to edit and create Wikipedia entries on women artists, ensuring that their presence is online for future researchers to discover.

But it is not just our history that needs editing to include the women whose contributions have been systematically ignored and devalued. Our capitalist culture demonstrates what it values through where it spends its money. Male art is considered more accomplished and desirable...and therefore more valuable. Still today the media gives most airtime to those with the biggest budgets and the best PR teams – usually male-led projects, supported by other powerful men in the industry.

In the major New York auctions in 2014-15, 92% of lots were by male artists.[xx]

> *While women artists are very slowly beginning to gain a fairer share of the art market, their male counterparts continue to outperform them dramatically at the highest end. [In 2015 a] $25 million Bourgeois was the only work by a woman to make the list of the top 100 lots sold at auction, [where] Picasso's Les femmes d'Alger (1955) sold for $160 million, an all-time record for an artwork at auction.*[xxi]

The echo chamber of celebrated male artists recommending, mentoring and extolling the virtues of other male artists still dominates our culture today. And it is not just the creative products of men that are valued, but the time and space which they need to create them. In an apologetic introduction to his second volume of the daily rituals of well-known artists, author Mason Currey speaks to the unconscious bias against creative women. "The side-effect of focusing on the most well-known figures in Western literature, painting and classical music is that they are overwhelmingly men." [xxii] I was gratified to see this acknowledgement, as I had noticed immediately how few women were featured in his first book – only 27 out of 161! As I read it, I had remarked to my husband how many of the world's great creatives had lives of immense privilege, unrecognisable to me. Even the poorest of male creatives still had their needs met by wives, sisters, cooks and housekeepers, who kept hunger, dust and interfering folk at bay, minded their children, and generally took care of the business of daily life, so that the genius could devote himself to his work of making Great Art.

Ah, how I long for a life like that. Not to wish my children away, but simply that being a creative mother is still very different to being a creative father. The unspoken rules and expectations on my domestic and parenting duties are still miles apart for me as a woman. My creativity is still in many ways a nice hobby in the eyes of many, a lame excuse for my messy house. As a woman, even though it is our main family income, my work is secondary to the needs of my children and home. And from reading the words of many creative mothers over the years, I know I am not alone in this frustration at the double standards our society holds.

We come from a long line of women whose creative needs have not been given the time and space they need to flourish. We have untold privileges and freedoms in comparison to our mothers and grandmothers, but still we have grown up not seeing women's work exhibited amongst the Great Masters of Western culture, not reading works by our sisters in school. Even today, women's works are only being rediscovered, a niche addendum to the mainstream of patriarchal culture, taught in Women's Studies to appease the stroppy feminists.

This is why, whether or not *we* think of ourselves as genderless in terms of our art, the world still sees our gender and sex first. We are still in the process of making visible what our culture has not seen, making valuable that which has been overlooked. There is still a very necessary place for women's prizes, women's publishing houses and exhibitions to right the historical imbalance, to make space for and give value to our creativity.

It is important to remember this larger context. Because when we attempt to reclaim time and space for ourselves to create what we have not seen before, chances are the patriarchal voices still bark in our minds: *shut up...get back in your box...you don't have anything worth saying...this is of no value...your viewpoint doesn't matter...you should be cleaning the house...*

"

For women poetry is not a luxury. It is a vital necessity of our existence. [...] Poetry is the way we help give name to the nameless so it can be thought. The farthest external horizons of our hopes and fears are cobbled by our poems, carved from the rock experiences of our daily lives.

Audre Lorde, *Sister Outsider*

Creatrix Speaks

I think that the nature of women's work is inherently transient. Much of women's creativity has historically taken place in the domestic sphere, creating things that are used and also creating with materials that are often organic and will disintegrate over time.

Perhaps this is why there is such a gap in artefacts depicting 'her' story. While men have tended to create more imposing and lasting objects: monoliths, stone carvings, monuments, literally making their mark on the world, far fewer ancient objects have been discovered that were made by women. I would argue that this is not because women were not creating, but that what we created and how we were creating was much more transient in nature.

I stumbled upon this idea when I was researching the history of my own craft: doll making. I believe that since women have had babies, they have made dolls for them. There are still remnants of this ancient craft passed down through cultures such as the American corn dollies.

But when it comes to archaeological evidence of domestic doll making, very little has remained. What has been found are bone and stone carved 'goddesses' often ascribed to be symbols of fertility, but little understood.

However, dolls lovingly made as a gift, as a plaything, have not survived, purely because of the fact that they were made of natural objects such as grasses, wool and fabric, and these objects would have been lost through the course of time due to their natural tendency to biodegrade.

Many arts and crafts traditionally pursued by women have this element of transiency: weaving, sewing, knitting, henna art, embroidery and doll making to name but a few. All these have been ways women have expressed their creativity and I have no doubt that they also told a story, they spoke of culture and knowledge, the natural world around us and our place in it.

Women have tended to create with what was at hand. Our creations have often had dual purposes: warmth, comfort, clothing for example, as well as creating a piece of art. Still today many women find it difficult to take the time out of their daily lives to create just for the sake of creating, so we can hide our creative outlet in objects required by the family, into the work that needs to be done.

I think also that it is the act of creating that is so important to many of us, not so much what has been created. The process is often of more value than the outcome and as a result we feel little need to preserve what we created. We needed to create...not simply to make a mark.

Generally, women are much more at ease with the transient nature of things, we are much more connected to change. We understand change within our bodies deeply. We know that change is not death: it is the bringing of something new. And thus, we are much more comfortable with the fruits of our creativity changing over time, being used in a different and new way or biodegrading back to the earth.

Laura

Creator/God

In the beginning God created the heaven and the earth. And the earth was without form, and void; and darkness was upon the face of the deep. And the Spirit of God moved upon the face of the waters. And God said, Let there be light: and there was light. And God saw the light, that it was good: and God divided the light from the darkness.

Genesis, Chapter 1, v 1-4

The roots of the silencing of women's creativity go all the way back far beyond Western industrial capitalism to the founding texts of our culture.

Within Judaeo-Christian cultures, the shadow of the Creator God (masculine) has loomed large over the creativity, fertility and sexuality of women for millennia: the denigration of women was seen as God's command, the decree of the Ultimate Creator.

However, I think it is interesting to note that in the first four verses of the beginning of the Bible (quoted above), God is genderless. The Creator is neither male nor female...simply a deity with immense creative capacity.

In all the passages thereafter, God is gendered, referred to as He. The almighty Creator is depicted as a Father God. And so begins his-story: sacred creative energy was claimed by male writers as masculine. We are then told that "God created man in his own image" (Genesis 1:27) and so males were appointed the de-facto cultural gatekeepers of creative energy in human culture.

After a global history of multiple gods and goddesses representing the myriad expressions of psychic energy and spiritual understanding, suddenly with the advent of Judaeo-Christian religions there was only One True God. And it was most definitely male. The fertile abundance of a birthing Mother Goddess was replaced by a wrathful Father. And men alone were able to commune with and embody the powers of this supernatural creator. Woman was only allowed the biological act of reproduction using her physical womb, a painful punishment for her inherently disobedient nature. Any use of her creative energies to do other than nurture was considered selfish and dangerous, an act against the will of God: a sin that could condemn her to eternal suffering.

For generation upon generation, virtually every aspect of Christian, Jewish and Muslim culture was built upon this foundation myth. It was strengthened, policed and judged by male voices, visions and perspectives.

Encouraged by these creation myths, we have forgotten, or rather we have been taught not to know, the centrality of women's creative contribution, not just to culture, but to human existence. As film director Jane Campion, the first and only female filmmaker in history to receive the Palme d'Or, said: "We are women, we are only half the world, but we gave birth to the whole world. No one on this planet should be ignorant of our views or our voices."

The Creatrix Archetype

***Creatrix:** A female who brings forth or produces. A female founder, authoress, creator. (Wikipedia)*

From classical Latin creatrix mother, creatress, authoress (of a situation), feminine form corresponding to creator – first usage 1620. (Oxford English Dictionary)

My sense is that the archetype of Creatrix is a more accessible concept for creative women as they reclaim the full spectrum of their creative powers and voices, rather than trying to fit themselves in to the archetypes of Artist or Creator, which have been forged in the male image for so long.

Because the term has so little cultural baggage, we can own Creatrix and define it for ourselves. Self-definition is the ultimate reclamation of our power from oppressive forces, both inner and outer. It can help us to make psychological and energetic space for ourselves to create in our own words and images, in our own way, with our own intentions. It can allow us to more freely incorporate our values, feelings and priorities into our creative work.

> I'm restless. Things are calling me away. My hair is being pulled by the stars again.
>
> Anaïs Nin

Does what we call ourselves *really* matter? I believe it does: how we define ourselves with words shapes our actions. How we think and feel informs what and how we create. Once we own the label of Creatrix, it becomes an innate part of our identity, rather than creating just being another activity on our over-long to-do list. Identifying with a role unlocks latent energy within us. Ian Taylor, a lecturer in sports psychology from Loughborough University, explains that identity is a great motivator, far more than willpower – we *do* because we *are*. Rather than making yourself go for a run, you think of yourself as a runner.[xxiii] The same is true of creativity. Our motivation, our reason for creating becomes far more than just required productivity. We create because we are creatrixes, not because we ought to write a thousand words today. When we embody the energy of the Creatrix, we stand in the fullness of our birthright, as two-way channels of the full creative power of the Universe.

We can fashion the term as a container for our reclaimed creative energy, free from any traditional definitions of what art or an artist is or isn't, what we should or shouldn't do. We can choose to ignore the man-made boundaries between 'real work' (work that is paid), heart-work (caring and nurturing) and soul-work (healing, ritual, sexuality and artmaking). We can do away with the artificial Western division between the spiritual and the mundane. We can merge performance with ceremony and visual art, healing with words and sculpture… We can finally allow our creative minds and creative bodies free reign to show us what they are capable of without outdated constraints that were never made for us. We can ignore the arbitrary boxification of high art and low art…and simply create, because *this is who we are and this is what we were made to do.*

Embodying Creatrix

In our culture the creative artist is often encouraged to be not much more than an entertainer – singing their greatest hits on loop, acting in the same play each night, creating more pictures like their beloved masterpiece. Or they are required to embody the creative direction of another: the words or music someone else has written, the moves someone else has choreographed. Self-expression is bottom of the list, as many who start out longing to be dancers, actors or musicians soon discover once they are bound by contract to their economic and stylistic masters.

The creatrix is not simply a performer or entertainer – though these are elements of what she does – she is a dedicated shaper of consciousness and energy, a culture weaver, a dreamer and midwife of new worlds. She is an asker of uncomfortable questions and a liver of taboos in a world that expects conformity. She is answerable to her own intuition and sense of authenticity, and The Work itself. She follows the call of her soul above the demands of the world. She knows herself more deeply and sees herself more clearly through The Work.

To be a creatrix is to dedicate oneself to the cycle of creativity – to embodying soul, through impregnation, gestation, birth, nurturing and death in a way that is not really understood in our culture. It is to consciously engage directly with the forces of the Universe on a daily basis. The creatrix gestates her own content and births it out: her art is an expression of her inner world and a reflection of what she has sensed in the outer world. Through this sacred birthing she is transformed, as are those who witness the process or its products. In this sense the act of creative expression is a sacred act of communion for the community.

I believe that a creatrix is more than just a fancy name for a female artist. She is artist *plus*...artist plus priestess, artist plus healer, artist plus activist: her work has both sacred and worldly dimensions. She is an energy worker first and foremost, weaving energy into form, colour, words, sound, making meaning from symbols, in order to transform herself and those her creations touch.

The creatrix is also a woman of earthly skills. In a *Late Night Woman's Hour*[xxiv] discussion of the legacy of soul singer Aretha Franklin, the host,

Lauren Laverne, made an important observation about the language that is traditionally used to describe women artists. She pointed out that we're quick to make Franklin into a kind of goddess, and to overly focus on her connection to the creative Source rather than acknowledge her very real skills and tireless hard work. She stresses that there is a tendency to do this far more with women artists, in a way that diminishes their agency and labour.

This is a vital point to remember. His-storically, so many of women's skills in healing, mothering, cooking, home-making, negotiating, nurturing, peace-making, aesthetics and community building have been dismissed as merely natural, instinctive or somehow divinely given and have therefore gone un(der)valued. We are not in the habit of crediting women for their hard-won misstery of skills. As women we play our own special part in this dance too, when we deflect compliments for our accomplishments or diminish the value of our contributions.

> "Blessed are the weird people: poets, misfits, writers, mystics, painters, troubadours for they teach us to see the world through different eyes.
>
> Jacob Nordby, *Blessed are the Weird*

To declare yourself a creatrix is to shift the very landscape you inhabit. It is to own your power to create and transform. By honouring your relationship with the creative energy that pours through you, as well as fully acknowledging but not becoming egotistically attached to your own agency and skill, you are performing a revolutionary act. By dedicating yourself to the inner process of exploring, and the outer process of expressing our creative energy, by committing to use it for the good of others, you, in your own small way, are contributing to re-writing our-story. This recalibration of your life force transforms you from powerless patriarchal consumer to co-creatrix – one who is invested in our culture and community, who takes responsibility for transforming it.

Dark Voyages of Soul

The creatrix is one who is drawn to the dark voyages of soul and the high flights of spirit. She is one who has committed herself to exploring terrains little spoken of in our culture and mapping them for others to see. This journey of descent into the realms of the unconscious and the body is little recognised or rewarded within a culture which deifies and glorifies ascension, and rising above the body.

The creatrix's job is to sink her hand into the dark places and pull gently on the tender threads she finds there. She must dive into the depths of being and bring them to the light. She has to re-learn (or never forget) how to remove the mask the world has fitted her with and work directly with her essential energy beneath, the raw materials of her humanity so long denied her: feeling, the body, the personal and collective unconscious, the ego, the divine, the erotic and the sensual – the 'dark matter' of our inner universes. By dark I do not mean 'bad' but unknown – that which has yet to be 'lit' by the light of conscious knowledge or understanding. We create from this place, just as the Universe itself is created from dark matter within mysterious black holes into which our scientific instruments cannot probe.

Being a creatrix requires that we slip on our soul skins on a regular basis, like the selkie, so we can be of and with the ocean of the collective soul once more. We learn to shapeshift as, time and again, we experience the many inner layers, worlds and energies that make us up. This is how we remember who we are beyond the roles that the world demands of us.

This can be terrifying, as we have lived so long in the denial of what we really feel and what we truly know and who we ultimately are.

But as creatrixes, we dedicate ourselves to learning the language of the soul, its signs and symbols. We learn to see beyond the daily world of forms and to travel vast tracts of internal space and time. Through the creative process we weave new languages, new identities, new worlds from these. We create a new reality that we and, if we have the courage and platform to share it, others can inhabit alongside us.

> "
> The call to the creative life is a call to dignity, to a life of vulnerability, and adventure.
>
> John O'Donohue

The Heroine's Journey

For most of his-story the path of the creative has been described, celebrated and mythologised as a Hero's Journey – both the creator and their characters epitomising the archetypal masculine journey.

The Hero's Journey was articulated most clearly by Joseph Campbell in his 1949 book, *The Hero with a Thousand Faces*. It has dominated storytelling from the very first myths and legends through Bible stories to the Hollywood blockbusters of today. Whilst it does also reflect an inner journey to a degree, its main focus is on the outer world: the Hero leaving home, finding a teacher, overcoming obstacles, slaying the dragon and returning home with the princess he has saved. It is so familiar to us all. And yet because of this we do not tend to see it as just one possible archetypal process, skewed towards the masculine, rather than The Ultimate Truth, as patriarchal culture has insisted it is.

This depiction of The Hero's Journey is adapted from Christopher Vogler's, *The Writer's Journey*, based on Joseph Campbell's work.

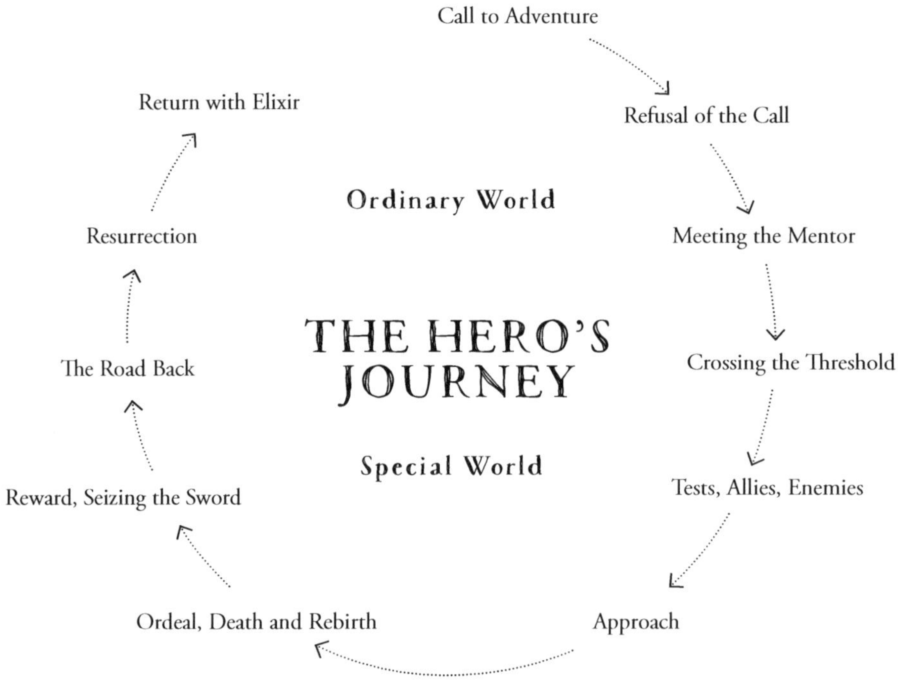

However, for many women this path of outer individuation is far less pressing or even relevant, within patriarchy, than the inner journey of reconnecting with the lost Feminine and the inner trials and tribulations that this incurs. And so another model was presented: The Heroine's Journey, that begins with separation from the Feminine and finishes with integration of Masculine and Feminine, as articulated by Maureen Murdock in her book *The Heroine's Journey*, from which this diagram is taken.

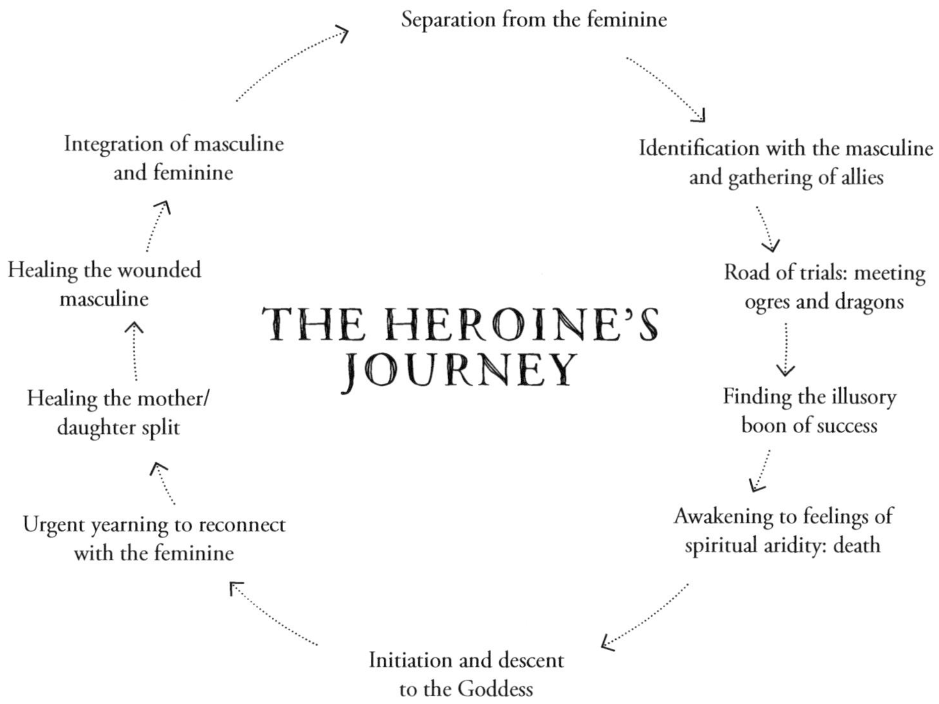

As illustrator, Alice Meichi Li, says in an article comparing the two,

> *A hero is coming from an ordinary world and already knows how to play by the rules and has mentors to help conquer any obstacles. A heroine starts a journey with disadvantages. […] A hero's journey is the journey of someone who has privilege. Regardless if the protagonist is male or female, a heroine does not start out with privilege.*

It is my understanding that the Creatrix combines these two archetypal paths: The Heroine's Journey, the inner journey of reclaiming and integrating our native Feminine creative process, with The Hero's Journey – the struggles associated with sharing our creative work with the outer world.

My intention with *Creatrix* is to help us rebalance the creative energies within and without, to support us as creatives, in letting the Feminine lead the way and then finding ways to integrate the Masculine in a supportive and empowering partnership.

Other Archetypes of Creativity

I want to take a moment here to briefly introduce some of the other archetypes that we'll meet along The Creative Way as we journey through our consciousness and the creative process. The first group are often elements of the Creatrix archetype, or appear alongside it. These include:

"

Archetypes [are] constantly repeating characters or energies which occur in the dreams of all people and the myths of all cultures.

Christopher Vogler, *The Writer's Journey*

The Storyteller – one who creates a narrative of our experiences using words.

The Entertainer – the part of us that loves to play to an audience.

The Shapeshifter – our chameleon nature that shifts from one form to another, refusing solidity or permanence.

The Visionary – one who sees with the inner eye and relies on intuition.

The Artist – one who expresses themselves creatively.

The Crazy Woman – often condemned, confined and medicalised by our culture, she holds a powerful rebellious energy and ability to embody the forbidden parts of the psyche.[xxv]

The Magician – one who makes the impossible happen, who makes things appear or disappear at will and has supernatural control over their surroundings.

Burning Woman – the incendiary Feminine power, our burning passion, that has often been condemned as witchcraft and burned at the stake to silence its heresy. I coined the term in my book, *Burning Woman.*

Medicine Woman – the soul of Feminine healing energy. See my book, *Medicine Woman.*

The Hero/Heroine – the central character around whom the story is woven.

The Hunter – one who tracks patterns and ideas, following hints and traces.

Archetypes that the Creatrix often engages with on The Creative Way include:

The Critic – one who criticises, for many different reasons. They can appear as the judge, the editor, or even the troll – the monster who hides under the bridge and seeks to destroy the Heroine.

The Witness – the wise, inner reflective nature.

The Mentor – a teacher or guide to the journey who imparts wisdom and helps the Heroine to develop their skills.

The Gatekeeper/Threshold Guardian – one who protects or guards a new stage of the journey.

As we name these archetypes here, we can begin to acquaint ourselves with the possibility that these are not the personal forces we have taken them to be when we previously encountered them (in ourselves or others). Rather they are archetypal roles: energetic, psychic forces that play out universally in each of our lives. Our job is to respond archetypally, and understand them in terms of the part they play in the larger story of The Creative Way. When they are no longer considered personal they cause us less upset and we can interact with them in a more conscious, less reactive manner. And our interactions with them can impart wisdom.

But chances are you will forget.

We all do.

Until we remember again.

"

You know that crazy heart of yours? The one with lightning crackling and moonlight shining through it. The one you've been told not to trust because it often led you off the beaten path. The one so many have misunderstood your entire life. Trust it. Feed it. Grow it. It's your greatest treasure and will point the way to your highest destiny. It is the voice of your soul.

– Jacob Nordby

The Creative Way as a Path to Psychological Integration

This is a powerful and necessary journey.

And you, dear one, are more than capable of it. You are so much greater than our culture allows for.

You feel deeply. You know more than you should. You are called by something greater than your individual self to engage with life more fully, on behalf of us all.

Your creativity is the bridge, the thread, the glue between your daily self and your individual soul.

You are destined for greatness.

For you are a Shapeshifter and a Magician. You are an Edgewalker and Time Traveller. You are a courageous and messy human ensouled, in a world that insists that you live the life of a machine.

The world will try to keep you on the surface. It will shackle you to the sink and the desk. It will try to keep your spirits up, to keep you from your soul. But your soul has come to claim you, so that you may know the fullness of your power, the brilliance of your body and mind that the world tells you are faulty or broken.

Your time has come.

Your destiny is waiting.

Will you answer its call?

Creative Inquiry

Labels

- How do you define creative? How much do our definitions align and where do we differ?
- Do you have a sense of *create or die* in your own life? What is it that drives you?
- What happens if you don't create?
- Who do you consider a real, proper Artist? What qualifies them as such?
- Have you ever defined yourself as an Artist, Writer, Actor…? What was your journey to claiming this for yourself like?
- Do you question your right to be creative? Why do you think this is?
- How has your family defined, supported, shaped or restricted your creativity?
- Have you ever questioned the right of another to define what they do as art? Why do you think this is?
- In what ways do you consider creativity a superpower? What challenges does it bring with it?
- What are the curses of creativity? What impact have they had on your life?
- Do other people define you as an Artist? How does that feel to you?
- How does the term Highly Creative Person feel to you?
- Have you come across the Creatrix archetype before? If so, where?

- What resonance does she have for you? What mystery does she hold?
- Which of the other archetypes are you familiar with and which are new?
- What creatrixes do you have in your life? Authors, teachers, friends…

Women and Art

- Do you think being female impacts the art you make?
- Do you think being female impacts how your work is perceived or valued?
- Do you like being defined as a female artist, or do you prefer your art to be seen as genderless?
- How is your life experience different for being a woman?
- What of your pain and pleasure is uniquely female?
- What has been silenced because it was too Feminine…or not feminine enough?
- Do you identify more with The Hero's or Heroine's Journey? Why is this do you think?

Creative Practice

The Creative Way

- What does The Creative Way look like and feel like for you? Can you draw, paint, write or collage it? These questions might help guide you when you consider how to express this.

- When did you first discover it?
- How does it make you feel?
- Are all parts of it visible?
- Is it internal or external to your body?
- What are its signposts?
- How does it correspond to or navigate the natural world?
- Where has it taken you so far…and do you have a sense of where it is leading?
- What does it feel like to be on it?
- What is the path made of?
- What landscape is it taking you through?
- What are the qualities of the path itself: wide, winding, overgrown, illuminated?
- Can you see any traces of where you have been?
- Is the path pre-existent or are you creating it as you go along?
- Are you alone on it? Do you have any sort of guide or companion?
- Are there any footsteps or tracks that you are following?

Creating an Image of Creatrix

Create an image of the Creatrix archetype for yourself out of whatever materials call you. Paint her, draw her, collage or art journal her. Sculpt her from clay or papier maché, needle-felt or knit her…why not dance or play her? What does she look like?

What symbols represent her? What colour and form suits her best? Where might you keep her so her presence is visible to you as you continue to read? Do you want to add her to an altar space, or make one in her honour? If so, what might you surround her with?

Lineage

> "Most of us are not raised to actively encounter our destiny. We may not know that we have one.
>
> Julia Cameron

Every artist has a lineage, a series of artists who have either personally taught or inspired them in their work. They may have taught you skills, or modelled what a creative life can look like. Tracing our lineage provides powerful insight, and helps to give clarity to previous mysterious facets of ourselves.

Where do you come from?

Try to answer this on as many levels as you can: geographically, genetically, culturally, intellectually – what are your roots? What do you love about this, and what scares you? Do you try to hide or ignore anything about your inheritance? What have you not been told about it?

On whose shoulders do you stand?

Write a list or a mind map, create an art journal page or collage of the artists, books, teachers, styles of art that have influenced you. Include photographs or sketches of them or their work. Add in some of their most inspiring quotations to encourage you on your journey. You'll probably want quite a big page! You might want to attach threads to each one and see how they interweave.

The Hero's/Heroine's Journey

Create an image or map to represent the stages of The Hero's Journey, or illustrate the one in this book. Create another to represent the stages of The Heroine's Journey. How do they differ? What parts have you struggled with in the past or been unaware of? How might you combine them visually? In what ways are they similar to your map of The Creative Way, and in what ways do they differ?

2

I am she who stands
One foot on the moon,
One on the sun,
Thread of time in hand
And begins to weave
Through the stars.

SPACE

> “The most regretful people on earth are those who felt the call to creative work, who felt their own creative power restive and uprising, and gave to it neither power nor time.
>
> Mary Oliver

Space and Time

In almost every interview I do, the question comes up: *what are your top tips for getting creative?*

I understand it. Creativity appears to be a mysterious force. When we first consider creating we think that we have to bring all of the energy and the vision. But the truth is that they are gifted to us…or rather activated in us. What is required of us is our body and consciousness as a container for the creative flow to pour through.

And so my answer is always the same: create space and create time and then keep showing up.

Making space and time to create sounds so simple. But for most of us, especially women, it is powerful work. And an on-going practice.

Creating a spatio-temporal container into which you can disappear, make magic unseen and reappear transformed is not to be underestimated. Before you make one piece of art, or write a single word, you have taken a quantum leap. Reclaiming your time, reclaiming your space, reclaiming your right to your voice, your imagination, your body, your own energy, every feeling and thought that has been denied or dismissed, reclaiming every form of expression…this in itself is revolutionary.

A Room of One's Own

The idea of a room of one's own resonates strongly with most creative women today. Having a physical space where your creations and materials are safe and untouched, where you can feel private and unobserved when you labour and birth your creative babes is not a given, nor to be taken for granted. When Virginia Woolf wrote about it almost a hundred years ago, having a room of one's own was a ground-breaking political statement of women's empowerment. The tragedy is that, for most of us, it still is.

We all know that making a space to create with materials and tools, good light, a comfy chair, a practical surface, a view perhaps, books, images, colours, fabrics and artefacts to fascinate and delight, and of course your own artworks and works in progress will help to activate the creative process. But most of us cannot afford to have a spare bedroom, let alone a dedicated studio, certainly at the beginning of our creative lives.

> A woman must have money and a room of her own if she is to write.
>
> Virginia Woolf, *A Room of One's Own*

Please do not let the lack of a dedicated studio space get in the way of your being creative. It's much easier to blame the lack of a room than our own fear of getting started. You must start somewhere. In fact, not having the financial overheads of a dedicated studio space is often a blessing in disguise starting out, as it allows more space and time to experiment and find your authentic creative voice without added pressure.

You will probably have to be both creative and flexible in finding a way to get what you need. So often the spaces we use are not our own. They are borrowed or shared. Your space might start as a box with a lid, a shelf or drawer or cupboard that is totally yours. Or perhaps the kitchen table after the rest of your household have gone to bed. Or a corner of your bedroom. You can create pretty much anywhere when you need to. And I have. In parks, on pavements, in cars, in cafés, in armchairs, whilst breastfeeding, in bed…

> An artist must either find or *make* solitude to work in.
>
> Elizabeth Barrett Browning

I remember yearning for a room of my own, but with three bedrooms for five family members and a husband also working from home, this seemed a total fantasy. I wrote on my blog about my dream for my own creative space. I had a fantasy of a little cabin in the woods, like Henry Thoreau, or one of my favourite writers Louise Erdrich. But we live on a housing estate and we own no woods.

Then two weeks later a friend who reads my blog, whose parents own the adjoining property, said she had a little shed at the bottom of their land which she used to use for painting but no longer needed: *would I like it?* It was just over our boundary, in the woods. That was my first room of my own. A place where I could shut the door and not be mama for a while. I could be free with my thoughts and my words. It was cold and damp and dark…but it was a creative space close to home.

Since then I have worked in a Japanese-style tea house at the bottom of my father's garden, in old offices, an unfitted house, a huge amount from bed, as well as on our kitchen table and the corner of the sofa. In that time I have written nine books and run a creative business. These have proven to me that you don't need money to have a creative space, or some beautifully fitted out, purpose-built studio in order to be productive. Just get clear about what you *need* right now, and get creative in finding it and assertive in claiming it.

> "In our Western culture, we're always rushing to fill something, do something, make something [...] As a result we are almost unaware of the space prior to the doing or making as being anything that is relevant or worthy. It's almost as if we can only see ourselves if we see what we've done to the thing rather than being in the presence of what we have yet to do.
>
> Day Schildkret, *Morning Altars*

Clearing Space

Each of us has a different understanding of what a space must look like in order to be able to work. Many of the creatives I spoke to talked about needing to have a really clean, clear physical space before they can even think about getting creative. They find that working in a clear space allows them to have a clear head, rather than being disorganised and constantly tripping over junk. But, and this is a big but, the need for a clear space can be a block to creativity.

If we cannot start until the house is perfectly clean and tidy, the chances are we won't start at all. We will spend so long cleaning, or making the perfect studio, that our time is over before we have even begun to create. Many people use the safety of the known, such as domestic cleaning, as a form of procrastination, so that they can further put off what scares them most: entering the process and getting messy.

Wherever we create, the primary focus needs to be not décor, but a safe space: a place where we can access the underworld of our psyches and immerse ourselves in the void.

If you have given birth or seen an animal doing so, you will know that safe space is a mammalian requirement, both to protect ourselves and our offspring physically, but also to allow our brains to shift from daily fight or flight living into the primal state needed to give birth.

Creativity is no different. We need a sense of core safety so that our daily persona can be put aside, our defences dropped and the shape-shifting of creativity can occur. Creativity needs the same conditions as birth or making love – a safe outer womb-space to protect the vulnerable power of the inner womb-space as it opens to life.

The creative soul simply needs a trusted empty space in which to try things out unobserved and make mistakes. It needs a boundary – even if it is psychological – to keep the world at bay.

Taking Up Space

The act of creating – or claiming – space is as much a psychological act of valuing our own need to create, as that which we create in that space.

We might have made space, or been given space, now we need to fully take it up. This is something I have always struggled with. The child of divorce and many house-moves, I have my belongings in boxes and bags, waiting for the next move. I find it hard to settle in, to make myself at home in any space. There is a constant anxiety and guilt at play, knowing that my being there is a potential imposition on the needs of others. And I worry that the moment I get attached to anywhere I will need to relinquish it. So it is easier not to get attached at all.

I know I am not alone. The conscious taking of space for ourselves and claiming what we need goes against much of what we have been taught as women. I have noticed that this happens not just in the rooms we inhabit, but also in our own bodies and personalities. We are encultured as women to take up as little space as possible and to apologise for any trace of ourselves that might intrude upon another.

So when we create space for creativity, yes, we put up shelves for our books, make room for our brushes and pens, make sure we have floor space to move, ensure the lighting is good. But the most important thing we make space for is ourselves. Making space for magic to happen, allowing enough space for The Work's quiet voice to be heard.

In time, as you learn what matters most to you, you will refine and evolve your creative space into a sanctuary, a container to hold you whilst you fall apart and weave yourself back together, a place to keep your stuff and yourself safe whilst you're playing with the stars.

> A sacred space is built around the heart of creativity; fortified by experience, it grows to become a safe space for us to be, make things and find our wisdom.
>
> Rachael Matthews, *The Mindfulness in Knitting*

Creatrix Speaks

> How huge it is, how empty, this great space for which I have been longing all my life.
>
> —Iris Murdoch, *The Sea, The Sea*

*Sometimes we have to sit in that excruciating place
of living into the edge of all that we are,
on the very brink of our own creation,
while the wind blows cold around us,
as we face the enormous task
of allowing ourselves to be unapologetically
as powerful as we really are,
allowing ourselves to ask unapologetically
for what we deserve.
Sometimes our fellow humans
haven't learnt yet how to fully see us,
how to truly behold us in all that we are.
So we stand alone,
courageous and afraid,
exhilarated and uncertain,
bearing the fierce winds of this frontier place,
where few dare to tread.
If you look far across, on your periphery,
you will see that you are not alone,
there are others standing on that edge,
equally called to be in the absolute autonomy of their aloneness,
as they too become so uniquely what they were born to be.
Enduring the absolute solitude
when even the people who love us
don't have eyes with which to see
the truth of who we are.
In this place we might become wild,
driven to the brink of madness and back,
a thousand times.
When we follow our innermost authority*

there is no external resource
to reassure and to placate,
just this almighty risk of one's own becoming.
That eternal journeying into the places within
where no being has journeyed before.
The wild frontier,
where hungry beasts howl in the darkness
and the insidious tricks of our shadows
loom and dance grotesque in the solitude.
The jeering voices deriding the innocence,
absconding creation back to the smallness of
How dare you?
and Who do you think you are?
As we rise and rise again,
journeying back into the wilderness
of our own innate wisdom,
relentlessly scratching the ground,
blood and earth in our fingernails,
desperately seeking the taproot
of our own succulent beauty,
our plumply radiant health,
our own awesome empowerment.
A lifetime of longing to be seen,
without ever truly seeing ourselves,
a lifetime of wanting love,
traipsing through the barren biology of loss,
without ever truly gathering up that frightened, hidden, dark one,
into our arms and loving her,
enlivening her,
filling her from our own overflowing breasts,
retrieving her from the darklands.
The wild rage of not having been seen,

and the soft question beneath
of how do we yet hide from ourselves
this deep profound potential of
all that we are
all that we have
as the veils fall
and the shackles crumble
in the face of our brave standing in that ferocious wind,
is the anchor of this softly radiant and precious body
and the deep nourishment of our own beauty
as we birth ourselves upon the Earth,
and Her deep thunderous birthsong
crooning to us from the deep,
as alone we emerge,
like the brilliant wildflower births herself
through the barren crust,
or a supernova,
alive in the cosmic throb.

Lucy

TIME

Claiming Time

Most of us have learned to be busy as a default way of earning our right to be here. We spend our time looking after others, attending to their needs, working hard, earning money. We do it consciously and unconsciously… not just because we have to, but because it is safer to. So that we aren't accused of laziness. So that we don't have to face what lies within. So we don't have to encounter the void. Busyness allows us to stay disconnected from the deeper levels of ourselves and others and run on autopilot, whilst gaining social approval for superficial success.

In order to create we have to make a conscious effort to step away from this busyness and the approval it garners us. Learning to untangle ourselves from the sticky web of daily life is one of the major challenges of creativity. Creativity takes time from the other demands in our lives. Usually lots of it. Time has to be carved out, negotiated, scheduled in and accounted for in order to create. We need unpredictable amounts for planning, gestating ideas, research, making, editing and sharing our work. Time that we can find it hard to explain or justify…especially when there is little product to show for it. But still we must, or we will find we have none left to dedicate to The Work of our creativity.

The agency to claim this time for our own priorities has been denied women for most of history. And so we are, still, in the twenty-first century, in the words of indomitable US public representative, Maxine Waters, *reclaiming our time.*

"

The great thing about being an artist is that you can create time, you are not ruled by it.

Josephine Meckseper

Experience

I am often asked what my days look like, how I manage to fit writing, art-making and editing into a life already full of children.

I understand this curiosity. For years I have been fascinated by the creative habits of others, not just to pick up hints and tricks from other artists, nor even to see if I was 'doing it right' but really just to see the invisible lives of fellow creatives, to get a glimpse of the creative process that tends to lie hidden.

> "If what it takes to create are long stretches of time alone, that's something women have never had the luxury to expect.
>
> Brigid Schulte

My days ideally start with time to myself. As I transition from sleep, I need my own headspace to process and integrate my inner world. If I have had a powerful dream, I write it down. If my emotions or mind are churning on something, I do a WORD+image piece to try and figure out what is going on for me. If ideas were coming to me as I fell asleep and I didn't write them down, I try to follow the thread and note them down. Most of the time I lie still and think. And then I read or knit as the thoughts percolate.

Whatever I do, I do it quietly and in bed to allow myself as much time before the others in the house wake. This is my sanity time. If I am jolted too fast from sleep to mothering my brain jangles for the rest of the day and I find it hard to focus on anything, I feel scattered and untethered. I am someone who finds transitions challenging in general, but for me the transition from the inner to the outer world is the hardest of all. I am still learning how to be able to embody both simultaneously. Ideally I would do some movement at this point, but this will make others aware that they need me. So I leave it until later.

Then it's breakfasts and making school lunches and putting up hair and signing homework journals and finding shoes and dealing with emotional upsets. If it goes smoothly then I come back and dive straight into movement and writing. It is rare that this happens. But I love it when it does.

I try to set my intention to write the night before. I focus my energy towards it and tell my family. When something comes up – with kids or the business – I feel frustrated and upset. My energy is now chaotic and pointing into a void. I won't pretend I don't get resentful. But sometimes – often – when I want to write, I try and the ideas come to nothing. Then it's myself I get frustrated at.

When I hit a block or a spell of procrastination I tend to push on for a while – usually much too long – before finally remembering that it never works. Then I might go for a walk on the beach, or read a book connected to what I'm writing. If I'm being lazy, which is much of the time, I'll stay where I am and trawl the internet, following an invisible trail of articles shared on Facebook. Sometimes I might let myself do some art (though it feels like a waste of precious time when I should be writing.) Sometimes I put on some music and dance – I always forget how good this makes me feel.

With each book I develop a playlist, and listen to the same songs each day before I start writing. I sing to them, move to them, meditate to them... I have another playlist of sacred instrumental music that I listen to with big noise cancelling headphones when I write – this is especially helpful when I'm writing in a café waiting to collect a child from somewhere. The music weaves into the fabric of my being as I work on the project and connects me with the energy I am trying to articulate through my words.

Chocolate has become an important part of my writing routine – dark chocolate eaten ceremonially – savoured and slowly. I don't drink coffee, but I guess it does the same thing: the hit of caffeine and sugar to kickstart the system.

Most of the time when I sit to write I have the 'bones' of my work ready – jotted notes on scraps of paper or in my journal that have landed as sparks of inspiration through the previous days. My job is to expand upon them, give examples, continue the flow

> ”
>
> Carve out the time. Notice I do not say find the time. That is an absurd and dangerous phrase. Time is never lying around waiting for us to find her. She is elusive. She wants you to sculpt her like clay, to mold her into exactly the form you desire your days to take. Time wants you to realize that she is the most precious and irreducible fact in your life. Make her into what you will.
>
> – Jennifer Louden

of them, find a place for them in the work. This is often quite a dispiriting process – what sounded profound at 3am sounds trite or downright obvious in the cold light of morning. Or, worse, I discover that this new inspiration is actually something I have written in almost identical ways twice already in the book. This happens a lot when you have such a broken up creative process on a large project. It is frustrating.

I devour words like a starving woman – from the internet, books and TV, so am always weaving in ideas that I pick up from there. I am a real magpie, as you have no doubt seen. Often they can be ideas reasonably disconnected from the topic I am writing about, but they give me a word, a pattern, a lead that I need to follow and incorporate in order to articulate my knowing more clearly.

And sometimes I literally run to my computer, shoo away any member of my family that approaches and write like a maniac until the flow finishes. It may be ten minutes or two hours. However long it is, it is magical. My family knows to leave me alone at this time: the flow cannot be broken and will not wait for me or anything else. When this happens in the middle of a busy day it is tricky. If I am out, I grab the nearest piece of paper to hand and disappear to a bathroom. If I am driving, I dictate to the child sitting next to me.

Because of how I work, a lot of the time my daily work is moving paragraphs around, reading through the work again and again and editing ad nauseum. Shortening sentences. Adding and taking away commas. Replacing … with – . There is nothing glamorous or even fun about it. It is slow work, tough for such an impatient person. But it's where the final magic is done: the polishing, the spotting of patterns, the dumping of dross, the honing of metaphor and theme, as I follow the invisible energy through the whole piece – be it book or article – to see where it gets stuck and how it can be freed.

Though you might find it hard to believe for a writer as 'prolific' as me, I am not someone who gets many writing days. I am just fast at channelling the initial work through. I spend far more time answering emails, promoting books, networking on Facebook and Instagram, parenting and being ill. My time is mainly spent on the business of being a working creatrix and the living of life, rather than the writing. And again, I find this frustrating, with so many creative ideas jostling to be born through me. But I remind myself gently that most writers just write...they don't also publish several other peoples' books each year and make art too!

Writing requires me to dive deep, and I have a life where that is not possible nearly as much as I want. Instead I must go and collect a child from the train now, and another from a different school and then do snacks, then dinner, and hang up the washing. And it is my writing that must wait. I will do a little here and there throughout the day, but the deep dives, I long for more, always. But I also know that when I finally get them it will be when my children are grown and I will miss these frantic days of motherhood filled with love, frustration and busyness.

> By marking time with beauty made from our hands and our words, we can slow down the moment so as to find our way back into it.
>
> Day Schildkret, *Morning Altars*

Chronos and Kairos

The ancient Greeks had two words for time. *Chronos*, from which we get the word chronological, which refers to the only time we in the Western world recognise: linear, sequential time. And *kairos*, a specific, opportune moment that stands apart – a time that is timeless, perpetual, "a passing instant when an opening appears which must be driven through if success is to be achieved." [xxvi]

The most crucial creative moments require *kairos*. And the act of creativity itself seems to happen in time out of time. "Artmaking as a practice stops time," notes Pat B. Allen in *Art is a Spiritual Practice*. Entering the creative realm seems to allow us to bend the law of physics...so we can step out of daily time, and into the universality of soul time. But the products of our creativity are often dictated by the constraints of *chronos*. This is the endless challenge for the creatrix moving between the two worlds.

Rhythm and Routine

"Habits have an undeserved reputation as unconscious, rigid patterns that stifle creative flow. But, consciously cultivated, habits can be the protective riverbanks that guide the effortless flow of your creative energy.

Hiro Boga

Much is written about having a creative routine: writing a thousand words a day, good or bad, in sickness or in health, come rain, shine or Christmas. And yet I find it ironic that one of the most celebrated authors who insisted upon this approach, Harper Lee, managed only two novels in over fifty years.

As creatrixes we certainly have to learn to show up again and again, even when inspiration seems far away. But if this is merely by force, I feel that there is some sort of violence against the self, which in the end will never lead to full and authentic co-creation with soul and Source. Connection cannot be forced – it is a two-way process. So yes, we have to show up when we receive the call. And yes, we have to show up when it's not all unicorns and daisies. But forcing ourselves is not a healthy habit to get into. The Feminine has been forced to bend to the masculine will for the whole of our his-story. It is important that this stops with us.

We certainly need to make our creativity a regular practice in order to keep our skills honed, and I think this is what the emphasis is on when folks say you have to write a thousand words a day. But it's like saying you have to cycle a hundred miles a day so you don't forget how. If you don't cycle for a year, you're bound to be a little unfit and wobbly when you get back on the saddle. And your bike will also be rusty. So, yes, frequent practice is a good idea for both vehicle and rider. But the chances are you'll choose to ride frequently because you need to go places and you enjoy getting out and about, because you enjoy the wind in your hair, the pounding of your heart and the feeling of using your muscles. So it is with creativity. And just as with sport, the active portion – practicing our skills and performing in front of others – is only part of it. If we do not incorporate resting and recovery periods we damage ourselves. A routine that focuses only on what we do and make will always lead to lesser work and more suffering.

When I was a young mother I wrote an article about the difference between routine – a mindless clock-based adherence to doing things according to externally appointed rules – and routine, an inner-driven motivation which works in response to the rhythms and cycles around us. At the time I was writing about it in terms of baby-care – but the same holds for the nurturing of our creative babies. The morality of routine has been pushed hard during the mechanisation of human culture and the drive for ever-greater 'efficiency' judged by external authorities. We have internalised this way of being which is not natural to us as cyclical creatures of flesh and blood.

You need to find your own tempo at different parts of the creative journey, different times of year and different periods in your life. Honour these changes of tempo, weave them into your work. This is the pulse of your creative work. Keep your finger on it and it will bring your art to life, and keep you healthy and productive at the same time.

Know yourself.

Commit to your creativity.

And be kind to yourself in the process.

"

Do not fast forward into something you're not ready for. Or allow yourself to shrink back into what's comfortable. Growth lives in the uneasiness. The in-between. The unfinished sentence. You are a season, a season of becoming.

Adrienne Watts

Experience

I know that others schedule in creative days, whole seasons in the winter or writing retreats at beautiful woodland artist colonies. To me it feels like scheduling in sex. I have learned from experience that there is one thing guaranteed to dampen my healthy libido than a planned romantic weekend. I feel the pressure to be 'up for it' and my desire shrivels up like last week's birthday balloon.

I am never in the mood when I feel under pressure. I am used to creating in the corners of my life, in the midst of business and busyness, curled up in an armchair with the kids careening around me, or in my room knowing that I have to be down in ten minutes for dinner. Just as even in my dreams sex is interrupted by kids, so it is with my creativity. If I have too much space and time for it, I am like a rabbit in the headlights: I feel the pressure and freeze. I prefer to sidle up sideways to it. To trick myself into creating.

Creativity for me is preceded by a feeling of agitation, a sensate formless urgency that longs to be fulfilled. Its expression is an inner journey along a clear but unseen path, mirrored by, guided by, expressed by external actions, leading to a sense of deep satisfaction and joyous emptiness of self on completion. Much like sex. When the inner agitant is gone, I can rest in the embrace of the Universe: I am an empty vessel, aware that something powerful, mysterious and magnificent has just passed through my body. Something that was both me, and not me at all. Something that I made happen, and yet was powerless in its grips.

And so I find myself snatching illicit moments in the corners of my days, for quickies with the muse. I have to be ready to drop everything and strip at a moment's notice. To devour and be devoured in the messy impromptu orgy of creative passion. And to be daring enough to play with myself in between times, to indulge in regular creative onanism to help keep my juices flowing and my desire fresh, when she's off visiting her other lovers. Just like me... she comes most magnificently in the darkness.

Deadlines

> One forges one's style on the terrible anvil of daily deadlines.
>
> —Émile Zola

A deadline – be it a publishing agreement, the date of an event or the need to exchange our work for money – requires that we fit the unknowable path of a creative project, with all its unforeseen twists and turns, into a time-based framework.

Rare is the person who is genuinely unfazed by a deadline. For many of us, the *create or die* energy kicks in internally at the beginning of the process when the invitation to create is received, and is only alleviated by the completion of the creative act. Others need the external imposition of an approaching deadline to rouse the creative juices and spur them to action. I could see both clearly represented by the creatrixes featured in this book.

I have noticed that each of us tends to have our own unique places of struggle during the creative process – and I wonder to what extent this reflects our experience of other deadlines in our life and how they impacted us. For when stress levels rise, often we revert to these psychological defaults.

The most profound of these was our own birth experience. As a surprise baby, I wonder if my own anticipatory anxiety is high because of not knowing how I would be received. In birth this played out as a forceps delivery, I had to be pulled out head-first by force. I would suggest that you consider your own birth experience, and also, if you have birthed babies, your experience of approaching their due dates: were they pre-mature, overdue, induced or on time and how did those involved respond to this?

With experience we learn that all projects, just like all births, have their own innate rhythm and that no matter how much we try to push and shove, some are slow-burns or simply need more time. This is why, as creatrixes, our deadlines must always be negotiated four ways: between ourselves, those we are creating for, the work and the creative Source.

A due date in itself is not inherently a bad thing. Rather it is the narrative that our inner Storyteller weaves around what it means that causes the stress. In many ways a deadline creates one edge of a much-needed container for our creative energy. It is a limitation imposed by the material world on the ineffable and expansive possibility of any creative project. However much we resist or resent it, a deadline becomes, by its very presence, a part of the final creation.

PROCESS

> “The creative process, so far as we are able to follow it at all, consists in the unconscious activation of an archetypal image and elaborating and shaping the image into the finished work. By giving it shape, the artist translates it into the language of the present and so makes it possible for us to find our way back to the deepest springs of life.
>
> C.G. Jung

Visualising The Creative Process

The internal emotional journey of creativity often tends to be made up of many periods of soaring highs and crashing lows that can be isolating, exhilarating and overwhelming. Like most things in life, we believe that we are alone in this unique experience. It can be truly scary and this fear of the unknown can stop us in our tracks at any point. Each new project can seem daunting, disorientating and directionless.

It looks something like this…

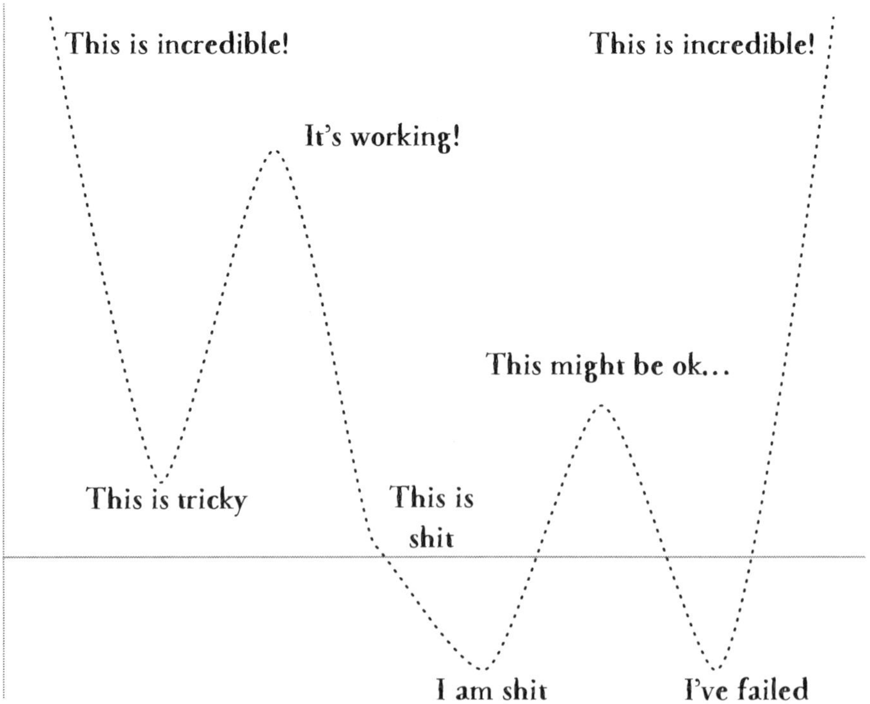

This graph reflects many similar diagrams of the creative experience which I have seen shared on social media over the years, accompanied by knowing comments from creative people relieved to find a reflection of what the unseen journey of creativity feels like. It feels personal, when we are going through it. But the fact that it is so universally recognised shows that there is obviously a common human experience of the creative process. Whether we are writing a book, designing a dress, painting a picture or composing music, the seemingly erratic emotional rollercoaster ride is actually an accurate reflection of an inner journey. It is an archetypal path known intuitively to the soul and collectively experienced. It is real.

Each time we begin a new project it is, of course, a unique journey – if we are making art that challenges and excites us and our audience. With each project we must find a way to build a bridge from the known world into unknown realms with this specific project: energetically, intellectually, technically and aesthetically. But the creative process itself does not change.

In order to begin to visualise The Creative Way, it is helpful to understand it as being divided in four energetic movements. These energetic shifts are the same whether we are thinking of the shift of the seasons, the rhythms of sex or birth.

	Energetic	Sexual	Seasonal	Birth
Stage One	Receptive	Arousal	Spring	Conception
Stage Two	Generative	Building energy	Summer	Pregnancy
Stage Three	Expressive	Orgasm	Autumn	Birth
Stage Four	Restorative	Refractory period /Rest	Winter	Fourth Trimester

How do we know that we have reached the next stage? We sense the creative energy shift, our inner energy, and our feelings along with it. At times the shifts are sudden and violent. At others, it is often not quite clear until we have passed through, where exactly the threshold is. This is why I prefer to understand it not in terms of discrete boxes, but rather a spiralling journey.

This spiralling journey has been expressed for thousands of years within many different spiritual traditions in the form of a labyrinth. Labyrinths come in many shapes and forms, from the simplest spiral path, to the complex rose-shaped labyrinth in Chartres Cathedral in France. Though they can have different numbers of paths (circuits) and take different forms, the anatomy of the labyrinth is innately simple: one entrance, one path and a centre.

At first glance a labyrinth resembles a maze, as both are made of winding paths. But there is a vital difference: "A labyrinth is a right-brain intuitional tool. The maze is a left-brain analytical puzzle." [xxvii] Mazes have dead ends, and wrong turns, whereas a labyrinth has just one path leading into the centre and out again. Unlike the maze, which is there to trick us into going the wrong way, in a labyrinth we cannot ever go wrong.

When we walk a labyrinth we are doing no more than spiralling in and out a number of times as we move ever-closer to the centre, and then following the same path as we head back out. However, the labyrinth design makes this seem less straightforward than a simple spiral, because we cannot anticipate the path ahead with our minds. We cannot visually or logically figure out where the path is taking us, and so we must trust ourselves and the path to lead us to our destination. Although walking a labyrinth might *feel* like we are going around in circles getting nowhere, in fact, we are always moving on through: we cannot lose our way.

In terms of its use as a metaphor for the creative process, the labyrinth is of course a simplified image. The Creative Way is multi-dimensional – taking us not just forwards and back, left to right, but in and out through physical and emotional space and time. It is a pathway that we traverse not just with our metaphorical feet, but with our whole selves, over the course of a lifetime or even several, spirals within spirals.

Just like a labyrinth, The Creative Way has both Circuits (or pathways), and what I call Moments of Transition (marked with an * in the following sections). The shape of the labyrinth echoes the graph that started this chapter. The swift shifts in energy – the peaks and troughs that make it look like a rollercoaster – are the Moments, the longer lines are Circuits.

At these Moments, the energy shifts quickly, the path no longer stretches ahead but takes an abrupt turn. We tend to have a big emotional experience at these Moments, as our energetic flow hits a point of resistance and has to navigate the bend before we can move forwards. We tend to experience these Moments as exhilarating or exciting when we start going up, and when we reach the peak. The creative energy is expanding, our bodyminds are too, our hormones and neurotransmitters are all helping the emergent positive feelings. Our hearts feel open, we feel lighter, clear-headed and can see the whole vista. Whereas when the energy starts to contract, our inner experience is a descent, we feel despair, frustration, negativity and out of control in a bad way. Our vision darkens and our ability to see options diminishes.

It is interesting to note that the first half of the journey is an inner-directed spiral led by intuition. It is focused on our own personal witnessing of the *vision* – the receiving of it, acceptance and commitment to it, and the first private articulation of it. This would traditionally be considered a more Feminine, 'passive' part of the creative process: The Heroine's Journey.

The second half of the journey, back out of the labyrinth, is the traditionally 'Masculine' part: the active process of refinement of the vision into matter, the overcoming of inner and outer obstacles, in order to express it into the world.

It is important to remember that we may experience certain parts of the journey in a slightly different order to what I share here. Or we may find ourselves revisiting the same parts of the process several times during one project. If we are working on a short project, then the separate Circuits and Moments may not be so pronounced, whereas on a book-, exhibition- or album-length project they will be more apparent. If we are multi-passionate creatives, we may be at one point of The Creative Way with one project and at a totally different place with another. We may even find ourselves in a couple of places simultaneously.

As a final note, I must caution you that the more aware you become of The Creative Way, you will begin to see that it is echoed in your outer life. It is a lover of synchronicity and irony: if we are not learning on one level, and insist on continuing doing what we have always done, it will reinforce the lessons of The Way in many other areas our lives.

So with that warning in place, take my hand, and let us journey through the Circuits and Moments of The Creative Way together.

"The richer and broader the inputs, the more the brain has to play with. Creativity doesn't mean making something out of nothing, instead it means refashioning what already exists: bending, breaking, blending...

Dr David Eagleman, *The Creative Brain*

The Inner-Directed Spiral

Creative Bathing

Walking The Creative Way sounds glamorous and exciting. But as creatrixes we inhabit the same world as everyone else, with the same demands on our time and energy: feeding ourselves, making a home, finding a mate, caring for others, staying alive... This is how most creatures on Earth exist. How do we move from here into the creative realm?

We must first immerse ourselves in the fullness of the world and nature, in the energy and creations of our wider community, taking them in through all our senses. And then we have to allow our own feelings and stories to bubble up in response. This I call creative bathing: consciously and unconsciously absorbing the world around us and combining it with the world within us.

If we take time to surround ourselves with diverse inspiration, our minds and hearts are naturally triggered into creative response. The entrances to The Creative Way are everywhere if we have eyes to see and a spirit of adventure…if we are willing to take an unknown doorway into the dark.

> Leave the door open for the unknown, the door into the dark. That's where the most important things come from. […] For artists of all stripes, the unknown, the idea or the form or the tale that has not yet arrived, is what must be found.
>
> Rebecca Solnit, *A Field Guide to Getting Lost*

Doorways in the Dark

Each time we state our intention to create, we enter the void: the dark unknown of the unconscious. As creatives we commit to returning time and again to this place. Sometimes the void looks and feels blank. At other times it is chaotic: a deluge of sensory inputs, fragments of ideas and competing energies. Whichever way it appears, it is a vital part of the process.

Facing the void feels so overwhelming because it is the birthplace of limitless possibility. It is the place of potential new life, and the repository of the old. It's not that there's nothing there…it's that everything that exists is there in its elemental nature.

The void acts as an echo chamber for whatever is in there with us: it can amplify the energy of a seedling dream…and our fears. We have to learn to listen with our inner ears to the voice we get to translate into our art and call our own. This voice gets louder and clearer the more attention we give it, the more we commit to showing up and listening to it.

In order to create, we have to find ways to be comfortable in the void. This tends to involve keeping our bodies and hands busy whilst our psyche travels through this space, doing something that requires a degree of concentration: knitting, sewing, cleaning, sorting materials, exercising, driving…tasks that novelist Kate Atkinson describes as "mindless yet purposeful." [xxviii]

What is required is that we have the courage to step out of our comfort zones, through the doorway in the dark and into the unknown. We must dare to lose ourselves in the void so that we can know a more expanded sense of being. It's a practice. One that, as creative souls, we commit to again and again. Showing up with no guarantees. And waiting. And listening. Again. And again.

> All creativity awakens at this primal threshold where light and darkness test and bless each other.
>
> —John O'Donohue, *Anam Cara*

Threshold Guardians

At the threshold to any important space is usually a person or animal that guards the boundary: a sentry, police officer, security guard, guard dog, passport control, bouncer…or dragon. Their job is to keep out folks unprepared for the journey ahead, or those who are not entitled to pass. In his book on The Hero's Journey, Joseph Campbell refers to these as Threshold Guardians.

The Threshold Guardian tests us for courage and commitment. They ensure that we take the process seriously, that we want what we are seeking badly enough and that we can show that we are eligible to proceed.

But it is not just the entrance to The Creative Way that is guarded, though the Gatekeeper at the threshold to the labyrinth tends to be the most testing of all. Each Circuit has an invisible threshold that we must cross, and each threshold tends to have a Gatekeeper. This may take the form of an inner psychological restraint, outer authority figure or cultural taboo that we must overcome in order to pass. Sometimes we must negotiate, pay our way or sign a contract. At other times we must make ourselves invisible or outwit them. We often need to act braver than we feel in order to move through. It is important to remember that the more fearsome the Gatekeepers we come across, the higher the stakes the project usually has, both for us internally, and for the world at large, so the more courage, resources and support we will need.

As we travel The Way, we find that some Gatekeepers are mentors or teachers in disguise, waiting to be discovered. Others are simply tests or distractions, out to confuse, bewilder, overwhelm or stop us. It is up to us to learn to distinguish them.

And finally, we discover that the greatest Threshold Guardian is our own self. We are the ones that ultimately stand in our own way, deciding whether the creative flow will pass through us and out into the world.

Experience

I often describe catching creativity as being like catching butterflies in the dark: fast-flying, bright coloured sparks darting here and there. It requires quick wits, good eyes and desire to net them. And once you have them, you need to act fast. An idea, like a butterfly, doesn't last long: it is ephemeral. It is here, and now it is gone.

When creative inspiration hits, I feel buzzy and slightly vibrating, my head is both racing and ultra-still. There is a tangible energy that rushes through my body, which is exhilarating. I am hyper-alive and full of knowing. It feels wonderful.

This surge of energy needs to be poured out. I stream it onto paper. Notes, mind maps, lists, doodles, sketches spill out fully formed and fast. It is as though I am downloading information. I am not in control of what it is or where it is coming from, my only job is to be a note-taker, not try to steer it or interfere, this only blocks it. My role at that moment is to step into the pure bubble of energy and inspiration before it pops, and to sketch out as many of the details as I can. My fingers are the ones typing, yet there is something just ahead of me: divine dictation, and I am struggling to keep up. This is the magic time. It is always thrilling. Like diving into icy cold water, I feel more alive than ever.

And once it's gone, it's like the flow is turned off by some unseen hand. I feel like a child again, as it's a tap that I cannot reach. I am left to work with the information that I have, to fashion it into something – an article, a picture, a project, an event, a book. A seed has been planted, I am pregnant with new life, carrying the soul of a new creation that I can only sense, but which haunts my days and nights, driving me onwards, exhausting my energies. I know when I am 'on the money' because the tap turns on again whilst I work. What was previously invisible becomes visible once more, what was unclear only moments before becomes obvious. Piece after piece of the puzzle falls into place as if by magic.

"

Making art can be a process much like ambling along through an untamed physical place. To begin, you need only a sense of an idea – a quiver at the edge of consciousness. [...] Catch it while you can. The path to what you may make or say has only to be a narrow parting of the grass, barely wide enough to enter. Begin with that first whispered thought; the next will come, and the next, thought following thought like raindrops chasing each other down from the sky.

P. Vecchione

Call to Action

> "
>
> The artist is a receptacle for emotions that come from all over the place: from the sky, from the earth, from a scrap of paper, from a passing shape, from a spider's web.
>
> Pablo Picasso

One day a door opens, a crack appears, a thread dangles before our eyes, a strand of potential…will we follow it?

If we do, we find ourselves at the mouth of the labyrinth, the beginning of this particular creative odyssey. We pass the Threshold Guardian and proceed with excitement and trepidation. At this point all we hold in our hands is some sort of a kernel of an idea – a mood, a medium, a colour, a feeling, a word or a few lines. We may have been gifted them by Source, or the call to action might be given to us by a teacher, client, family member or event. Wherever it comes from, this is a powerful moment. A sacred calling. An invitation. One which we can choose to honour or ignore.

This starting idea has an energy that sucks us in. We need to learn to hop on this initial wave of excitement and then sustain the energy ourselves. Like a lit match on a windy night, we hold the flame close and lend it the shelter of our body so that it may grow strong and bright. It will show us the way past the threshold. But only ever a few steps ahead.

If we dare to follow its flickering light and see where it takes us, then the magic, the journey of creativity in the labyrinth of the bodymind begins. In the memorable words of Sherlock Homes: *the game is on.*

Getting Down the Bones

We take a pen and jot down the beginning of the idea, the vision, some lines of the story, a rough sketch – these are usually very rudimentary, broad strokes or tiny details. We do not begin at what will be the beginning of the finished work…but at the beginning of the process of discovering it. The first words to a book are often written last.

This is not a rational process. Like palaeontologists we are digging down into the strata of life, unearthing bones. As we continue finding the bones and shifting them around, a more solid shape begins to emerge. We become able to develop a reasonably firm working plan that will guide our steps. Or rather two plans – one for ourselves, a work schedule of what needs doing, how and when. And a plan for the structure of the work itself, its skeleton, that will support the emotional, sensory or narrative journey for our audience.

We might write an outline of the themes and motifs, make a plan of the chapters to include, create a story board, do some preparatory sketches. We figure out what we know...and what we don't. This helps us know how to proceed, what we can start to get down...and what still we need to discover to fill in the blanks.

We let the dreamtime and intuition help to add details to the basic outline. As more comes we become more able to translate it into the material realm. Some will be false starts, some will be major parts of the finished piece. Most of it will probably be in the wrong order. What matters is that we get everything we can down, without worrying too much about it making sense or even looking good at this stage.

"Everyone has talent. What is rare is the courage to follow the talent to the dark place where it leads.

Erica Jong

Hunting and Gathering

We head out and wander and wonder. We follow the scent of new leads. We gather what we find along the way. We track down our prey. We search and research far and wide.

As we begin to process everything we feel and see and do through this new lens of the project everything becomes a potential lead. We take in so much information we feel we might burst. Then we realise that there are layers beyond layers. We process more and more until everything we thought we knew when we started out is a blur. And yet still there is more.

False Starts

Eventually we find we are lost. The plan no longer fits. Instead of the glimmering perfection of our vision, our scribbles are messy and incoherent. What was whole and beautiful in our heads doesn't look right on the page. There are big gaps in the plan that we don't know how to fill. We doubt our abilities.

We fumble to find a way outside of our comfort zones, whilst simultaneously trying to stay safe. We try to find a new way whilst following the old way.

And so we begin again. Turning the paper this way and that. Trying this colour. That word. Ripping it into pieces. Screwing it in a ball. Aiming it at the bin.

Cursing.

Crying.

Failing.

Trying again.

> Begin to weave and the Divine will provide the thread.
>
> Old German Proverb

Surrendering to the Process

We have entered the process.

Or perhaps more honestly, the process has entered us.

No, that is not it. We have become the process.

No, that's still not quite it…

We remember that we are and always have been the process.

We recall how joyful it is to play.

We reclaim how we were always meant to be.

We become our creative selves.

This is a stage of deep faith, of surrender to flow and playfulness, of openness to quantum leaps and seismic shifts. Magic is happening within, but miscarriage may only be a breath away. Life and death hang in the balance. And all we can do is to trust the process and release our desire to control everything. It is vital that we share this precious secret with only our most beloved and trusted people. Allow it to develop and grow unpressured free from too many expectations.

Chipping Away

Each day we take our hammer (keyboard, paintbrush, needle…) and set to work.

It requires patience and skill and focus.

And time. Lots of time.

Nothing hugely interesting happens these days. No big spiritual epiphanies.

Just lots of work. We keep on pushing on through. Getting covered in dust.

Occasionally discovering something new.

Tap.

Tap.

Tap.

Getting Stuck

And then one day, for seemingly no reason at all, we get stuck.

Trying to find the last crucial bones.

At first we keep pushing on, looking in the same places. Sifting through dust.

Then we look further afield.

We look at the maps of others. Take our hammer to different spots marked on them. And chip away there.

Until we discover that there is nothing there.

We get frustrated.

And give up.

But occasionally come back and start chipping away again.

And then we give up again.

Then we really give up. And tell everyone we know that we've given up.

Until the only thing left to give up is our insistence that we know how it should be. If we knew, we would not be searching.

Rabbit Holes

“

She'd been to Narnia, Wonderland, Hogwarts, Dictionopolis. She had tessered, fallen through the rabbit hole, crossed the ice bridge into the unknown world beyond.

Anne Ursu, *Breadcrumbs*

Just as we really, really give up, and decide to do something completely different, suddenly we find that the ground has given way and we are tumbling down a rabbit hole.

Rabbit holes are at the heart of creative genius. They disorient us, changing our perspectives, making the small appear massive, and the enormous insignificant. They may open up in our dreams, or in altered states of consciousness. Or simply by reading a line of text in a book. Or driving down the road.

The internet is a notorious enabler of this process – for good and bad. Go to Google to check the spelling of a word, and you'll find yourself there an hour later following hyperlinks about cats that have saved firemen and ancient Sumerian goddesses and why cranberries can cure cancer.

You need to learn to become aware when you have fallen down a rabbit hole. When you do, take a moment to:

1 – See where you have ended up.

2 – Assess if it is a useful, fun or interesting place to be right now...or if you are allowing it to be a distraction to hard or boring work you would prefer to avoid.

3 – Notice how much time you have just spent down the rabbit hole.

4 – Is it a common rabbit hole like Facebook or an online newspaper? Do you need to make it a little harder to fall down it next time by working offline or using an application blocker?

5 – Retrace your steps. What was your starting point? Why were you drawn down here in the first place? Have you found what you initially came for?

6 – Did you find anything useful that you can bring back with you and apply to what you are working on? Can you bookmark it for another time?

7 – Do you need a physical or mental break?

At many key points in a creative project when we are looking for new information or connections or if we have hit resistance and find ourselves stuck, rabbit holes can be our tunnels to new worlds. However, when we are up against a deadline, when we are tired or anxious, rabbit holes tend to be our bodyminds' way of trying to take a much-needed break that we are not allowing them because we are pushing ourselves too hard.

> Thoughts will lead you in circles. Silence will bring you back to your centre.
>
> —Rasheed Ogunlaru

Creatrix Speaks

Could something as unappreciated as procrastination actually be of great service to an artist and her creations? There is a good case here for inquiry.

I believe procrastination is an under-appreciated tool for creators. Yes, you read that correctly: I see procrastination as a part of the creative process. I link it to divine timing. It serves a purpose and initiates a gestation period.

When my intuition tells me to rest, I put whatever it is down, until it tells me to pick it back up again. This can take days, weeks and sometimes years. I await the inspiration before starting again.

Marsia

M(o)usetraps

If a rabbit hole is where we fall into the void, with the potential of reaching the Creatrix, m(o)usetraps are our way of luring her towards us. Just as the Creatrix leaves creative breadcrumbs for us to follow, so too can we leave offerings for her.

My offerings of choice are peanut butter, cheese and chocolate! These nutrient-rich, fatty snacks are what I crave pre-menstrually, when pregnant and when writing! I had never made the connection until I realised that they are all times of my creative womb-space being deeply active. Incidentally they're also the tasty morsels that we pop into our (humane) mousetraps at home!

But lures don't have to be calorific. Symbolic lures include:

- writing down a key word that you want to understand more about,
- focusing on a symbol that you feel is significant to your work,
- meditating on an image,
- creating an altar space,
- flicking through a book,
- moving your body to a certain piece of music on the theme you are exploring...

All these are ways of calling the m(o)use to your side.

Like a mouse she seems most active at night. She visits regularly in your dreams, daydreams and deep pleasures, but unless you consciously call her into your work, she respectfully stays away and leaves you to it. If you have it all sorted, you have no need for her input.

We often steam arrogantly ahead, believing that we're in control of the creative process and know where we're going...only to find somewhere along the way that we have hit a metaphorical brick wall. This is when the ego has taken control and we've forgotten her. And so we need to call in Creatrix once more – with gratitude, respect and more than a little humility. We create our ritual, we make our offering of peanut butter and chocolate, and open ourselves to receive her delicious presence and guidance once more.

Experience

The creative process for me is about energetic resonance. Although from the outside it probably looks like a lot of lying in bed with my eyes closed! However, the internal process happening is delicate and deep – and the furious writing that happens afterwards is enough to tell you that I wasn't just having a nice nap!

When I find myself getting to the end of my energetic stream of writing, I tend to go and read or watch something. Often it only takes a couple of minutes, but if the resistance is stronger, or I've chosen the wrong thing, it takes longer, a day…a week, until I can let go of my insistence on how it should be and allow space for what is to emerge. A word, the way the light falls, a mood and suddenly a word or phrase flashes in my mind. I feel the resonance, like a deep bell tolling. I know when it is right. I close my eyes and consciously toll that bell again and again, repeating the word or phrase in my mind, whilst my body relaxes, becoming like deep, black water, waiting for the echo to come back to me. I also use this process almost every time after sex or waking up from a memorable dream. Then, whilst the phrase echoes like a foghorn far off, I travel around and through my body, looking for resonance, looking for a point of energy or tension and keep my attention there as the resonance between them grows and sentences begin to pour. I stay with this, never running for my pen at the first moment. Instead I let the sentences join other sentences allowing the flow to build up, as I try to record it in my mind, until each becomes part of a larger whole.

The quantum leaps between subjects that happen in this place are breath-taking. In this space of pure energy, with no boxes to contain them, it is often the simplest of connections, and I am always left wondering why I hadn't seen this before.

A-ha Moments

Instances of immense clarity occur throughout the creative process. Like hearing the heartbeat of our baby for the first time, or feeling the first kick, a-ha moments are miraculous. We get a sense of the bigger picture, and how it all fits together. And for a moment or two we can hold it all in our minds.

A-ha moments usually emerge a little while after complete despair has set in, or after we have looked beyond ourselves for answers and direction, set our m(o)usetraps and waited. And waited. It is as though we need to fully surrender our own answers and possibilities, to really say *I don't know*, before the co-creative power will step in to assist.

These moments tend to be short and glorious. A sudden flash and the whole vista is visible, shimmering in front of our eyes, as hypnotic as a mirage to a thirsty woman in the desert.

Trust these moments completely. They are literal revelations of The Creative Way. This is the magic made visible.

> One part of creativity is the ability of taking an idea from one place and applying it in an utterly different context.
>
> Nathan Myhrvold

Creatrix Speaks

Riding my cherry red Conch Cruiser, it came to me. First as a gentle murmur, then as a force I could not deny. Get home now! I said to myself.

Zooming past the beach and all of its happy tourists, I headed into the wind through the area of Key West known as Bahama Village. I hurried to get back to my house at Blue Heaven, so I could jot down all that I was hearing. The lyrics were coming rapidly and I was afraid I might forget them, so I repeated them over and over as I pushed the pedals of my bicycle faster and faster. Soon the melody came in and commanded all of my attention with a strong and pulsating beat. I married the two in my head and pedalled harder. "Could you be someone who, can see beyond the thick of blue..."

As I reached my yard, I jumped off the bike, ran full speed into the house, grabbed my guitar, paper, pen, and a handheld recorder. Sitting at the kitchen table, I quickly found the notes on the guitar and played them into the recorder. Next came the lyrics, one after another. Before I knew it, voila! A song was born. This is how I wrote the tune, "U R What U R."

There have been other songs that have come fast and furious like this one, but most, have not. The muse is funny that way. She enjoys changing it up, and sometimes she really makes me work for it. Often I joke, "The muse can be so damn demanding. And, I love her for that!" Truly it is my honour to co-create with her. I am grateful. She has given me many great melodies over the years. She lights the fire in my belly. She is the voice in my head. Without her, there is no creation. There are no songs. We work together. As one. She is the source, and I the channel for her musings! We make a good pair.

Occasionally the muse will leave me to my own devices and that's when I find myself meandering around the house, going from my living room to the kitchen, back to my studio where I bang out a few chords on the guitar or piano, then up again to visit the bathroom or get something from the fridge. Upstairs, downstairs, back to the studio, out to the porch, the yard, and back to the studio again in hopes of coaxing out the melody and lyrics swirling around in my head. This is often what my songwriter self looks like. This, my creative process.

Recently, while playing with a painter friend, she made a comment about how she was surprised that I, a musician, didn't have any music playing in the background. We were painting in silence. She told me that she always 'jams out' when she paints and that it gets her creative juices flowing. I told her that I am in silence a lot of the time, and not only when I am painting.

What I didn't say to her, was that for me, silence is music. From it, I hear everything. Quiet, to me, exists in that mystical space in-between. In-between here and there, and everywhere. Between this *world and that world. Between you and me. It is fertile ground for learning, for listening. I am comfortable with it. It is the place where my melodies come from and my rhythms are birthed.*

Silence is the river moving through me right now as I am writing to you, hoping that I can say something with these words to encourage you to paint, to draw, to sing, to dance or do whatever you can to create something meaningful and beautiful and specifically from you. Do it because it makes you feel good. Forget all judgment and criticisms, open your heart and create and be free!

Personally, my art has been my greatest ally. In a world that can be especially challenging to navigate for us empaths and those of us leading from our hearts, my artistic endeavours have buoyed me again and again. This thing we call the creative process is something that I have learned to trust. No matter how laborious it feels. As long as I stay open to the flow of artistic energy moving through me, creation is inevitable. I love that. The process is very consistent.

To an outsider, my creative process most likely looks a lot like chaos, procrastination, and day-dreaming. Truth be told, they all play a role. The chaos can come at any point, and it is sure when I lack trust and question where I am going, unsettled by not having the slightest clue as to how I will get 'there'.

Through the years I have learned that it is much better to approach things with the curiosity of a child. When I am successful at this, creating is easeful and filled with wonder. Even the chaos can be a fun ride! At age fifty-five, I've come to understand that from chaos, comes creation. Today, I remind myself to embrace it and not be overwhelmed by it. To make space and allow the waves of labour to crest and fall, and do my best to prepare for what's coming.

Marsia

(Listen to 'U R What U R' on the Creatrix Spotify playlist **tinyurl.com/MotherTurtle**)

Filling in the Gaps

We must first make our intuitive leaps before filling in the gaps with research and experience.

But now we know what we need to do, we shift our sails, adjust our course, our direction now clear and understood. Sail on the newfound energy and inspiration from your a-ha moment for as long as possible – it will take you far!

Now is the time to build the main body of the work, fleshing it out, sewing it together. Discovering what works and what doesn't. Trying and trying again. And again. And again. Sometimes we are following the pattern we have drawn out, and sometimes improvising. The most important thing is to fill in the gaps, flesh out the bones, even if we know that what we are doing will not make it into the final creation. We need to make a coherent whole at this point. Once we have we add depth, we add in new colours and shade, building the drama and contrasts of the piece.

> These things are already writing themselves in me, and they're asking to be brought outside of myself to share with others.
>
> Alice Walker

The Turning Point

We have reached the turning point, when we see our work as whole for the first time. This is where we step back from the details and the process and bear witness to the work.

We see it as it is.

And often think that it is finished. But in truth we are only halfway there! The baby might be fully formed at twenty-four weeks, but it is not yet ready to be born. Once out in the world it would struggle to survive. There is still so much more strengthening, growing and refining to go.

In the words of Florence Scovel Shinn, artist and author,

> *Every great work, every great accomplishment, has been brought into manifestation through holding to the vision, and often just before the big achievement, comes apparent failure and discouragement.*

"

The difference
between a good
artist and a
great one is:
The novice will
often lay down
his tool or brush
Then pick up an
invisible club on
the mind's table
And helplessly
smash the easel
and the paint.
Whereas the
vintage man does
not hurt himself
or anyone.
And keeps on
sculpting light.
Hafiz

This is why people who consider themselves 'not creative' are generally unhappy with their work. They will get this far and claim to be finished, and give up, either because they are not experienced or confident in the next act of refinement and polishing, or because they think that the quality of their work at this point is representative of what they are capable of.

It is not.

We may find that we have to leave our creative baby half-formed in the centre of the labyrinth. If so, we come back out of the labyrinth alone, except for feelings of grief and loss, as we realise that we cannot – perhaps just now, or ever – carry this creative baby to term. We mourn that we will not get to share it with the world. But this does not negate its preciousness to us, its fleeting vulnerability: its brief life has changed us indelibly.

If we are able to continue with the creative process we commit our energies to the second stage of refining, growing and birthing our creative work out into the world.

This place of transition between the 'passive' and 'active' energies is something most humans find hard. In the birthing process it is often where we feel most emotionally overwhelmed and physically exhausted. We have laboured for hours, only to discover that the pushing still lies ahead.

This is the place my therapists, physical and psychological, are telling me that I need to pause and give myself some breathing room, rather than charging through and damaging myself in the process. Or running away in fear.

When we have been close to our work, working intensely on it for a long time, it is really hard to step back, to take a break in order to really 'see' it as it is now. Especially as we know how far it is from what we envision it finally being and how much it has taken us to get it to this stage. We wonder if we will ever be finished with it, if we have what it takes.

This is an important time to remind yourself that the most powerful shifts happen in the dark, rather than the active doing. If we make space for this at each part of the process, the mystery and insight that emerge will shape our creation in ways we could never have expected. Allow this. This is what will make your work transformative for others. But it takes courage to surrender to this.

Step back.

Give it time.

Give it space.

For the magic to enter.

The Outer-Directed Spiral

”

I begin with an idea, and then it becomes something else.

Pablo Picasso

The Path Out

Our job as creatrixes is to build strong containers that can hold the energy of The Work. We need to craft seed pods that will travel far and spread the magic.

This is where our craftswomanship, our artistry, our technical skills and knowledge of materials and structures come to the fore. As we craft, we know what has worked well in the past for ourselves and others, as well as what hasn't. We know what is expected, and what has never been attempted and why. Or we find out through trial and error.

At this stage we will hopefully be clearer in our own vision for the final product. We will also be guiding it from the limitless realms of the imagination towards worldly expectations through many limitations – deadlines, costings, functionality, length and dozens of other imposed obstacles.

This part of the process can be taxing and time-consuming – it always takes far longer than you expect. You may begin to empathise with Sisyphus. Each day you push the rock of your work to the top of the hill. But when you return the next morning and start again, you seem to be starting from the bottom of the hill. However hard you work you seem no nearer to the summit.

Keep on, creatrix, you can do it!

Spiralling

As we edit, shape and adapt the container of our creative expression, we spiral in and out,[xxix] constantly shifting perspective, physically and psychologically, witnessing it from many angles. As we do so we continually compare what we see in front of us to the initial vision we had.

Spiralling in and out requires that we look closely, focus our attention on the tiny details, and then zoom out and see the bigger picture. We shift our focus from micro to macro, from individual stroke or word, to entire work, again and again. In and out our attention goes as we find some sort of order, ensuring that all the individual parts function well together.

At this stage we must allow ourselves to be compassionately critical of our work, make decisions, then work some more. We are comparing what we perceive with our inner vision with what our outer vision is observing, comparing the inner voice to the outer expression. We witness it as ourselves. We witness it as our audience. Again and again, though we may feel overwhelmed by details, we are called to hold the bigger picture in our minds and hearts, seeing where our creation is resonant, and where it needs further refinement.

"

When you seem farthest from your destination is when you suddenly arrive is a very pat truth in words, but a profound one to find with your feet.

—Rebecca Solnit, *Wanderlust*

More Moments

We experience the recurrence of the Moments from the inward spiral with ironic bewilderment – false starts, getting stuck, rabbit holes, a-ha moments. We thought we had overcome these. Yet here they are again. But this time the stakes are higher, we have more time and resources invested in the project, more people know about it. Continuing seems impossible. Giving up also seems impossible.

Refinement

This is the part of the process when we sift our work through finer and finer mesh, like archaeologists. First we pick out the larger rocks and discard them, then the smaller pebbles, until only what should be there exists: the treasure. Or like in woodwork when we move down through ever finer grades of sand-paper.

This is where we refine our articulation and expression until we are at the very limits of our own potential. In doing so we allow as much of the light of The Work to shine through the container we have crafted, rather than be obscured by the structure. We ensure that we have removed all of the scaffolding that we have used to construct this creation, allowing its final structure to be internally self-supporting once we remove ourselves.

"

You do not
have to be
good.

You do not
have to walk
on your knees

for a hundred
miles through
the desert
repenting.

Mary Oliver,
"Wild Geese"

Sharing

This is the stage where it is advisable to share the emerging work with our trusted inner circle – our creative group, mentor, editor, close friends or partner – to gain multiple further perspectives. Then we sit with this feedback and our own intuition before taking drastic action. Sometimes we only need small tweaks, sometimes we might need a total structural overhaul. This takes immense courage.

Are you willing to risk losing what you have worked so hard for, in the faith that something even better will emerge at the end? So that the essence of The Work can be experienced more distinctly and profoundly by the audience.

Rest and Retreat

Be aware of the natural pauses that exist in the process. And allow yourself to rest in them. Often we try to run a creative marathon as though it were a sprint. Be respectful of your human self and its needs. Just as a human pregnancy cannot be fast-forwarded by will-power, however intense or uncomfortable it is, neither can a creative pregnancy. We have to learn to pace ourselves, to allow the intensity to subside a little, rather than pushing ourselves through without rest.

Experience

> "Begin at the beginning," the King said, very gravely, "and go on till you come to the end: then stop."
>
> Lewis Carroll, *Alice in Wonderland*

When I was editing each of my 'big' books (The Rainbow Way, Burning Woman, Medicine Woman and now Creatrix) I found that it was far too intense an experience to be close to them for very long in their primal energetic states. For me, the process of researching, channelling and editing the material was physically and mentally deeply uncomfortable – a little like getting too close to the fire, or staring at the sun. The only way I could manage the process was by doing a little bit, then darting away to do something else – play a computer game, go for a swim or a drive to recover my energies – before diving in again. Even so, I would find my mind still editing as I ate and slept.

I know that this 'bigness' has translated into the experience of reading these books. I have received countless emails from women speaking of feeling taken over by the energy of the books as they read, of crying, throwing the book across the room, staying up all night and reading it in one sitting, carrying it everywhere with them or knowing that they were not in the right mental space to embark on reading it.

Ready to Burst

The energy has been building and building, and our bodies are barely able to contain this extra life force: we are ready to burst. We are now heavy with the weight of our creation (and perhaps a little too much peanut butter and chocolate!) Like the thirty-ninth week of pregnancy, we are so close to the end that we can almost touch it. It keeps us up at night and haunts our dreams. *When will it be done? What will the response of the outside world be? What will we do when we are not giving every living moment to gestating this creation? Will we love it? Will it be as we hoped?*

We need to carry our baby to term to be sure that it is fully ready to meet the world: plumped out and beautiful. This is the time for a final polishing: a proofread for any remaining spelling mistakes or punctuation errors; the varnishing; the dress-rehearsal; tidying up the loose threads. Don't rush this. You will feel more able to release the work fully into the world if these have been done to a high standard. But be gentle with yourself, it can only ever be good enough. Don't torture yourself with perfection. At some point you will have to let go.

How can we gauge when we have done enough? How do we know if one last touch might perfect the work or ruin it irredeemably? How can we tell if we are doing vital polishing work, or procrastinating to avoid sharing the work? This is the tightrope of creation.

We can stay tight and second-guess ourselves. Or we can trust ourselves and the process for the last few steps. We can learn to trust that The Work has its own pattern and that we have done our best. We can remind ourselves that there is no such thing as a mistake or failure. But this is often easier said than done, especially the more of our time, energy and money we have invested in something. The more public it is, the more our identity is connected to it, the higher the stakes, the harder it is to fail.

And so we can play it safe, stepping out of the creative danger zone and into our comfort zones just a little too soon. We can leave a piece when it is pretty or familiar. Or we can take a risk, and chance what happens if we take an extra step into the unknown.

Listen and watch for the small signs, from the work, from the world, that the time to release this work is here. We are seeking that elusive moment of perfect balance – *kairos* – where everything is in harmony. Land artist, Andy Goldsworthy, describes these as "astonishing, inexplicable moments of complete clarity…when it feels very clear and very beautiful and it all makes sense." [xxx] These moments are what we are always aiming for, but can never force into being. And sometimes it just has to be good enough. Sometimes it just has to be now.

"

You must do things you think you cannot do.

Eleanor Roosevelt

Moment

No doubt you will have a Moment here. Perhaps several.

Take a break.

Centre yourself.

Gather your energy.

Focus on the bigger picture.

You've got this.

"

Where we end up will not look like where we began.

Pat B. Allen, *Art is a Spiritual Path*

Birth

The moment of birth is here. We move down the birth canal of The Creative Way and out into the world once more. That which we have been gestating in private, will now be unveiled.

Birthing can be exhilarating, exhausting, daunting or terrifying…often all at once, depending on the support around you and what sort of labour you have. Though you emerge on the same path, you are not the same person that entered the labyrinth at the beginning of this journey. The seed of the vision that you carried in your heart, hands or womb has transformed into a reality that you can finally share with others. It is time to gather the fullness of your energy for the final push. Keep breathing.

Witnessing

Sharing our work with the world is a vital part of the creative process. Though we might feel very vulnerable, we also tend to feel deeply affirmed when our creative work is witnessed and received with love and gratitude. This, after all, is one of our main human motivations for creating. Seize this moment of glory and completion to celebrate your achievement. Acknowledge the hard work, the commitment and the courage it has taken to get here. Take time to give thanks, to yourself, The Work and all who have made it possible.

As creatives we often struggle to really 'see' our work as we are too close to it – we are usually simultaneously too generous and too harsh with our creations, rather like our children! We tend to see the errors, or rather our own fallibility in it, rather than The Work itself. It is time to make peace with this creation, with its imperfect perfection, to begin to perceive it as something in its own right. It is no longer a work in progress. The combination of gratitude and witness consciousness allows the beginning of detachment of artist from her creation, mother from her child.

On a grander scale, The Work comes into being so that the creative energy of the Universe can be consciously beheld: consciousness may witness itself in form. Allow this magic to happen. Allow the Witness to be awoken within you. Observe how your work touches others. And then allow yourself to experience the work fully yourself and receive its medicine. Be sure to come back to it again in a few months or even years to experience it from a more detached place and see what new things you receive from it.

Spaciousness

Allow yourself to experience the spaciousness of the void at the other side of The Creative Way. It might feel odd, confusing, lonely and boring. But really let yourself to sit with that feeling of emptiness, and allow yourself to experience how you have been changed by the process. Try not to go flying into the next project or manically catch up on all the things that you've had to let slide (note to self!) The intensity of jumping from one creative project to the next becomes addictive: living with the big energy is exciting and a welcome distraction from the struggles of everyday life and relationships. Creating gives us a sense of misstery in a world where we might otherwise feel small and out of control. But try to step back before your bodymind takes the decision for you and burns out or gets sick.

Give yourself permission to rest and recoup your energies, knowing that the energy you have released into the world is out there doing its work. Its being released has allowed space and energy and time for new possibilities to emerge. Know that your work will seed other creative works – in your life and those of others – whilst you are resting. Through you The Creative Way continues flowing, onwards, onwards… You have played your part. New life has come to being through you. It has expanded you and now comes the contraction. Rest well in the darkness before you begin to soak up beauty and colour and begin the process once more.

"This process is not linear but one of discontinuous leaps into new plateaus of reality.

Jeremy Johnson, *Seeing Through the World*

The Process at a Glance

The whole process looks like this. Note the expansions and contractions of energy, like the contractions of the birthing process get closer together as birth becomes imminent.

Stage	Feeling	Activity	Moment/ Circuit	Energetic State
CREATIVE BATHING	At ease, relaxed, curious, joyful	Information gathering, sensory experience without conscious intention	Outside labyrinth	Expansion
DOORWAYS IN THE DARK	Excited, thrilled, daunted	Meditation, reflection, thinking	Approaching entrance	Expansion/Pause
THRESHOLD GUARDIANS	Resolute, determined, committed, courageous, fearful, bold	Decision and commitment to proceed	At entrance	Pause
CALL TO ACTION	Excited, trepidation, anxious, thrilled	Making first notes or sketches – themes, motifs, first inspiration	Circuit	Expansion
GETTING DOWN THE BONES	More solid sense of the reality of the project	Planning, early structuring	Circuit	Expansion
HUNTING AND GATHERING	Focused, engaged, information overload	Researching, information gathering, interviewing and inviting contributors	Circuit	Expansion
FALSE STARTS	Frustrated, false hope, despair	Throwing away ideas, starting again	Moment	Contraction

Stage	Feeling	Activity	Moment/ Circuit	Energetic State
SURRENDER TO THE PROCESS	Surrender, relief, enjoyment, surprise	Play, improvisation, experimentation	Circuit	Expansion/Pause
CHIPPING AWAY	Resolve, bored, satisfied	Working with our medium	Circuit	Expansion
GETTING STUCK	Frustrated, despair, despondent	Procrastination	Moment	Contraction
RABBIT HOLES	Distracted/ frustrated at self. Or awe/wonder	Reading or watching unrelated material	Moment	Expansion
A-HA MOMENTS	Awe, wonder, excited, thrilled	Lightbulb moment of illumination	Moment	Expansion
FILLING IN THE GAPS	Confident, determined, resolute, driven	Getting down final structure and content	Circuit	Expansion
THE TURNING POINT	Relief, frustrated, proud	Resting and reflecting, recouping energy	Centre	Pause
THE PATH OUT	Confident, determined, resolute, driven, anxious to finish	Beginning to refine and edit the work	Circuit	Contraction
SPIRALLING	Constantly shifting emotions – it's great, it sucks…	Major edits and restructuring. Moving from focusing on big picture to small details again and again	Circuit	Expansion and contraction, alternating rapidly
REFINEMENT	Focused	Editing – focus on ever-smaller details	Circuit	Contraction

Stage	Feeling	Activity	Moment/ Circuit	Energetic State
SHARING	Courageous, excited, anxious, self-doubt	Sharing our work with friendly critics	Circuit	Expansion
REST AND RETREAT	Despair, exhausted, frustrated	Get away from the work	Moments	Pause
READY TO BURST	Fullness, bored, anxious, frustrated, exhausted, building excitement	Very final polishes	Circuit	Expansion
BIRTH	Terror, exhilarated, numb, anxious… ALL the feelings at once. Intense	Launch – sharing work with the world	Emergence from the labyrinth	Full expansion
WITNESSING	Reflective, celebratory, empty	Reflection	Outside the labyrinth	Pause
SPACIOUSNESS	At peace, joyful…or agitated and frustrated!	Rest and retreat	Outside the labyrinth	Contraction to pause

Creatrix Speaks

For whatever reason, this thread I follow, this creative force is in my DNA and I know will ebb and flow throughout my life. And so I work to find both a rootedness and a flexibility to be able to keep it moving. Because I don't want to wait until the end of my life to share what I've made. I don't want to live an uncreative life – I need it now and I need it to live. If I waited until I'd arrived, I would never begin. If I waited until I'd gathered the wisdom of an elder, I would never learn. If I waited until I produced something of the perfection or wholeness I wanted, I would produce nothing. If I waited until I was thick-skinned and self-assured, I would be waiting forever.

I want to see my whole life as a piece of art – that only at its end it can be viewed as complete, and likely not even then! I want to take the pressure off and view each piece of writing or song or whatever I speak or do as a one brush stroke in a greater painting. And maybe the ideas will dry up, maybe I lose the means, the space or time or desire to create, maybe it will morph into something else other than songs. I hope it will. I don't want to stagnate.

In the meantime, it feels important to keep letting go. To not be motivated by fear, not feel tied into running an endless treadmill or be another voice shouting into the cacophony just for the sake of it. To devise a creative life that works for me, so that what is given out to the collective is coming from overflow not emptiness. And to let go of old paradigms.

As with so much of life, it seems we have to spend it unpicking patriarchal and neoliberal narratives that we have been conditioned to see through and face the shadow of that, rather than pretending it isn't there. None of that is easy. Unpicking ingrained lessons of success or failure, of good and bad or begin-

nings and ends. To get away from the story that there is a right or wrong way to be creative or be an artist. Away from thinking that art is not valuable, or that its value must look a certain way. Away from individualistic thinking that we must say and do it all ourselves, or even that we must be original. No piece of art ever exists in its own orbit, nothing does: no human, nothing on this Earth. We are interconnected, and woven from and into a billion other threads. Where I think we find our own unique piece, is telling our own story in some way – that is what I want to celebrate in myself and others.

It's a privilege to have a channel for that. To write songs, make records. Like markers in the sand and windows to the soul. I love that I have contained myself at different times in every decade and I get an insight and understanding into who I was and how I felt and what I thought in a way I could never access just through memory. Then I can learn forgiveness and compassion towards my past selves, to inform the person I am now and who I want to be.

Creativity is never done, just as my healing is never done. I create to keep becoming. I create because it helps me live. I create to document the process of living. I create for the healing and for what cannot be healed.

The only thing I know for sure is that life wants to grow, and creativity is life. Creativity is our birthright. It's a way of being. Pushing up through the cracks, even in the harshest conditions. It keeps cycling round its different seasons, grows and blooms and dies and pushes up through the dirt again.

Eleanor

The Embodied Spiral

The Creative Way is not just a metaphor. It is wired into us on every level of our being as a physical reminder of how the life force works.

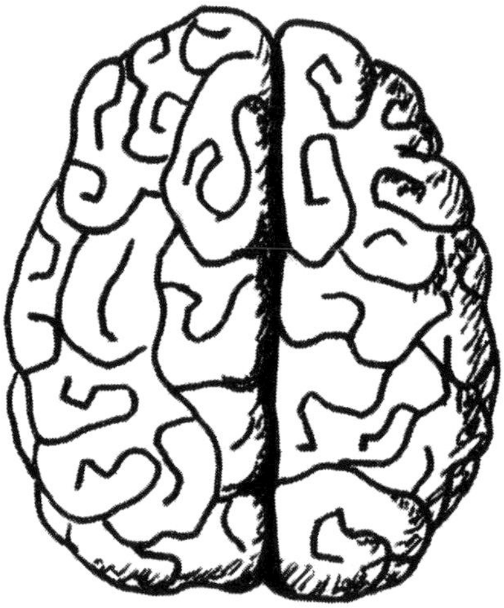

> The evolution of consciousness is not a ladder but a labyrinth.
>
> Jeremy Johnson, *Seeing Through the World*

Look closely and you will see it in the squiggling pathways of your brain, the smaller structures of neurons and dendrites, the twists and turns of your intestines, the twisting downward journey of birth, the spiralling umbilical cord of a newborn, the patterns of your outer and inner ear, in the whorls of your fingertips, the double-helix of your DNA. The Creative Way is a holographic fractal, the blueprint of creation encoded into living things from the micro to the macro.

The labyrinthine form of The Creative Way represents both the physical brain structure, and consciousness itself. The creative process that I describe in this book is a metaphorical explanation of physical and metaphysical reality. It is what part of your consciousness is doing as it changes tracks from its daily mode of functioning to being in the creative zone.

When we allow ourselves to align with The Creative Way, it is a homecoming to our most primal way of being.

This is the pattern of our menstrual cycles and the galaxies, the storm and the whirlpool – the spiral journey of expansion and contraction *is* the creative blueprint of the Universe itself. All we are doing is remembering. Learning with our conscious minds what our souls have always known.

Creative Inquiry

Creating Space and Time

- What does your creative space currently look like? How would you like it to be? Where does this desire come from?
- How are you at taking up space? What did you learn about taking up space as a child and young adult? Are there unhelpful things you learned that might be better to let go?
- How do you feel about mess?
- Is cleaning a good way for you to sort through issues internally before you start work, or do you use it as a way to procrastinate? Where did you learn this habit?
- How are you with deadlines? How might you re-vision them?
- Do you have a creative routine? What does it look like? Does it work for you as you are now, as your work is now?
- In what way might it help you to think in terms of rhythm rather than routine?

Creative Process

- Which parts of the creative process do you enjoy the most?
- Which parts of the creative process do you struggle with?
- Are these the same parts of pregnancy, the spiritual journey or relationships that you find difficult?
- How might you make them easier or more enjoyable?
- How might you leave yourself reminders of these stages, for next time?
- Have I missed any parts of your creative process out?
- Can you describe catching creativity from your personal experience?
- Do you believe in the muse? What does the muse look like or feel like for you?
- When and where do you tend to get moments of inspiration?
- What do you attribute them to?
- How well do you listen to your intuition?
- Have you ever been led astray by it?
- What is your experience of the void?

Creative Practice

Labyrinth

I invite you to trace the labyrinth at the beginning of this chapter with your finger – perhaps whilst imagining the creative process of one of your most recent projects. Be sure to pause in the middle.

There are many different shapes and types of labyrinth. You can see my Pinterest boards for more ideas.

Labyrinth: **pinterest.com/dreamingaloudnt/labyrinth/**

Spiral: **pinterest.com/dreamingaloudnt/spirals-unfurling/**

Why not create your own labyrinth or just a simple spiral? You could make one on paper, out of wool or clay, in sand or snow, out of leaves or paint. You might want to make a small one to keep in your creative space. Or make a larger one and walk or even dance it.

Mapping the Dark

Can you map the terrain of the darkness as you move through it?

Can you paint or draw what the void looks like to you? Try using a variety of media to do so. What is the relationship between the void and what lies beyond it? Is there a way in or out? What feelings, words or metaphors emerge for you as you create this representation of the void? How might you represent these?

3

This is the song of your soul,

Calling you back home.

SOUL

> Your soul knows the geography of your destiny. Once the soul awakens, the search begins and you can never go back.
>
> —John O'Donohue, *Anam Cara*

Psyche

At many stages of the creative process when we look at someone 'being creative', there is very little to see. We cannot witness the inner creative process of another. So, when I speak of The Creative Way, what part of us is actually traversing it? It is not our bodies, and neither is it our logical minds.

I believe that creativity is the physical expression of soul. By soul I mean the invisible, innate *beingness* of each of us beyond our physical human bodies.

The ancient Greeks used the term *psyche* to express "the soul, mind, spirit; breath; life, one's life, the animating principle or entity which occupies and directs the physical body." [xxxi] But for many today the term *psyche* brings to mind the modern usage by our medical fields, where it is really just a synonym for mind and usually associated with mental health, or rather, mental *illness*. Using the term *psyche* might mean that you think I am only focusing on creative (as in divergent) thinking, which is only a small part of the creative process. And so, in this book I have chosen to stick with soul, that, for me, retains the sense of the myriad untouchable energies of being far beyond just the mental. I am fully aware that some folks struggle with this term. In our modern, Western scientific and materialist context, soul is not considered a real thing. There is no diagram for it in our biology textbooks, no chemical equation. You cannot prove soul. And yet, you know it. You sense when it is present, and when it is absent.

You do not need to have a religious or even spiritual leaning to understand soul: you do not need to *believe* in anything. We all have an intuitive sense of it. Most of us are aware of the difference between a work of art imbued with soul, and a product manufactured as an item to be consumed.

Think of a factory-produced cushion cover and a handmade patchwork cushion cover. The latter may be battered, faded, and unless it was made by a well-known artist, worth less money, but it would have soul to it – the energy passed into the materials by the craftsperson as they worked, and the history that it carries with it from all the people that have sat on it, all the places it has been. Both do the same job, but one has soul, and one does not.

The Iceberg

> What we see isn't in things but in our souls.
>
> Salvador Dali

Soul tends to be conceived of as an energy force residing within us, an individual energy within an independent body: the ghost in the machine. I would suggest that in order to fully understand our creativity we need to expand this understanding.

If we were to think of the bodymind as an iceberg, as Freudian theory has taught us to, the conscious mind makes up the seen part above the water, and the larger unconscious parts of the psyche lie beneath the surface. In Western thought, the self is only the iceberg. Some seen, much unseen.

But this is all we are.

We do not speak of the water. Just focus on the ice.

Nevertheless the water is there.

Surrounding the iceberg, there is a vast ocean. It is the medium within which the berg exists and of which it is formed. One is always becoming the other. Sometimes the iceberg melts, sometimes more water freezes on. But they are in fluid relationship with each other. You cannot say where the iceberg ends and water begins on a permanent basis.

This is a useful metaphor for the soul. The soul is not just a ghost trapped in a body, but part of a larger soul or energy that is constantly changing form: sometimes freezing onto the individual form, sometimes melting off.

The soul is woven from images, rhythms, words, movements, gestures, dreams, memory residues, colours. It is both personal and collective, shared between us as cultures of humans, across periods of time and geographical places, but also shared with the supposedly inanimate world of landscape and nature.

Through creativity we enter this knowing of our expanded being. We consciously experience a merging with the greater soul. This *oversoul*, which is an integral part of the ecology and environment around and within us and is a medium of energetic interaction and communication, becomes accessible to us.

> Behind your image, below your words, above your thoughts, the silence of another world waits.
>
> —John O'Donohue, *Anam Cara*

Art is the *language* of the soul. It is a product of the communication process between the individual soul (from various times in our own lives), the collective, transpersonal soul and the divine or sacred oversoul. Each time we take part in creative practice we enter into dialogue with each of these elements of our being. We give expression to them. We learn from them, hear them, see them, share them. We bear witness to our greater form of being that is usually hidden to our conscious minds.

In the West we are encultured to live detached from our souls. The only permissible entry points to them being patriarchal religions, witnessing works of art by others, experiences in nature or more recently analytical psychology and dream analysis.

Once we have experienced contact with our soul, a desire to respond tends to be kindled in us. For those who are blocked in their own emotional and creative expression, the response tends to be destructive and deeply critical – seeking a way to destroy that which has unsettled them. For those open to the possibility, an emotional and psychological release is experienced as catharsis – a sense of deep relief, bliss and profound homecoming to which we are drawn back again and again.

Soul as Guide

A creatrix is a student of soul. She learns to trust an unseen energy that guides her hands and steers her mind. She dedicates herself to following its traces, these snail trails, the quicksilver twinkle of the invisible currents, the eddies and whirls of life force that bind us all.

When we create with soul we are following the blueprints of creation. To make something 'inanimate' come to life and have a resonance, as we do when we create, I believe that we capture the soul of The Work itself and combine it with some of our own individual soul. We then imbue the soul of the materials with our own life force as we work with them. This is how and why a work of art can communicate across time and space to the souls of others we have never met: it is triply ensouled.

I have an intuitive sense that when we create in this way, we must be following what Aboriginal Australians call the Songlines or Dreaming Track – the paths the creator-beings followed during the original Dreaming.[xxxii]

My understanding of this dreaming place that we enter when we create is also heavily influenced by the archetypal psychology of Jung and his idea of the collective unconscious. That is, a collective human field of dreams, ideas, thoughts and feelings – an invisible, shared realm – from which artists weave story, music, dance and images. We access it through night dreams and daydreams, waking visions, heard voices, flashes of inspiration or trance – all soul states. Dreams forge new pathways between the day's sensory experiences and memories, and resonant places in our subconscious. Laid down in our sleep, these dream-roads weave together our levels of consciousness, which we then strengthen by working through the material in waking consciousness, exploring the images and themes that have emerged.

The Dreaming is the state of being that we unconsciously inhabit, just beyond our daily lives and our doing selves. But it is a state that earlier cultures lived in constant, undifferentiated connection with. This is the repository of psychic energy – our own and others, the homeplace of the unspoken, the invisible, the unspeakable. It weaves through us all, not only humans, but animals, landscapes, historical eras of the Earth and Universe beyond us.

> Dare to dream again.
> For dreaming is the language of your soul.
> And nothing your soul truly desires could ever be wrong or impossible.
>
> —Jacob Nordby

Those who navigate this world superficially with ease, manage to be almost entirely unaware of this other dimension. But that does not mean that it is not real. It is as real, more so, than our surface world, as it is the energetic framework that underpins all being and existence. The creatrix is highly attuned to The Dreaming, it is her communication interface with the sacred. As she develops her skills, she weaves her dreaming and her waking lives into closer and closer connection.

"

The dream is a little hidden door in the innermost and most secret recesses of the psyche.

C.G. Jung

Creatrix Speaks

"You are such a Dreamer," the Critic chides. When did dreaming become so frowned upon? Why are we admonished for this awesome skill? Humans have this unique ability to dream and create.

Dreaming is sacred. It's an act of faith. A dance with possibility. Humanity would not evolve without dreams, without imagination, there is no discovery and life would cease to be of any great interest.

Dreaming is a huge part of my creative process. It all starts with a dream and ends with another. My paintings, I feel, are representative of that dream state. Mystical and magical, abstract and enchanting. It's hard to describe what happens when I paint. I am somehow suspended in time and the real world is completely shut out. I hear only the conversation between myself and Spirit, the canvas, and the paint.

This dream dance is invigorating. I love every minute of it. When the painting tells me it is complete, I awake to my surroundings and am always surprised when I finally look at the time and realize that I have been engaged for hours. Dreaming led me here, to this outcome, to this creation. It is not foolish to dream. It is a gift, and if you begin to make time for it, there is no limit as to what can manifest.

Marsia

Magic

As creatrixes we are often acknowledged as magic-makers: the circus performer seeming to suspend the laws of gravity and human biology; the actor or musician assuming god-like abilities on the stage in full costume; a book or film that transports us to an entirely new world; a shared creative experience that makes us feel that we are one organism with the others around us. Magic is unleashed in these moments.

Creativity involves a harnessing of unseen powers, a making possible of the impossible. An act of creation that leaves all parties changed is a form of deep magic. It is transformational alchemy.

This, I think, is why creatives are experienced as dangerous: we don't follow the accepted laws of existence. We bend and break the rules with daring, rebellious abandon. We see the structures of our society as optional and malleable. We work with the very matter of the Universe.

> Magic is the art of changing consciousness at will.
>
> Starhawk

But what we call magic is simply a power that our culture is yet to understand or harness. Much of what previous generations of humans would have seen as magic has been explained away by science and harnessed by our technologies. But still there is so much that we do not understand. So much mystery. Despite our increased logical understanding of the world we live in, still we long for magic. Our human desire for the awesome, the incredible, the breathtaking, the impossible has not diminished.

Our culture has always grown because of visionaries, risk-takers, question-askers, artists, writers, philosophers, prophets: those who commune with the unseen. Yet still The Creative Way is a hidden path, often considered occult, and discouraged by a culture that wants conformity, conservatism and control.

As our culture's appointed conduits of soul, creatives could be considered independent priests and priestesses both of an emergent world and the timeless world's soul. We are the holders of the vision. We are the magicians.

We must live in such a way that our contact with magic and The Dreaming is prioritised as a vital way of being and the voice of the soul is louder than the voices of the world beyond.

We have to believe in the possibility of what calls to us in our dreams and visions, and pulses like electricity through our veins. We have to believe in that which no one else can see. And we have to believe in ourselves and our abilities to bring this forth.

Ritual

Ritual is most commonly associated with religion, magic and spirituality as a way of opening channels of communication between the seen and the unseen levels of self and Source. It is a declaration of intent that lets each level of ourselves know that we are here, listening, and ready to engage.

> *Ritual is the form and structure that enables your spirit to fly free. Ritual is the safe space you create that allows you to open to the deepest parts of yourself. [. . .] Ritual contributes to your wholeness by letting you swim and scamper with the Sacred.*[xxxiii]

"

Ritual is a routine that is sanctified by intention.

Stephanie Serrano, *Demystifying the Artist*

Rituals known as rites of passage ceremonies have tended to be held at significant parts of the life journey, to help ease the individual's passage through times of momentous physical and spiritual change. It feels important that we do the same to honour the significant parts of The Creative Way – both by ourselves and with our communities. That we take time to mark the completion of one stage and the entry to a new part of the process of any significant and lengthy creative project that will contribute to our body of work. We already do this through: 'turning of the sod' ceremonies at the beginning of significant building projects; launch parties; award ceremonies; cracking open the champagne when the first copy of our new book arrives; framing a good review or burning a critical one.

If you think again of the map of The Creative Way, what we do before crossing into the labyrinth and again at the centre, is to pause, to allow our mind and body to 'yoke' together. We root into ourselves, slow down our thoughts, assume the witness presence and allow ourselves to start to listen to the voice of intuition. When we are centred in ourselves we become aware of our inner senses as clearly as our outer senses: we can be guided by both.

Ritual can intimidate many, who feel that they need to be elaborate ceremonies led by an expert with fancy accoutrements. If this all sounds far too esoteric for you, please know that these practices help to shift the energy and brainwaves from the faster, multi-tasking, beta waves which govern our daily lives to the slower, alpha waves that are more receptive. They also awaken our senses, relax the body, heighten our intuition and quieten the chatter of the mind.

Many people have remarked how helpful they have found my sharing of my own personal creative rituals on social media. Seeing how mundane they can be seems to take away some of the fear. I am a firm believer that what matters most is your intent, and the symbolism of your actions for you. You need nothing more than your genuine intention and some sort of symbolic gesture: whatever sound, movement, special objects or words seem meaningful to you. You can certainly learn from the rituals of others, but the greatest power comes from creating your own, rather than following someone else's recipe to the letter or having a cupboard full of ritual items.

For some folks simply picking up their creative tools or entering their creative workspace brings them into connection with the Creatrix within. Other people or other times need a conscious centring practice and way of marking sacred space or sacred times in the creative process.

As I started on my final edits of this book I was feeling stuck and finding it hard to focus on a couple of chapters that needed a lot of restructuring. And so I decided to stop trying to edit on my computer and use some old-school cut and pasting techniques as well as a little ritual to help me make progress. I cleared my bedroom floor and put a cushion down in the middle. In front of it I placed two candles, and an image of rainbow-coloured tree branches that I had painted during the process of writing as a mini makeshift altar to the Creatrix. In front of these I laid down the printed pages that I had been struggling to structure. I put my shawl over my shoulders and dripped an essential oil mix called "Passion", gifted to me by a reader, onto my wrists. Then I put on the playlist that has carried me through the writing of the book and lit the candles with some words of intention.

I sat in silence for a few minutes, witnessing the pages that I had been getting so frustrated at. I picked up the first page and began to read and cut the work apart with scissors, dividing it into paragraphs and laying them on the floor, moving them here and there, weaving a new path through them, scribbling notes in the margins. When I found the order that felt right I stuck them together with Sellotape. When I was finished I uttered a few words of thanks, blew out the candles and tidied the space.

I find that this symbolic disconnection from modern technology in order to connect with Her via ancient technology through ritual, needs to happen at key parts of my work. I use ritual as my direct line to Source. As hundreds of generations before me have done. But I don't do this every day. Most days my ritual is as simple as shutting the door to my room, turning on the computer, and as I wait for it to start up I put my blanket on my lap, shawl on my shoulders, gather my books by my side, and slowly eat a square of dark chocolate as I focus on what I intend to do that day.

If you are yet to find or develop a ritual that works for you, here are some ideas that myself and other creatrixes find useful:

> Any sufficiently advanced technology is indistinguishable from magic.
>
> Arthur C. Clarke, *Profiles of the Future*

- Close the door, which is a symbolic way of shutting the world out. Lock the door if you want. Or put up a sign. Turn your phone off...or at least silence it so that you are creating uninterrupted space.
- Put on a piece of clothing or jewellery which you associate with creativity, imagine it contains within it some way of accessing your creative self. Some writers have a favourite hat, necklace, ring or shawl. Some take their shoes off.
- Try to have a chair, cushion or way of sitting that you associate with your work.
- Turn on some music which inspires you. Put on some headphones to make an instant creative bubble for yourself. Develop and play the same playlist which will help you enter your creative zone quickly each time.
- Use scent – incense, a scented hand lotion, diffuser or an essential oil mix that is calming, invigorating or helps you to focus...
- Sound a chiming bowl, light a candle or turn on your desk lamp.
- Dance, stretch or shake your body out.
- Have a cup of tea or coffee or glass of water or eat some chocolate.
- Write down or think of an intention for the session – make it as general or specific as you need. It might be to open up to your creative Source... or to write the introduction.
- Take out a previous piece of your creative work, or your work in progress and drink it in without judgement, through all your senses. Just spend some time with it.

- Briefly tidy your workspace.
- Lay out your tools in front of you, so that they are inviting you to work.
- Pull an affirmation or tarot card.
- Start by doodling, especially with your non-dominant hand.
- Take ten minutes to free write or draw.
- Do a visualisation or short meditation.
- Take a short walk in nature.
- Flick to a page in a daily book of inspirations…or your favourite poetry or art book.

Once we become more familiar with the sensation of creative energy coming through, we can set ourselves up for success more easily. We know what we need and we know what Source needs…and so we make these methods of connection a priority.

Ritual is about taking moments in the busyness of life to allow magic to seep through the gaps.

It's about clearing space for ourselves – our bodies, our voices, to show up as they are – and start listening.

It's about making space to spend time with what we have already created, so that we can soak up its medicine.

It's about opening ourselves to the possibility of the dark, and what happens when we let go of forcing and control.

It's about showing up as ourselves, willing and open, making space for the magic and mystery to meet us.

> Ritual and myth are like seed crystals of new patterns that can eventually reshape culture around them.
>
> Starhawk, *Truth or Dare*

THE WORK

"

Creativity is the way I share my soul with the world.

Brené Brown

Calling

If you are creative, the layman's understanding goes, then surely you should be happy doing anything creative. But we know that this is simply not the case. Whilst many different creative activities may be pleasurable, soothing and enjoyable, this is very different to finding and committing to creative work that engages us on every level, makes us feel alive, drives us incessantly forwards, and transforms us…and those we share it with.

Whilst I applaud so many books on creativity – they share beautiful and inspiring ways to begin to reconnect with the creative flow – what most are doing is saying that this is *it*. Creating *anything* is enough.

But that is simply not true for those who seek self-expression and transformation through their creativity, those to whom creativity is not just a pastime, but also their life's work.

For example, I enjoy knitting: the colours and repetition soothe me. I enjoy it as a way to pass time on winter evenings. It clears my mind and calms my soul: it is a form of profound meditation and at many times psychological survival. When I am stuck with my writing, I often pick up my knitting, and after a while the words flow again. It has also added much beauty to my wardrobe. But knitting is not *my* Work: it is a way *to* my Work.

That is not to say that knitting is not *The* Work for others. But it is not mine (at least, not yet). It has been a strange and winding road to discovering exactly what was and wasn't my Work. I am not a gifted poet of iambic pentameter, and no literary mistresspiece is calling my name. No, my Work is sharing words and images that express the unseen energies I struggle to navigate, illuminating the path of the depth psychology of the Feminine. My calling appears to be exploring and expanding the boundaries of creative non-fiction in a genre non-conforming manner, giving voice to the liminal, the unspoken and the unspeakable and sharing this with women. This is my Work.

We each have to find The Work. Or rather, open ourselves to it…to follow the breadcrumbs of our bliss. That is the job of The Creative Way – to lead us closer to that which our soul hungers to make real in the world. Not just to make music, but *this* song. Not just make art but explore *that* symbol.

In the beautiful words of Joseph Campbell,

> *If you do follow your bliss you put yourself on a kind of track that has been there all the while, waiting for you, and the life that you ought to be living is the one you are living. Follow your bliss and don't be afraid, and doors will open where you didn't know they were going to be.*

I am the voice that always is calling you.

Brendan Graham, "The Voice"

This is The Creative Way.

Hearing Your Calling

Your Work sings a song

That only you can hear.

You may be too distracted, too scared,

Too caught in the mirror of others to hear it.

Until one night,

As dusk falls and the blackbird sounds its homecoming call,

Behind its voice

You hear the calling which is yours.

Beneath the rustle of the leaves and the dulling gold of the sun,

Under the silver voice of the rushing stream,

There it is,

Calling, calling

You.

Dare you follow the call?

Though the night be dark and your home be safe and warm.

Dare you seek out the sparks that light your way

To the flames within?

Dare you give yourself to that which longs to be born into this uncertain world through you?

Dare you finally listen to that which has been calling your name all your life?

"An essential portion of any artist's labour is not creation so much as invocation. Part of the work cannot be made, it must be received... There are few artists who have not had the sense that some element of their work comes to them from a source they do not control.

Lewis Hyde, *The Gift*

What is The Work?

I have mentioned The Work in passing many times so far, but what exactly do I mean by it?

I believe that The Work has its own distinct form, energy and agenda. And I believe that The Work chooses us. Our duty as creatrixes is in finding ways to connect with The Work in order to understand, collaborate, embody and express its energy and message most authentically. Through our creativity we map the invisible shape of The Work, bringing it into form: we are conceptualising the inconceivable – not so much making it up, as making it real for others.

This is what artists mean when they say that they are a channel for their art. It is not a dereliction of responsibility or a desire to seem mystical. Rather it is the truth of their experience: that they discovered the soul of each work of art, or rather it found them, and they laboured with the unseen to bring it into form.

The Work must move through us intact. It is a process of birth-giving as much as any physical birth is. And just as new parents may long to shape a child in their own image, we creatrixes quickly discover that our creative babies are not amorphous blank slates, but each has a definite character. Each pregnancy is different. Each birth is different. Each parenting experience is unique.

Our relationship with The Work is dynamic and alive. It is as real and complex and consuming as any we might have with a partner, parent or child, but without its being visible to anyone outside of us, except through our distraction and the fruits of our labours. The Work transforms us as we in-form it into the material plane.

Staying in right relationship with an entity that neither we, nor anyone else, can see or hear, and that has little respect for the human concerns of time, expense or deadlines can be an extremely challenging experience. But it is what we sign up for when we become creatrixes. In order to stay connected to The Work, we must tell the truth about it. However hard we may find this. It cannot be faked or forced, or the connection dries up and our creation reaches a dead end.

For those who inhabit only the daily world, The Work is invisible except through the works of people like us. The Work is often attacked, misunderstood or actively blocked, perceived by those in power as threatening to the worldly sphere. It is often considered too strange, too discomforting, and those who bring it through too uncontrollable, too weird, too dangerous or unreliable. By committing ourselves to bringing it through we are doing an act of incredible faith and service, making visible the invisible – bringing other worlds and visions into this daily world. It is work that is not always rewarded in worldly terms of money or acclaim.

To commit to The Work is to answer your calling.

It is an act of immense courage.

And in the same breath it is hardly a choice.

We committed to it long before we remember.

Our only real choice is how long we are prepared to live in denial or active avoidance of doing The Work.

It is willing to wait lifetimes.

We have only one.

Experience

I totally believe in my Work (most of the time, except when I doubt everything about it and my own abilities, or when I've had a nasty critical comment about it).

I am totally committed to it (except for when it seems the most insane thing in the world to trust my family's financial security to).

I do it pretty much every waking moment that I can (except when I need to give my energy to my children or I'm sick or burned out and have to simply try to stay alive).

It has my yes and confidence (except when I doubt my sanity, or try to explain what I do at dinner parties).

I invest a large part of my time and energy into it.

My job is to make notes on the process in words, images, colour... Even if it's the middle of the night or I have a deadline for something completely different.

Even if I know I can't do it.

Even if, especially if, I find it weird and deeply uncomfortable.

Over the years there have been a number of problems with this set up for me:

1 – I do not know where this 'Work' comes from. Or rather, I do not have the words or the confidence to share what I do know.

2 – I feel very weird talking about it this way. I would find it much easier to say "yes, it's all mine" and be in control of its content and direction!

3 – I am called to do Work which I would not consciously choose. It often scares me and freaks me out to have to stand up and put my

face and name to something that others will criticise.

4 – By doing The Work, I have to put myself out there when really I am much more in my comfort zone being private and small. I am not after ego trips or fame or fortune. I have anxiety attacks and autistic meltdowns when under the public gaze, I am terrified of most people on a daily basis, without having to try and sell strange books and odd paintings.

5 – I feel my skills are lacking for what I am called to do. Not-so-friendly critics never miss the opportunity to highlight these failings with words that lodge in my brain and refuse to shift.

But what I have realised is this: the resulting work reaches many, many people who have been hungering for something like it. It heals me too. I trust The Work that comes through me implicitly. I am blessed to have it.

My feelings about myself are beside the point. And in a way are an insult to The Work. My discomfort cannot and must not step between it and the world. It is not my role to censor or seek to control the feelings it provokes in me or others.

It is truly not about me! (But trying telling snarky reviewers that, when they're trying to take you down!) I need to get out of my own way and show up. Taking care of myself in the process. For no other reason than to let The Work happen through me.

This is not to say that I only turn up to my work when my golden telephone to the heavens rings and I float to my desk. I work whether or not I can hear its guidance. Though often that means a lot of U-turns when I find I've been taking it in totally the wrong direction. There are a lot of days looking blankly at a computer screen. But the days when it is there in the room, in my body, in my brain with me, when I am fully connected to creative flow: it is the most wonderful feeling in the world. I described it once as being invited to take tea with God. It's not an invitation you turn down for anything.

It is up to me to be there for flow when it comes. It doesn't matter that I understand exactly where it comes from, and if I believe in this or that. The Work is there. I can feel the immense transformation it makes in me, I am privileged to be told of the magic it weaves in the lives of others.

And that is enough for me.

I am here. It is calling to be born. And I can hear it. So, the question is not: how or why me? – but rather...

Where is my pen? My paintbrush?

Am I listening fully?

How can I stay connected?

How can I care for my human self so I am able to be of better service to The Work?

These are the only questions that matter.

"Creativity is sacred, and it is not sacred. What we make matters enormously, and it doesn't matter at all. We toil alone, and we are accompanied by spirits. We are terrified, and we are brave. [...] Make space for all these paradoxes to be equally true inside your soul, and I promise – you can make anything.

—Elizabeth Gilbert, *Big Magic*

Source

If you have a clear idea of where The Work comes from and what your creativity is *for*, it is often far easier to accept its incessant call and bewildering drive. How we understand the source of our creativity in turn informs our relationship with it.

For those who have been raised in a religious background and who believe their talent is a gift from God, and who have both an established language and ritual to draw on, understanding and accepting the role of artist can be relatively easy. That is, as long as the messages and images coming through are congruent with their received beliefs and are acceptable to those in their community.

For those who have been raised in a very individualistic culture, who believe that their art is a valid form of self-expression, and is accepted as such by their family and community, and whilst what emerges is not contrary to their own beliefs or cultural norms, again the role of artist is reasonably unchallenging.

For those who hold a belief in spirits, souls, the Universe or the muse and can identify the voice coming through them as belonging to one of these, then, again, once this entity remains consistent (though it may be ridiculed on the outside) it can be easier to follow.

What others call it is irrelevant: how you understand and build your relationship with the source of your creativity all that matters. Through your art-making you learn to trust the unseen Source more fully in sacred acts of co-creation and enter into partnership with it.

When we don't have a clear understanding of the source or purpose of our work, then all we have is strange voices in our heads telling us to do weird shit. Then we are more likely to ignore or sabotage what calls to emerge from our pens or paintbrushes or bodies, especially if it is challenging to us or those in our culture. This is when we can really struggle with sharing what is coming through.

As creatrixes we tend to be aware of our connection to the greater mystery, to the realms that lie hidden to most. This can be hard to articulate and can make us sound crazy. We know, through personal experience or the tales of others, the potential cost of this: ridicule, insanity, hospitalisation, medication, loss of reputation… The fear of these things often makes us resistant to living in full communion with the mystery. So, we often try to live with one foot in this world, and one – secretly – in another.

Experience

In my understanding, the Source is the font of what Liz Gilbert calls "Big Magic": a greater than human energy that propels us and demands to be expressed through us. Not being human itself it has little respect for our frailties and vulnerabilities – it is pure energy. Its only desire is expression. Its only drive is to flow outwards: spreading, flooding, watering everything it touches.

I have made a deal with this energy: its gifts and vision, for my body as a channel.

Many of us have. Consciously or unconsciously.

This Creatrix energy pours through us in paintings and poems, *dances and rituals, novels and protests. She is streaming through us, out into the world. Each artefact and object, each ceremony and circle a way for Her energy to emerge, so that the world can be filled with beauty, wisdom...Her.*

For me creativity is a path of devotion: reclaiming my connection to the Feminine Source, to myself and to the world. It is a path of extreme vulnerability and one which has immense gifts both for myself and for the people I share this planet with. It also feels extremely dangerous, because these realms have been considered occult for so long.

As I look deeper, question norms, explore that which I have left hidden in this lifetime or other lifetimes I feel great fear. But as I continue to look and paint and write the voices which are not allowed in our world, I become more fully alive. I become more fully myself.

And I know that this is why I am here.

Skills

Many of the abilities used by creatrixes are not the sort that we are taught in school. In fact, for many of us, they are skills we were educated and corrected out of. They include:

- intuition-led decision making,
- awareness of flow states,
- hyper-sensitivity to feeling, colour, sound and place,
- the ability to perceive or translate one sensory experience through a different sense – synaesthesia,

- the ability to travel energetically and psychologically backwards and forwards in time,
- the ability to sense and communicate in a non-embodied manner, or with non-physical entities,
- the ability to source information from the unconscious mind, through dreams, trance and visions and bring it into conscious awareness,
- the ability to step partially out of the way to allow a larger energy to cohabit our body and influence our actions,
- the ability to project our visions into material form,
- the ability to share our deepest vulnerability,
- the ability to join our energy with that of others around us and work as a community being,
- the ability to recreate ourselves at will.

These are the native skills that every creatrix must remember and reclaim.

Vocation

So much of our busy, noisy, automated world is soul-less. To devote oneself to bringing soul into form is a vocation.

We may be familiar with the idea of a vocation from many religious traditions around the world. Priests and nuns are often described as having such a 'calling' to this work of service. Teachers and nurses often experience a sense of vocation – calling them to challenging and poorly paid roles of healing and growth. And so, too, do most artists.

A vocation means that you have a knowing that this is what you are *meant* to do, that you are in service of both your community but also a higher power. There is some larger purpose at play. Your work is not just free choice, your living is not just – or even – about keeping a healthy bank balance or worldly renown. You are living on purpose, guided by something greater than your own desires and ambitions. You have both been *chosen* for this role, and have actively committed to it: you are sacredly contracted to work in partnership with unseen forces.

I am aware this can sound very strange to our modern ears. If you are not religious, having a vocation can seem extra unusual…because you have no clear name or image to define this 'divine order-giver' with.

> “
>
> Art is kind of an innate drive that seizes a human being and makes him its instrument. The artist is not a person endowed with free will who seeks his own ends, but one who allows art to realise its purposes through him.
>
> C. G. Jung

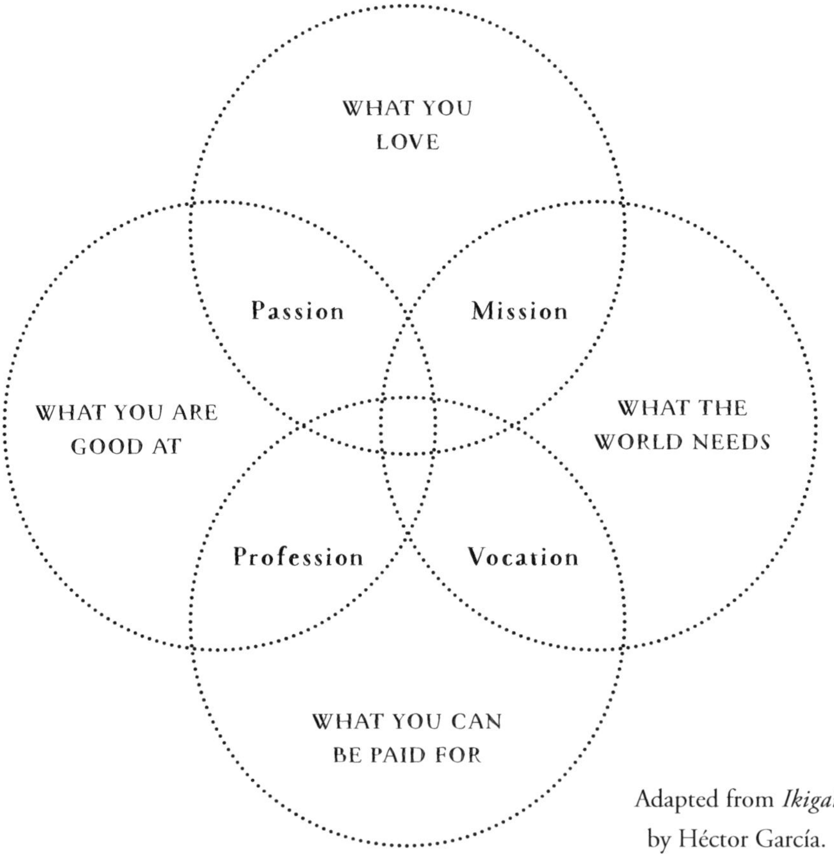

Adapted from *Ikigai* by Héctor García.

If it does, then I find this diagram a very useful, and totally non-spiritual way to understand the concept of vocation.

Because, in the end, most of us on The Creative Way at some point acknowledge that our work is not just of us or for us: it is not just ours.

However strange that might sound. However uncomfortable it makes us feel. The evidence is right before us.

Creatrix Speaks

Your creative muse gives ZERO fucks about your opinions regarding your capabilities or training when you make art.

She doesn't care if you think you are a shitty artist. Or not talented. Or never enough.

She doesn't pay any attention to when you compare yourself to others and fervently believe that you are lacking.

She takes none of that nonsense seriously. And neither should you.

She just wants you to create. Over and over and over again.

What you create is her department and none of your business. Showing up to your art is all YOU need to do.

All she ever asks of you are these three things: Trust her. Trust yourself. Trust your brush.

Nothing else matters. Nothing else NEEDS to matter.

Chris Zydel[xxxiv]

Channelling

The term *channel* has many meanings. It can refer to a structure which allows something to flow through it, such as a riverbank. This is the most common understanding of the term in relation to creativity and spirituality. This definition focuses on our emptiness and ability to yield.

But another meaning of the word channel that we use today is connected to media – a TV or radio channel is a dedicated frequency that broadcasts information to an audience which is congruent with its mission.

We as creatrixes are both. Our role is not just to allow The Work to come through us, but to amplify, transmit and share it as well. And when we begin to understand ourselves as both extremely sensitive receivers and powerful transmitters of soul-level information, we understand our role properly.

Both aspects can, however, be deeply unsettling as they are involved with unseen forces coming through the bodymind of the individual: forces that our culture denies exist. I find this denial strange, as we do not doubt the existence of radio waves, phone signals or the internet. Even though we cannot see them, our modern world is based on them. The energy signals that a creatrix receives and transmits are embedded into the fabric of creation. They pre-exist man-made radio waves by billions of years. And yet to claim to hear voices or to see visions (in non-religiously prescribed ways) has historically been dangerous for the individual, especially if they are female. And still today the dual aspects of channelling bring artists into the realm of the insane, the heretical, the magical, the generally untrustworthy.

“

Could it be that emptiness is a channel through which your creative ideas can be conducted and transformed into action? [...] your essential function is simply to keep the channel clear.

Day Schildkret, *Morning Altars*

It is right to be cautious. Channelling is an ability that can be abused if the ego takes over. It confers us with an unverifiable source of information and the potential power to influence the beliefs and actions of others. In order not to abuse this position we must be accountable and responsible to others and ourselves, we must reality-check wherever we can. Remember: the ability to channel does not mean that you are any more special than anyone else. Nor does it confer you with infallibility. It does not mean that every word that flows from you is perfect and unquestionable.

To deny that this ability exists is to deny the Source of virtually every creative and spiritual act since the beginning of human existence. It would be easier if we could say for sure what we were doing and why, and what this ‘energy’ was that came through us. And soon I think we will. In the past century niche researchers have sought to prove the existence of certain unseen energies used in psychic communication and ‘seeing’ experiments.

But for now, we have to accept that the experiential proof is overwhelming: we can see the results of it through the creative arts and advances in science, philosophy, religion and technology throughout the whole of human history. But most importantly we know it to be real in our own lives. We can choose to believe ourselves first and foremost. And let the power and truth of our work speak for us to those who find it harder to believe.

Experience

Looking back, I know I naturally channelled creative work in childhood and as a teen through drawing, painting, directing and writing. I would sit in front of a blank sheet and just start writing or drawing without planning, and it would just pour from me. But the second I would try to direct my ideas according to some preconceived notion it would dry up.

As you can imagine, trying to explain this to art teachers as I got older, who were versed in the need for us to produce dozens of preparatory drawings for each painting, never went down well. A-level art was supposed to be intellectually contained, not intuitively led. Needless to say, I found this very frustrating. So, I developed a technique of creating my art intuitively, backtracking to practice how to draw each of the elements contained within it, and then creating the end picture with these improved skills, but little of the intuitive freedom of the initial piece.

> There is a voice that doesn't use words.
>
> Listen.
>
> Rumi

My first experience of channelling as a young adult came out of the blue at university. I was in my second year, and suddenly an urgent idea came to me as I sat in a lecture. I wrote it down. But the information kept coming. So, I kept writing.

I moved from the classroom to a café, and stayed there writing for several hours, buying the occasional drink or cake to keep the café owners off my back. Lunchtime became early evening and still my pen was flying across the page. I walked back to the university and continued writing in the toilet until my next lecture. Still the writing poured through the lecture, and then the bus and train journey home.

This was totally unlike my usual experiences of writing essays where I would choose one of two essay questions, then make a logical plan, read some books and then write step by step. This was urgent and driven. There was energy and impetus to the words that poured through me, which were not planned or even thought: they were heard. Sentences appeared fully formed. I was neither initiating nor directing this flow of information, which wove together ideas I had never considered before: my only job was to keep up with this outpouring and not try to be clever.

When I am channelling there is an intangible energy which guides me. I can sense it. If it is there in the work I am doing, it flies. If it is not, it is like wading through treacle: slow and frustrating. When I write without the energy there, I fish around for each word making self-conscious sentences. Whereas when the energy is there, I fill page after page until it is done. A light edit and I have some of my strongest work: heartfelt, honest, and usually the most popular with my readers. And when I read it, it touches me too, because it is better than what I can write myself. It is inspired. And I can take little credit for it. This is not great for the human ego…and is pretty tricky to explain to others.

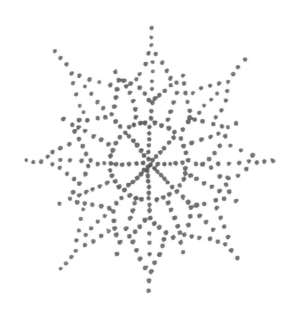

VOICE

Originality

Whatever your chosen artform, your voice – your unique form of expression – is what marks you out from other creatives. Your mission is to hone it over the course of your creative life, making it more true to The Work that pours through you.

We each have our own unique voice. But when we start to create we first have to work through the layers that we have accumulated:

- How we have been taught to create.
- What is correct.
- What is acceptable to express, when and how.
- What is out of bounds, wrong or unacceptable.
- What is impossible or undesirable.
- How everyone else creates.
- How our favourite artists create.

We have to slough off these layers to find our own unique voice, hiding beneath. This takes time and practice.

Most of us start out sounding like other people: our families, teachers, mentors or creative heroes, the people we have learned, consciously or unconsciously to emulate because we respected or feared them. And it is

> Your truth is your song rising up from the depths of your soul [...]
>
> If you're not speaking your truth, whose are you speaking? If you're not honouring your medicine, who will midwife it into being?
>
> C. Ara Campbell, *The Goddess Circle*

important to honour these influences. We are not, after all, the isolated individuals that Western culture leads us to believe, but rather are woven strands of our heritage and experiences. But, and this is the vital point, we are not them either. We are the only ones who are exactly like us.

The more you allow yourself to create freely, to deviate from some of the rules you have been taught that do not serve, to honour those that do, the more opportunity your own voice has to peep through the chinks of the armour of convention and acceptability. To find your voice allows the unique prism that you are to shape the light that pours through you in a way that hits the hearts and minds of others in a new way.

This is why it is so important not to censor ourselves: our creative soul is often different to what we have seen before and what we have been taught.

> "So long as you write what you wish to write, that is all that matters; and whether it matters for ages or only for hours, nobody can say.
>
> Virginia Woolf, *A Room of One's Own*

The Wild Voice

Your voice is a wild thing of immense power. She lives where the waters of endless creative possibility run clear and deep. She roams the world beyond your body, bringing back with her whispers of other lives, times and places.

We know her truth because her words send shivers down our spines and force a sharp intake of breath as she hits us with a powerful truth. She makes us cry or laugh, even at our own work. And she startles others too – people will respond strongly, emotionally to our work when it contains our authentic voice.

But how do we hear her? Where do we find her? How do we make her show herself in our work? She is wild, she cannot be forced or tamed, but must be lured and tracked with great respect and openness. It is often only in hindsight that we recognise her traces in our work, we see her footprints in the snow white page and know she was there. When we identify her, we can track back and try to recall, what was it that brought her out? Who is she talking to? What does she like to talk about?

You will find that the more you dare to risk, the deeper you go with her, the more you discover, the further you can go. It is an on-going and endless adventure, out into the wild edges of being.

Dare you go to the edge with your wild voice... and bring us with you?

Creatrix Speaks

I feel that my connection to the voice that lives at the sacred interface within is something that has evolved over time through my deep listening to the mysterious, elusive, sometimes nonsensical promptings of the mytho-poetic realms of life. This relationship has slowly grown as I have learnt how to honour and woo my own unique language of dream, deeply listening to the shapes my body wants to make as I dance, or the pictures or visions that bloom in my mind as I meditate or muse on themes or stories, in ritual and through the deep creative unconscious, untethering myself from the inner critic and the hyper-rational mindset of our culturally indoctrinated mind. I feel that to begin with, my relationship to the words and images that arose within me was tenuous and in contrast the voices within me that would belittle or diminish my attempts to articulate these offerings were strong. But over time, in saying Yes, again and again, to the half formed or strange-seeming offspring of my relationship to my deep inner muse, I feel I have made a more robust connection to my inner voice and to my creative narratives.

There has been a need to find an inner tenderness towards the particular way I receive information and a need to quieten the ideas of how I am 'supposed' to vision, of what it is 'supposed' to look like to receive from spirit. Almost as though we must learn to accept that the way in which we see/feel/hear, however humble it may at times seem, is the perfect way for us to receive. It has taken me a while to accept that often for me knowing is born of my kinesthetic sensing, of the sensation within the body. The imagery is often a delayed translation born of my coming to surrender to the receiving of sensation. A question I see I have been seeking to understand is: How can I receive myself as the sacred conduit that I am, that each of us are in our own unique ways?

Over time I have seen the gifts this conversation with the numinous interface has offered me, gifts of meaning, making and insight, not always in the moment of receiving, but in the timeless realm of intuitive becoming, imagery speaking to imagery, the body opening more deeply to receive the reciprocal tapestry of cohesion, of psychic symmetry, receiving the self as co-creatrix of the universe. It has also been my experience of suffering, of not belonging, of somehow feeling fundamentally unmet by what my culture was offering to me, that has helped to forge a deeper connection to my inner voice, a sometimes desperate cleaving to what authentic, embodied meaning I could make of life, in my own small and fumbling way, as a means of staving off the threat of meaninglessness, desperation or helplessness.

The tools with which I have courted the mystery in my life have included dreaming, ritual, dance, birth, eroticism, craft, art-making, women's circles, sweat lodge, story, drumming, meditation, prayer, song, chant, the labyrinth, poetry. It has felt important to me at times to fully immerse myself in the soulful, to saturate my life with the life-giving fruits of my fellow travellers of the beauty way, their words and pictures and song, in order to recalibrate my inner culture to a more deeply attuned reality.

Most of all it is the returning again and again to drink at that well, because of my deep love for that place, where I am in direct contact with the source within me, deeply receptive and diffuse and attuned, and then calling in my will to action, to direct the energy of what has been received into an offering back to life, of my love. This is something to live for I feel, the sense of belonging that is embodied in this process of listening to the unique lan-

guage of life that is speaking through me. It requires this deep unity between the masculine and the feminine it feels to me, the formlessness to receive the seed, the spark, and then the will and the direction to bring it to form. Both aspects need forging and tending, such a dance and one that I am still learning to trust and to read, to be mindful of feeding the voices that connect me to life and to the sacred weave and not to indulge those voices that would have me believe I am unworthy of belonging to the great cosmic dance of creation.

Lucy

> Being gifted simply means having gifts, having things to give. We all have things to give, because we have all been given things. So, how can I clear away all the nonsense that stands between this whole-hearted, full-bodied sense of generosity that I have about offering myself to life and allowing life to offer itself to me, without any stories about what that means?
>
> Dave Rock, *The Embodiment Conference*

Gifted

Your authentic soul voice has been replaced by your civilized voice, your trained voice, your mundane voice, through a mixture of fear and forgetting. You have forgotten your giftedness. Your creative talents have been gifted to you. Your voice has been gifted to you. They are an intimate and essential part of you which, for whatever reason, have become fully or partially disconnected from your sense of who you are and why you are here. You have forgotten that your very purpose of existence is to share your gifts generously with the world.

Your creativity is a gift to you and the world. It is a blessing. When you first hear your own authentic creative voice or see your gifts you may not recognize them. And then sometimes, you may be blessed to witness yourself in flow, without ego or judgement: to see yourself as you are. Like catching sight of your reflection in a shop window and for a moment you don't recognize yourself.

To reconnect with your authentic creative voice is deeply healing. A deeper part of yourself recognizes this lost part as its own – and every cell lights up and listens intently. You have received the gift of yourself.

Now it is your work to offer this gift to the world.

Creatrix Speaks

There are people waiting to hear your truth
People lying stranded on the shores of their desperation
Shaking for you
Aching for you
For your medicine
For the message in your bottle. [...]
You have been given a gift
The gift of artistry
Of illustrating the darkness
The mundane and monotonous
With the beauty of poetry and the grace of rhythm
Your voice is a gift
Use it
It is sacred
It is powerful
It is needed
So unravel the shackles around your throat that choke you into obedience
Into the solitary confinement of your silence
Pick up your pen
Open your mouth
Let the truth pour out
Unclog the coils of our interconnection
Your truth is my truth
Your story
Is my story
Is our shared story
Of our shared humanity
We are all a part
Of the one beating heart

Of the rhythm of life
And your darkness is so welcome here
So take the pain of rejection, the fear of never fitting in
Toss it into the simmering pot of your wholeness
Where your shadow dances into divinity through the light of your soul
Where the juicy fruits of your sexuality climax with the salty pungency of your intensity
And the warm dynamic spices of your deviance bubble and boil with the creamy innocence of your angelic faith
Filling the air
With the unique flavour
The aromatic essence
Of You.
Open the windows, darling
Let the world know just how exquisite you are in the messy beauty of your authenticity
Because goddammit sweetheart:
You
Are
Fucking
Delicious!

Dawn

(Watch Dawn sharing the full poem here **tinyurl.com/DawnCreatrix**)

Discovering Your Own Symbology

If we are to access the richest seams of our creativity we must allow ourselves to cut ties with the language that the world has taught us and allow our own inner vocabulary, our native soul language to emerge from our depths. The language of the soul is formed not of words, but symbols. Our most powerful magic as humans is the ability to decode and recode energy symbolically. No other creatures do this.

Discovering what our souls long to express is a process that is not random but carefully guided by a code of resonances: symbols. According to artist Allyson Grey, who has spent her creative career exploring symbology through her art, in *Women of Visionary Art,*

> *Communication through mark-making is sacred. Visual artists are symbol makers. [...] Symbols are evidence of consciousness.*[xxxv]

Learning to be able to decipher and read our own soul's language of symbols is a core part of the journey of The Creative Way. We discover them through physical feelings, intuitive hunches, night dreams and day dreams, through the metaphors we use, the images we are drawn to. When we create, we leave the literal world and its 'sense', and enter the realm of the mythical, the symbolic, the poetic – a realm of meanings within meanings.

When you see symbols emerging on a regular basis either in your creative work or in your dreams, or when you find yourself repeatedly drawn to one, do explore their meaning, both in your personal life and more universally. A book such as *The Book of Symbols* can offer fascinating insight.

As your body of work develops and you weave these symbols through, you will work deeper and deeper with these motifs and themes, and begin to see how they influence each other. You may start with a superficial or aesthetic interest in them, but after a while you will realise that they are leading you on a journey. They are the signposts on The Creative Way, your personal guides, taking you through the layers of your being and knowing. In the words of Shaun McNiff in *Art as Medicine,*

> *We [can] imagine paintings as a host of guides, messengers, guardians, friends, helpers, protectors, familiars, shamans, intermediaries, visitors, agents, emanations, epiphanies, influences and other psychic functionaries.*

Your images are leading you home to yourself and to more fully understanding your place in collective consciousness.

Follow them.

> Artists and writers whose work touches us deeply instinctively access collective symbols. They 'dream' for us; they bring images and stories from their own depths that could be our own. Seen from this perspective, artists or authors are our contemporary versions of shamans who have visions for their tribes.
>
> Jean Shinoda Bolen

Experience

I discovered my own personal symbology as I started painting again. Images that had previously meant a lot to me, that I was drawn to in my life: peacocks, pregnant bellies, hummingbirds, spirals, rainbows, labyrinths would keep emerging on the canvases. Especially spirals. In whatever medium I worked spirals kept appearing. I didn't really get why...in fact, truth be told, I wasn't sure I wanted them there at all, they seemed a little...clichéd.

It was only later that their deeper, subconscious meaning began to unfold for me. I started to track them back through my life, through my lineage, exploring their meanings and associations, and their wider archetypal and mythical significance.

But at the time I was simply painting what emerged from the patterns of colours on the canvas, following the energy that came through me in the way that felt 'right'. I am so very glad I did.

> The Universe buries strange jewels deep within us all, and then stands back to see if we can find them.
>
> Elizabeth Gilbert, *Big Magic*

Soul Archaeology

The process of finding our creative voices is one of soul archaeology.

Your authentic voice is rooted in the intersection between your unique and personal experience of place, time and being human – and your ability to find the universal, the part that connects us all: to walk this tightrope of the intensely personal and our shared sense of humanity.

For centuries women have been denied our own unique language of symbols. Our words, our images, our feelings, our stories, our fields of expertise have been policed. We have been told how to write, how to dress, how to speak, in order to please others, not to honour ourselves. We have been told to be seen and not heard. We have been told that our feelings are dangerous. We have been coded in the masculine for the masculine.

So be gentle with yourself and understand that in unearthing your own creativity you are entering an archaeological apprenticeship, digging down into self-expression which generations of your ancestors most probably have been denied.

Be aware that what you find in the depths of your psyche might be strange and unsettling, it might be hard to decipher.

And know that some of what you find there might not even be yours. In our depths lie the bones of our forebears, of all those that have been lost or silenced. With each creation, with each act of expression, you are reclaiming your own authentic voice, your soul, your birth-right…and you are releasing the ghosts and voices of those who went before you, those who may have constricted or controlled your life force or had their own held tight. As we reclaim our own voices, we may use them to honour our ancestors, celebrate our lineage, speak gratitude for opportunities that they would never have received. But may we also remember that our work must be our own, we do not need to live their unlived lives, either from guilt or fear.

CONNECTION

Connecting

Creativity is all about connectivity, on every level.

Creativity does not occur in a vacuum, rather it happens when two or more previously separate ideas, feelings or objects fuse or react against each other to create something new. A nuclear reaction occurs, when the essences of two existing structures are combined in a novel way, releasing the stored potential energy of both. When a new connection is made, a channel is unblocked, new understanding flows, new possibilities emerge: energy is unleashed. This natural process, which happens in the world on a deep time scale, is accelerated and more consciously controlled through the bodymind of the creatrix.

As creatrixes we are open to potential new connections. We sense them, just below the surface of our waking consciousness, see them as synchronicities, as flashes of insight… We live with all our senses activated, with a visceral connection to history, geography, culture, spirit, energy, and the inner world of thoughts, feelings, dreams, hopes. In doing so, we discover new ways to think, feel, see and be, that we pass on through the connections we cultivate to the wider community.

> The world of the soul is glimpsed through the opening in a veil which closes again. There is no direct, permanent or public access to the divine.
>
> John O'Donohue, *Anam Cara*

Connection to Body

Within Western understanding, we create from our own heads and hands, through the use of our logical, individual brains. But in many other cultures, creative energy is believed to be channelled through the womb-space, which is why women, by dint of their female bodies, are believed to have a direct, embodied connection to the creative force.

I believe that the entire bodymind is a channel for creative energy. What we do when we create is ancient. Primal. A vitally embodied act. Therefore the more connected to each layer of our physical and energetic bodies we are, the more we can harness its powers of sensation, manipulation and expression.

Part of the work of a creatrix is learning to reconnect with each level of her physical and energetic self, each interwoven stratum of her own being. She learns to descend consciously into her own darkness. She becomes accustomed to connecting and communing to the life force within.

> "We write, not with the fingers, but with the whole person. The nerve which controls the pen winds itself about every fibre of our being, threads the heart, pierces the liver.
>
> Virginia Woolf, *Orlando*

Our souls speak through the bodymind in myriad ways that we have been taught to disregard: in shivers down the spine, butterflies in the stomach, a raised heart rate, flashes of insight, slumps of energy, breath that catches in the throat in wonder.

As you begin to pay attention to your body, you will notice that any time you create – or witness – something which is connected to your soul work, your body will give you the signal. Just like that game we played as children:

You're getting warmer, warmer, hotter

YES!

You've found it!

Creatrix Speaks

I love intensity. If life is not visceral and alive, be it in movement or stillness, then I feel bored and frustrated.

I used to judge this. I read other people's reactions. I was too much. I needed to be less intense.

But restricting myself limits my aliveness. That feeling when the Universe can pour through me. I can feel the rushing through my tissue, sensation flooding in. And I LOVE feeling this! So, I decided to stop worrying about others and love what my body loves.

I have always danced. I feel totally alive, totally connected, totally in flow and open. Although there were a few points when I thought about becoming a professional dancer it just never seemed to work out. Looking back now I think that perhaps becoming disciplined and having a trained body just wouldn't have worked for me. My 'good girl' might have usurped my 'flow body'.

As my work as a performer took shape I experienced Butoh for the first time and this radically changed what I understood as dance. It was the first time I danced very slowly and I was hooked immediately. There is a richness in the intensity of moving slowly. If I bring all of my attention to my body I notice there is so much going on, so much available to me. Two years ago, I took this one step further by undertaking a somatic movement training course. I had always thought I was fairly present, but this work has brought whole new depths to that experience.

What I know now is that to let the body speak we have to slow down. The rhythm and processes of the body are so much slower than the mind. And when we can slow our thinking down to allow our experience of the body to come to the fore, then we can also encounter the Other so intimately.

I have encountered Grace in the softest of breezes across my face. I have been intoxicated by a golden-gorse-cliff-Beauty, whose vanilla-coconut scent has filled every cell in my body. I have been filled with the sound of a roaring jet engine above me as I stretch my hands upwards.

"I will die if I am not filled by It," I whispered. I had no idea what I meant, but once I uttered the words, I knew it was true. For me the experience of the Divine is a bodily experience, not metaphorical and not merely spiritual. It is exquisite, sublime. I don't know yet what to 'do' with it all, but my sense is this is about living a richer life, filled by spirit, experienced by flesh so I am more fully human, more radically alive.

Tracy

Connection to Cycles

> "Our only choice in each moment is whether to be part of the creating or part of the unravelling.
>
> Tracy Verdugo

Our bodies are not machines or unchangeable lumps of clay, but deeply connected to the cycles of energy around and within them. Learning to read and ride these energies, rather than resisting, ignoring or working against them (as we have been encultured to do) empowers us as creatrixes.

We inhabit a digital and mechanistic world that focuses on endless, linear growth models. A world where things – and now people – are supposed to be at 100% productive efficiency 24/7, 365. But creativity hasn't got the memo. It still plays by traditional rules.

Creativity is a cyclical process, which is probably why it has traditionally been associated with the Feminine. It has its own seasons of expansion and contraction. The emergence of the first buds of inspiration as the thaw of the bitter winter of nothingness begins. The unfurling tender leaves as a project emerges. And then the glorious summer when ideas drip from us like honey, and all the world is alive. The body thrills to the fizz of creative delight and we emerge in our native colours, whole and complete. For a moment we are one with the flow. And then comes the autumn, when we gather in the harvest and share it, seeing the fruits of our labours ripe and full, people sinking their teeth in and the juices running down their chins. And then winter comes once more. Sometimes desolate and bitter, at others a time of quiet, rest, retreat and repose, where we can allow the magic of gestation to happen and the energy to return to our roots once more.

What you will notice is that all the aforementioned energetic cycles correlate. So, for example, new beginnings are found in the early hours of each day, when there is a sense of the energy being fresh, young, vibrant and building. This rhythm is repeated on a monthly cycle in the energy of the waxing moon and during the pre-ovulatory part of the menstrual cycle. On a yearly cycle it corresponds to spring time. And when looking at creative projects it refers to the beginning rush of energy, seeds of ideas and excitement.

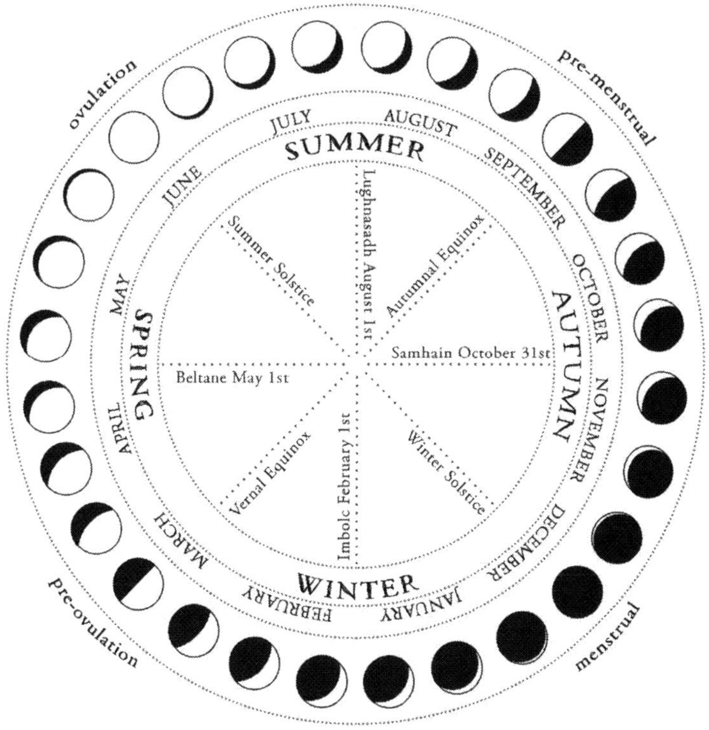

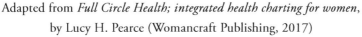

Adapted from *Full Circle Health; integrated health charting for women*, by Lucy H. Pearce (Womancraft Publishing, 2017)

On the flip side, so many people hit a creative winter, or are pre-menstrual, menopausal or depressed, and want to know what the magic spell is to turn it instantly to summer. The truth is there is none. Anything forced will be superficial and will drain you of energy. Creativity needs to come from our fullness. It might be a fullness of ideas, or words or joy…but also anger or sadness. But we need to be bubbling over with it.

Your Guide to Creating Through the Cycle

Stage of the Menstrual Cycle	Optimal Creative Acts
Pre-ovulatory	Signing contracts, planning, working, research
Ovulatory	Launches, working, sharing new work with others, reading reviews, networking
Pre-menstrual	Editing, decluttering, proof reading, cutting, making space
Menstrual	Reflection, rest, intuitive leaps, research, doodling, dreaming, witnessing

"

This is my art.

This continual ebb and flow of life.create. death.create.

what is more art than life and death?

what is more art than being?

Erin Darcy

Your number one duty to yourself as a Highly Creative Person is to keep yourself in flow with the cycles within and without, to harness their creative energy and combine this energy with your own, honouring both the expansive and contractive phases of the creative cycle.

Creatrix Speaks

As a mother of four, single-mothering two little ones at home (the others have flown the nest) and heading into my moon-pause, my creative moments have become a haven for me.

I've always drawn, painted, sewn and made things, but the last nine years or so I noticed an almost monthly call to create.

Coinciding with my pre-menstrual and bleeding time my creative juices get flowing and I need to carve out quiet me-time alone to create. What I have found is that when I can make the space to do this, I'm a much calmer mother, the creativity feeds a need that supports my mothering.

Now don't get me wrong, I don't always manage to get the time to do this, some months the timing just isn't right and I look for other avenues of self-care that can work around mothering. Plus, I've had to work hard at letting go of guilt and my mother's voice in my head telling me I'm being lazy and selfish. Self love, self care and self kindness aren't selfish, they are preventative health care!

Over time my creative offerings have woven more and more into my work, and I feel blessed that there are people out there drawn to my books, art, cards, drums and rattles.

Last year I was diagnosed with cancer, which has thrown me even deeper into my healing journey, and the need to create has become more frequent. I notice that around the full and dark moons I'm particularly buzzing with ideas and so I began channelling healing intentions – along with the moon and earth energies – into my drums. I began to experiment with natural dyes on the drum hides, mixing pigments in a big pan on the fire in the garden, some nights under the full moon, feeling like an age-old crone that has been doing this for many lifetimes! And what I have truly loved is the feedback from those who become the owners of these medicine tools, telling me they can truly feel the loving intentions I have woven into their making.

On so many levels, creating heals me and keeps me sane on the journey of juggling motherhood, cancer, perimenopause and life. I have realised that if you don't get the quiet, alone time, how can you hear your soul's calling?

I have a sense that the journey of perimenopause is a calling to the self. I'm sitting in the 'void' and instead of wondering where *life is taking me, I've stepped fully onto a path of deep healing. This time I'm getting it, and it's deep, deeper than I ever thought possible. Healing ancestral pain, trauma, historical sickness that's trapped in our cells, passed on unknowingly. I'm the 'lucky' one that gets to say, "No more, it stops here."*

Rachael

Connection to Feeling

> Tell the truth to yourself first.
>
> Maya Angelou

More than anything else, creativity reconnects us to our feelings. In a culture that requires repression and suppression, our creative urges insist on expression. Rather than the enemy within, we discover that emotion is the ultimate flow state, ever-changing and becoming. It is the superhighway to the unconscious self and the key to transformation.

Often the emotions we experience feel so conflicted and deeply personal that we do not know how to begin to express them: the grief and hope we feel for our species' future in a dying world; the love and tension we feel at a family gathering; the exhilaration and fear we feel when we are alone in wild nature. The art we create that stems from these paradoxical emotions can bring them into conscious awareness for others, expanding our ability to feel into the chaos and integrate it.

The artist has always been one that feels deeply and channels feeling. One that dares to exist in their beautiful vulnerability in a world too scared to feel fully. In the words of poet, Victoria Erickson,

> *An artist is typically a being that is filled with so much passion, love or pain for certain lands, people, ideas, or images that all they can do with that overflow is bleed it out by creating. And with this type of art, the energy will be shifted from the depths of them and into the depths of the audience to be felt. It is a dance. A transference. An intimacy. It is to touch and awaken another human in a place they hadn't known was aching, or sleeping. Both are opened. Both are nourished. Both are transformed.*[xxxvi]

Often it is not until the communal experience of our feelings, through reading or singing or dancing or protesting together, that we experience the totality of their essence. We experience a collective witnessing so much more powerful than anything we can know alone. And furthermore, where feelings in our own bodies can be crippling and isolating, when shared they are often both magnified and yet more manageable – we are able to flow and transform through them more easily, and focus the released energy into collective action.

Creatrix Speaks

I have been working professionally as an artist for sixteen years, at first as an actress and theatre maker, jumping through the fringe, West End and international touring theatre hoops before focusing on creating my own work.

In recent years my personal artistic practice has shifted to music and I principally work as a singer songwriter now. During my mum's illness and death, music and my musical practice became driftwood for my sinking sailor: the most resilient flotation device you could imagine. In a sea of desperate sadness I could hold onto something that held me. And we'd be off, on a treacherous journey. I would sit at the keyboard with my cavern of bottomless sadness and go around in circles, asking the same questions of the same chords: What do we do now?

I cried a lot
I sang
I'd play the keyboard
It heard my cries.
The guitar danced with my sadness,
I fell in love with my guitar
it held me and allowed me to hold it
with all the pain surging through my body

I wrote songs
some too personal to share and some that needed to be heard.
I sang to other people.
I was terrified to share my grief
but as soon as I did
the people I feared
held me.
The social mask disappeared
and we stood in our mutual experience of loss.
They cried
I cried
They shared their stories
I shared my songs
I was held by their honesty – they were held by mine.
We connected
without trying to fix or change anything
we shared our humanity.

Lewis

Connecting to Place and Time

Our creativity is a means of weaving us more deeply into the web of existence. Through it we learn how to be part of the land of our ancestors and community once more. We experience our own present – the zeitgeist, the themes and concerns that make up our historical time, and our presence (individual and collective) – both their immense power and complete insignificance – in a more visceral way.

As creatrixes we learn more fully how to belong to our world and ourselves in a way our dying culture cannot teach us. Creating, we follow the Dreamlines that our ancestors once lived by when the land was understood to have wisdom and soul was known to be real. As we create we re-member a time when each individual enjoyed a native connection to the divine through their own bodies. We re-embody earlier points in the development of human consciousness (known by Swiss-German philosopher Jean Gebser as the mythical and magical) through creativity, simple ceremony and ritual. Doing so, we reconnect to many levels of what it means to be human that Western culture has forgotten.

This state of being is always there, but simply dormant. It is what the Australian interdisciplinary scholar and author David Tacey refers to when he observes the Australian land as,

> *activating a deep layer of psyche in white Australians that has been overlaid by civilisation. [...] In this context a descendant of the Celtic world is likely to discover that a version of ancient Celtic spirituality is awakened. [...] It is as if the psyche, automatically realising that a bridge must be constructed between the colonising consciousness and the primal landscape, reaches back into cultural memory to find an answering image of aboriginality.*[xxxvii]

"

There are subtle and intangible bonds that connect us with nature and place.

David Tacey

I am sure that this is why so many creatives find themselves needing to be in a certain place in order to create. To enable themselves to overthrow the internalised colonist mentality, they need to connect to a greater power: the soul of the place itself, which pours through them into their work. Their work is of the place, it is the voice of the place: its landscape, its history, the energy contained with it, the living beings that have inhabited it, coming through the human channel of the creatrix.

Rather than just walking over a place, rather than being in charge of it, the creatrix comes into direct relationship with it. We discover who we are in relation to the natural world, rather than what it means in relation to us. We begin interacting with it in reference to a deep time scale[xxxviii], rather than our small human timeframes of minutes, hours and even lifetimes. Places become alive to us. They are no longer inanimate, but ensouled in their own right. They become more deeply woven into our stories about who and how and why we are as individuals and a culture. We move deeper down into the Earth, her soul, her stories, rather than trying to ascend her through our minds, claim her for ourselves and mine her for our needs.

Land artists such as Andy Goldsworthy, David Nash and Day Schildkret and creatrixes like myself respond directly to place – gathering materials direct from the environment within which we create, responding to the landscape and climate in a direct co-creative act. Andy Goldsworthy describes works of ephemeral or nature art as "containing memories of human presence" [xxxix] in the land: our work is the way we leave our human presence in places that have touched us…and we in turn touch it. We communicate what it means through its raw materials, we weave ourselves into interbeing with it by working with its essences. We connect with the soul of ourselves, through connecting with the soul of a place.

"

When I carve, I look for the Buddha in the wood. And, when I am carving, I need to bring the Buddha out of the wood. I have to be very careful not to cut the Buddha.

Kyoto wood carver, *The Creative Spirit*

Creatrix Speaks

I feel that at its best, the experience of making art, song, poetry, or at least the receiving of the inspiration for these things, is a deep listening at the interface of self and that which is beyond the self, a moving towards what is vulnerable and unformed, tender and ephemeral, in order to receive something new about oneself or the condition of life. Often the things received in this place are far from grandiose visions of salvation but rather gentle and intimate homecomings, private revelations of understanding about the patterns and shapes of our wounds and our gifts, and a sensing of what the balm might be.

Lucy

Connection to Materials

Through creativity we look beyond our knowledge of materials, into the possibility of what they could be. A glass bottle, for instance, transforms from a utilitarian vessel for holding water into a musical instrument, raw material for a mosaic or jewellery, part of a window, a rocket ship… Using the power of the imagination and creative thinking, basic materials are transformed. The more we create, the more we soften around what we know and enter into an expanded space of curious openness to possibility, where the material world is full of infinite potential. Through our honed skills of craftswomanship, our ability to manipulate materials increases to a point where our control of them appears magical to others.

This is the opposite of the Western mind's desire to categorise and name everything, break it down into ever smaller constituent parts and place these in known boxes, which once categorised become fixed, set and 'owned'. The creative approach leaves space for the infinite becoming, shifting, changing and unbecoming of energetic states that happens in all things – sometimes so slowly as to be invisible to the human eye. It accepts the reality of the Universe that all is in flux, all is in a constant process of coming into and going out of being. It allows space for chance, and for co-creation with the mystery.

As artists, we tend to have both a sensual and psychic connection with, and experience of, the materials we choose to work with: clay, wood, fibre, paint… We literally shape them with our consciousness when our cells touch their cells. There is a connection and energetic exchange as we transform each other. This is now being recognised by female physicists, including Dr Elisabetta Matsumoto who observes that "knitting is coding and yarn is a programmable material." [xl]

Our materials cannot be forced by will alone but must be respectfully softened, retrained, persuaded with our hands and vision. On a literal level we are breathing in the sawdust, soaking the ink in through our fingers so that the materials, for a time, become part of us, just as we imbue them with our own dynamic energy, bringing them to life for the moments that we work with them.

I believe that each material holds a soul within it that we are working with alongside the soul of The Work itself. There is an exchange of beingness, of soul, when we work with materials, inter-informing each other. In this sense we transcend the material world and actively experience the essence of things. We get an experience of the changingness of things, the alchemy of existence and an awareness of the magical moment between forms, when all is potential.

Even with man-made materials, the very essence of them, the qualities that each has, is central to the art that they make: the viscosity of acrylic paint, the fragility of glass, the rigidity of plastic... In the end, even these are rooted originally in the oil and the sand of the earth. Each process of creativity adds a layer of new meaning and possibility to the materials. We learn to cooperate with materials, to be in communion with them as we co-create. We learn to respect their limitations, approach them with playfulness and curiosity as to the unseen potential they hold within them. Just as through this interaction, they help to release the unseen potential within ourselves. Through them we process the textures of our inner emotional experiences and visions.

Well-crafted, the materials of many works of art can outlive their creators by centuries or even millennia, and are able to transmit the artist's vision through time and space. Enduring artworks are containers not just of the energy of their original creatrix but also repositories of the memories, witnesses and temporal events that have happened in the intervening period. They become, as Andy Goldsworthy observes, "containers" [xli] of time, and containers of soul. In a culture that worships the man-made, the shiny, the new, the artist once again is at odds, valuing the ways that materials continue to evolve over time – the cracks and crazing that add character to wood or clay.

When we create, we are only partially aware of the impact we have. We have our own intention for the piece, but we are unaware of the unpredictable and unforeseen ripples that occur when we release it into the world. When we put our energy to the materials now, in this moment, we do not know what other quantum unfolding this act will precipitate. We can only work in blind trust. Perhaps more than anything else this is what is the most thrilling part of creativity – when everything is in alignment and fractals upon fractals of chain reactions unfold. Knowing that we were an intimate part of it, and can remember at the exact moment when the unfolding was initiated and the materials danced with us in such a way as to create a greater magic.

Creatrix Speaks

Creativity leads us beyond what we know in our minds, to what we know in and through our bodies and our unconscious selves, that we did not know or trust that we knew. This is our superpower.

I don't create sculptures like this because I am so 'Zen' and have life all figured out, I make them to remind me what is possible if I listen to my soul.

The goddesses I make are all about three to four inches tall and there's a reason for that: they fit in the palm of my hand. When I create them, I feel as if I'm part of an unbroken lineage stretching back 30,000 years to the person who originally carved the Goddess of Willendorf. I feel connected to the priestesses of the Mesopotamian temples who sculpted hundreds upon hundreds of tiny clay goddesses.

Someone commented on my sculptures once saying, "echoes of Mesopotamia." And, I said, "exactly." I feel the connection between the clay in my hand and the clay in their hands, running through the ripples and eddies of time.

The ancestry of my goddess sculptures may not be the same energy that raised temples and built monuments (or walls), it is the energy that carried a baby on one hip and a basket of supplies on the other and needed a goddess just the right size to tuck down the front of a shirt...

Sometimes I describe my life in the woods as being held in the hand of the goddess. And, I make goddesses that I hold in my hand. Am I in the palm of her hand or is she in the palm of mine? The answer is both.

Molly

> Be around the light bringers, the magic makers, the world shifters, the game shakers. They challenge you, break you open, uplift and expand you. They don't let you play small with your life. These heartbeats are your people. These people are your tribe.
>
> Attributed to Danielle Doby

Connection to Community

Though many creative people are lone wolves by nature or habit, most of us benefit from connecting with other dreamers, darers, doers, artists, rebels and counter culturalists to feel, for a moment, a little less strange in this world. This collective aspect of creativity is powerful.

Have you felt the power of creating together? For most of the creatives I spoke to, creating together is an integral part of their practice and one which they would not be without. The energy that a group of creative people can raise is more than any one individual can – and greater too than the sum of its parts. In communion with each other and the creative spirit, creative energy is enhanced and possibilities increased. Together we create a slipstream that carries us all further and faster.

The possibilities for creating together are limitless:

- Creative companionship: writers' circles, art groups, knitting groups…

- Creating together: improvisation clubs, choirs, bands…

- Collaborations, either between folks with similar skills…or complementary skill sets: writers and illustrators, singers and songwriters, dancers and choreographers, costumiers and directors…

- Collaborative creative events: shows, summits, festivals, protests, podcasts, exhibitions…

- Creative classes, retreats and workshops…

> The circles of women around us weave invisible nets of love that carry us when we're weak, and sing with us when we are strong.
>
> SARK, *Succulent Wild Woman*

A creative community can be a makeshift container and mirror for your creative self, a womb where you might nurture your seedling ideas and share the vulnerable joy of your newborn creative children. With a shared language and set of experiences, it's often an alternate reality where you can feel safe, have fun, learn new skills and experiment. Your community gives you the first place to share new work, and to practice being in connection with an audience.

In the digital age, we don't even need to leave home to join a vibrant creative community. For all the talk of social media causing isolation, for creatives, if used well, it can be one of the most powerful tools for connection.

Whether online or in person, for many creatrixes being part of a creative group provides more than just creative support, but a real community of lifelong connections that weaves them more deeply into the world. It provides a human heart for their art.

Creatrix Speaks

For many years I had been looking for a centre to what I do– there are threads that go across all the work I have done in the past twenty years: people, communities, creative expression, opening/learning/transforming. But what is at the heart of this?

I realised that it's the bringing of people together that I am most interested in. And as I picked through this in more detail, I discovered that it is the experience of communitas (or at least the opportunity for it to arise) that I am most passionate about.

From latin, communitas refers to an unstructured community in which people are equal, or to the very spirit of community. I first came across the word when I was studying theatre at university. It was used by anthropologist Victor Turner to describe a non-ordinary state that occurs when we are in relationship with others, encountered usually in a rite of passage. But from my experience spontaneous communitas is also possible at cultural events such as performances, concerts, workshops, community feasts and processions.

There's something about the shared intention of a large number of people gathering in one place for the same purpose. The collective energy and attention forms a kind of node-of-beings, which allows each individual to access more power than we can on our own. Some of my teachers call it the Field.

We enter into the Field with others and the Field also works through us. I have a felt sense of this connecting force: something invisible weaves the group together. It connects me more fully to my own body, heart and spirit. The connection can nourish and restore me. Whether I'm performing, producing, attending or collaborating in an event, I have found both simple and explosive joy being in community with others. It has healing, transformative powers for all involved who are open to it.

Tracy

Creative Inquiry

Soul

- What is soul to you? Is there any unlearning or expansion of the term you want to do, based on what you have read in this chapter?

- How do you know soul is present or absent in an object, being or work of art? What are the clues? Can you perceive them in your own work? Do others perceive them? What effect does the soul of your work have on the souls of others?

The Work

- Do you feel called to your Work? Or do you have a sense that there is something you should be doing. Something clear and defined. You just have no idea what it is yet?

- What do you understand your role and responsibility to The Work to be?

Source

- Do you have a clear idea of where your creativity comes from, what it is?

- Do you have a sense of its source?

- What is your relationship to your audience, to the human community?

- What guides you?

- What helps your connection and what severs it?

Voice

- What does it mean to you to find your voice?
- Have you ever heard/witnessed/expressed it before? When and how?
- Have you witnessed others expressing their authentic voices? How did this affect you?
- What do you fear might happen if you express your authentic voice?

Gifts

- Do you consider yourself gifted? Have others considered you gifted in the past? How was this communicated to you? Did you consider it a blessing or a responsibility?
- Do you value your gifts? How, or why not?
- Do others value your gifts? How?

Magic

- Is magic a concept you feel comfortable with?
- How do you feel about the idea of comparing art to magic?
- When have you experienced magic?
- How did it make you feel?
- Have you ever made magic happen? Did you do this consciously or unconsciously?

Ritual

- What memories or associations does the word ritual bring up for you?
- What ritual practices do you currently use?
- Do you practice them regularly? If not what is getting in the way?
- What practices might you like to try?
- How might you use ritual and ceremony to further support your journey along The Creative Way?

Connection

- Which places do you feel drawn to create in?
- What material do you love to work with and why? Do you work with certain materials because you feel you 'should', but have no connection to? Why do you do this?
- When was the last time you tried a new creative medium?
- Do you weave cyclical understanding into your creative life? What impact does it have on your work? In what ways could you do so more?

Creative Community

- What type of creative community do you currently have…and what type of creative connection do you long for? How might you access this?
- What is out there already? What kind of creative groups are there in your local area that you know of? How can you find out about more?

Which friends could you ask? Which local publications run ads? Where are there good bulletin boards?

- Are there online groups that have caught your eye?
- How do you feel about starting your own group?

Creative Practice

> It doesn't interest me what you do for a living.
> I want to know what you ache for and if you dare to dream of meeting your heart's longing.
> Oriah Mountain Dreamer, *The Invitation*

What Calls You?

In your journal make a list of everything that inspires you, fills your heart or draws you in. This includes all the things that you collect, feel attracted to, that are recurring themes in your life...what flowers, animals, symbols, myths, characters, artists, places in the world, natural forms or elements do you resonate with? What images, colours, symbols, music, paintings or poems feel as though they were made just for you and have accompanied you through your life or recurred at regular intervals? What stories or associations do you have with each? Follow the vein of a couple of these through free association. Write the word down and then just keep writing, all the words and ideas that you associate with it. Don't worry about punctuation, making sentences, or even sense. Just let the ideas flow out onto the paper.

Another time, take yourself back on a sensory memory journey – think back to your happiest, most indelible experiences as a young child, and then moving forward through the years – what hobbies engrossed you, what colours sucked you in, what images have called to you through the years, which stories really resonated? What did you love to do when you were five, nine, twelve and seventeen? These seem to be common dates in my own and other creatrixes' timelines – moments of the creative soul breaking through before we learned to censor our passions for the benefit of others' comfort. Create a collage of your favourite books, characters, music, hobbies, people, animals, places, colours and objects for each of these key ages. Reflect on which threads have carried through, which have evolved, and which you have overlooked.

Surround yourself with the things that have emerged for you. Dive deep into them again and again – journal about them, sketch them, perform them, make an altar of them, hang them on your wall. Explore them inside and out, inhabit them, embody the medicine they offer you.

4

I am she who weaves new worlds,
From the gauze of creation.
She who is made of rainbows and shadows
Flesh and blood
And dreams.
I am she.

FLOW

“

Artists learn to live on, dance on and surf in the wild wave of unfolding that greets us moment to moment. Artists feel deeply and magically grasp the intangible, catching snippets of the unseen and bringing them life, form and meaning.

Eila Kundrie Carrico

Fluidity and Solidity

Creativity is composed of two opposing but equally important parts – flow or fluidity, the dynamic creative energy from which our work is woven, and structure or solidity, that which contains, directs and gives form to the energy. This echoes what we know from quantum physics, that all energy can have two forms – particle or wave. In the daily world we tend to work on a level of particle physics, but when we create we enter the world of waves.

Fluidity has traditionally been associated with the Feminine – biologically, emotionally and culturally, whereas solidity has been associated with the masculine. Most of us, consciously and unconsciously, have been taught to embody this polarity and its behaviours according to our biological gender and to prioritise the masculine over the Feminine. It is necessary for our wellbeing and success to learn to cultivate and navigate both.

Many of us are stuck in solidity, too trapped in the world, unable to contact or stay connected to or fully honour our inner flow. On the whole the 'Feminine' aspect of flow is that which has been shamed or ignored in our culture, and it is why this book focuses so insistently on it. However, some of us, regardless of our gender, are too stuck in flow – unable to structure our work, apply will and determination to it, too scared to bring it out into the world. For these folks, their focus needs to be on building the structural aspects of their creativity – their ability to shape, edit, market, sell or commit, which is covered in more depth in the second part of the book.

For the first group, the focus needs to be on connecting to and staying connected to flow, allowing playfulness and surrender once more. To do so we need to identify and allow the fossilised layers of our defences to crumble, unblocking the dam so that flow can emerge.

> I would love to live like a river flows, carried by the surprise of its own unfolding.
>
> — John O'Donohue

Finding Flow

The Creative Way is not a static path but a dynamic river of energy, always flowing, contained within ever-changing boundaries – here a chasm, there a narrow riverbed, here rapids, there a waterfall and now a floodplain. This flow is entirely independent of, and yet responsive to, us: a constant, ever-rushing stream of ideas and images, where it comes from and where it goes we do not precisely know.

The river of creative energy runs through our unconscious minds and bodies. We all have access to it. Any time.

Just like a river, you don't need to force it to flow. You are not the river. You are the vessel that holds the water, that carries and shapes it. You do not create independently, but cooperatively with it, channelling the flow of energy through your consciousness and body and into form, making it visible through your words, images, sounds and movements.

Artists often freak out about drying up and losing the flow. But whilst our bodyminds can become stuck, blocked or shut off with fear or exhaustion, the river is always there. Every single moment that we are alive, we have potential access to the flow: the river of images and ideas, inside and outside. Every moment.

How can I be so certain? Because that flow, which we long so desperately for, is life herself: the basic flow of energy from which all things are made. To think that we as humans are somehow separate from it or subject to other laws is our own strange madness.

We have become so full of misinformation about this energy flow and ourselves. Most of us have been taught to some degree to keep the hell away from its deep, rushing waters if we want to stay safe. This is why I'm here to reacquaint you with the experience of touching the flow, of keeping yourself open to it, of learning to swim, to float, to dive in and drink it, how to navigate the rapids and follow the stream when it runs underground.

Imagine this river. You may start out sitting on the grassy bank beside the river, you can paint it, you can record its sounds, you can stack the pebbles on its shores. Perhaps you stay here. Perhaps you take a kayak or a rubber dingy and explore its tributaries and rapids. Maybe you even decide you can walk on water, get a translucent Zorb and do it. This is your art, you get to choose your medium, you get to choose how you interact with the river. And you get to keep choosing. Again and again.

Eventually you get braver and don't need something to stand between you and the flow, and you decide to dive in and swim…swim naked even.

“

You are a river. A river creates her own pattern. She starts with a fews drops of curiosity in one direction, followed by a trickle of play in another, and eventually the route is engraved for greater surges of creativity and streams of delight to follow. She carries herself across the land with the untamed joy of her own emergence.

Eila Kundrie Carrico

The Flow State

Flow is not just a metaphor or concept – it is an accurate description of how information travels through our brains and bodies.

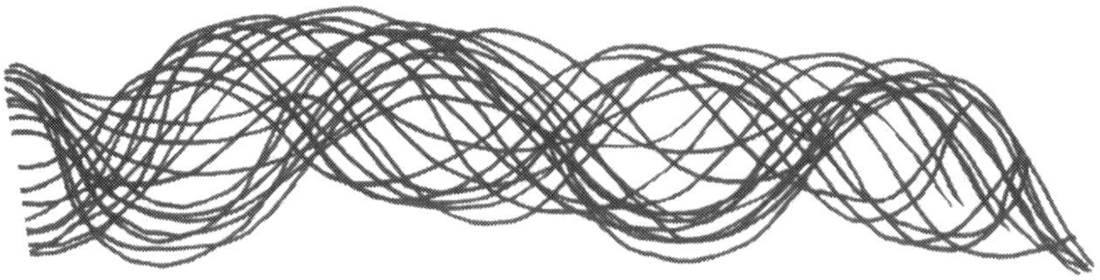

Flow is a positive psychological state that makes us capable of superhuman things: an expanded state of consciousness, where our senses are heightened and our perception of reality is shifted. According to Professor

Mihaly Csikszentmihalyi, former Chair of Psychology at the University of Chicago, who studied this state for over twenty-five years,

> *Flow helps to integrate the self, because in that state of deep concentration consciousness is unusually well ordered. Thoughts, intentions, feelings and all the senses are focused on the same goal. Experience is in harmony. And when the flow episode is over, one feels more 'together' than before, not only internally but also with respect to other people and the world in general.*

Csikszentmihalyi examined the optimal experiences of painters, rock climbers, musicians and athletes from around the world to discover the universal elements of flow.

He identified the main elements of the flow state as:

- A challenging activity that requires skill.
- The merging of action and awareness.
- Clear goals and feedback.
- Concentration on the task at hand.
- A sense of control.
- The loss of self-consciousness.
- The transformation of time.

There is no reason why flow should be an unusual or peak experience. Flow is the underlying principle of life, our most natural and potent form of consciousness: we do not need to make it happen. It can be reached in meditation and experiences such as birth, dreams, out in nature, and of course through creativity. We can align ourselves with flow processes arising naturally within us, and in the world. The more aware we become of flow and how it feels in ourselves, the more we are able to align ourselves with it.

"

When in flow, the creator and the Universe become one, outside distractions recede from consciousness and one's mind is fully open and attuned to the act of creating.

Scott Kaufman, *Wired to Create*

Being internally and externally aligned with creative flow gives us the sensation of freedom from external pressures and demands. It gives us what our souls long for: freedom from the restraints of time and the material world. As creatrixes our main work is in being able to reconnect to this state, more and more frequently, to learn to work, and in time live, from this place.

Flow is where the spiritual side of creativity comes to the fore. These peak experiences can feel like the most incredible meditation session, except we are actively engaged with an activity, rather than sat passively. For a moment it feels like we are suspended outside of time and space and reality, at peace with ourselves and the world. This is the 'high' that creatives and spirituals throughout history have quested after. The flow experience puts us directly in connection with Source energy. We become one with it, and for a moment experience the deeply pleasurable sense of self-transcendence.

Flow experiences tend to happen when our bodymind and soul are in synch – rather than the body or mind racing ahead, and the soul being left behind, all are working at the same speed, in unison. It is our natural state of being, but one that we have to reclaim deliberately, rebelling from the exhausted automaton state our culture cultivates, where both mind and soul are disconnected from an overworked, or completely passive body.

As you may have guessed, flow and the experience of kairos can be replicated or enhanced by other consciousness-changing methods: caffeine, alcohol and illegal drugs... This is perhaps one reason why many often take these short cuts.

So what are healthier ways of getting into the flow state?

- Minimising or eliminating sensory interference and stressors, maximising pleasurable sensory experiences.

- Regular creative practice.

- Cultivating creative rituals.

- Using trance, exercise or meditation as regular practices to help the bodymind enter this state.

- Allowing a sense of openness and softness in the bodymind by following the relaxation response.

- Fluidly moving from the flow state of dream and sexual arousal into creative work.
- Immersing yourself fully in the medium you are working in.
- Following your intuitive hunches.
- Taking breaks when feeling tired.

> I feel that I am transcribing verbatim from a flow of language running through the room, an ink current into which I dip the pen. It is a dark stream, swift running, a twisting flow that never doubles back. The amazement is that I need only enter the room at those strange hours to be drawn back into the language. The frustration is that I cannot be there all the time.
>
> Louise Erdrich

Direct Encounter

Flow is the deep satisfaction of experiencing life in its fullness – an allowing of all its sensations and emotions to pour through us undifferentiated. We experience flow during sexual, spiritual and creative engagements when we allow ourselves the opportunity to become physically or psychologically naked, in order to fully partake of and be changed by the experience. But so often these acts are merely done at a performative level, in order to enhance the ego or placate another. The appearance of communion is made, but nothing transactional occurs on the soul level. This is the faked orgasm, the trite spiritual meme, the popstar's carefully choreographed routine. In performative experience there is no place for vulnerability, no opportunity to leap into the void and risk failure or glory: the ego and persona are fully in place.

Authentic, transformative sexual, spiritual and creative communion require this leap in the dark. They require surrender, vulnerability and openness to something beyond ourselves, and the willingness to journey into the unknown towards it. The ultimate two versions of this experience are birth and death. And so we find, once again, that creativity is inherently connecting us to the life-death cycle, providing hundreds of little practices and remembrances of these major life events.

Each time we enter flow, we shift from the sympathetic to parasympathetic nervous system, from the stressed, fear-based daily state to a relaxed, receptive state. This can only happen when the bodymind can trust that it is deeply safe and is not under immediate threat. Only when we are able to switch off our basic fight, flight or freeze survival instinct, that most of us in the modern world inhabit as normal, can we shift into a state where we have deeper connection to our intuitive selves and the Source.

For some folks this may awaken echoes of trauma memories of soul dislocation or dissociation. The key difference is that trauma is unchosen, and is triggered in a state of high fear arousal, whereas the creative state is triggered by feelings of wellbeing and pleasurable arousal.

Experience

In creativity I find complete focus, the harnessing of mind and body towards an unknown, yet passionately yearned for, goal. I get a sense of making something new, meaningful and beautiful, seeing thoughts and feelings that I have not even previously guessed at writ large before me in my own hand. I find a deep intellectual stimulation, a harnessing of heart and mind, like the fluttering of first love, the adrenaline rush of a sky dive, but all from the safety of my own chair. And I feel connection, a deep soul connection, to those whom I am creating for and with, as I imbue the best of me into my creations.

At times there is the most precious moment of getting lost in the process. When my hands and the medium are one: the knitting is doing me, the piano is playing me. It has the strength and depth and clarity of an orgasm. But just as I realise what is happening, it is just me again, sitting by myself knitting or playing.

Every time I sit to write, or hold a paintbrush, the possibility is there, just a heartbeat away, if only I can fully bring myself to it with all my being and surrender myself to it. If I can let go of my ideas and flow with it, then, for a moment it is holy. I am holy. I and it and everything are pure, undivided energy and colour. We are one great beauty, pulsating in joy.

Through my creativity, be it painting or birthing my babies or making love, I have felt that I am connected to something greater than myself. That there is a heart in all things and, for a moment, I have touched it, been held by it, known it intimately.

This is what I long to share with you.

Creative Flow – A Neurobiological Reality

Picture in your mind a river, its twisting course, all the dozens of tiny tributaries running into it, and the way it can braid out into dozens of tiny streams when it forms a delta and runs into the sea.

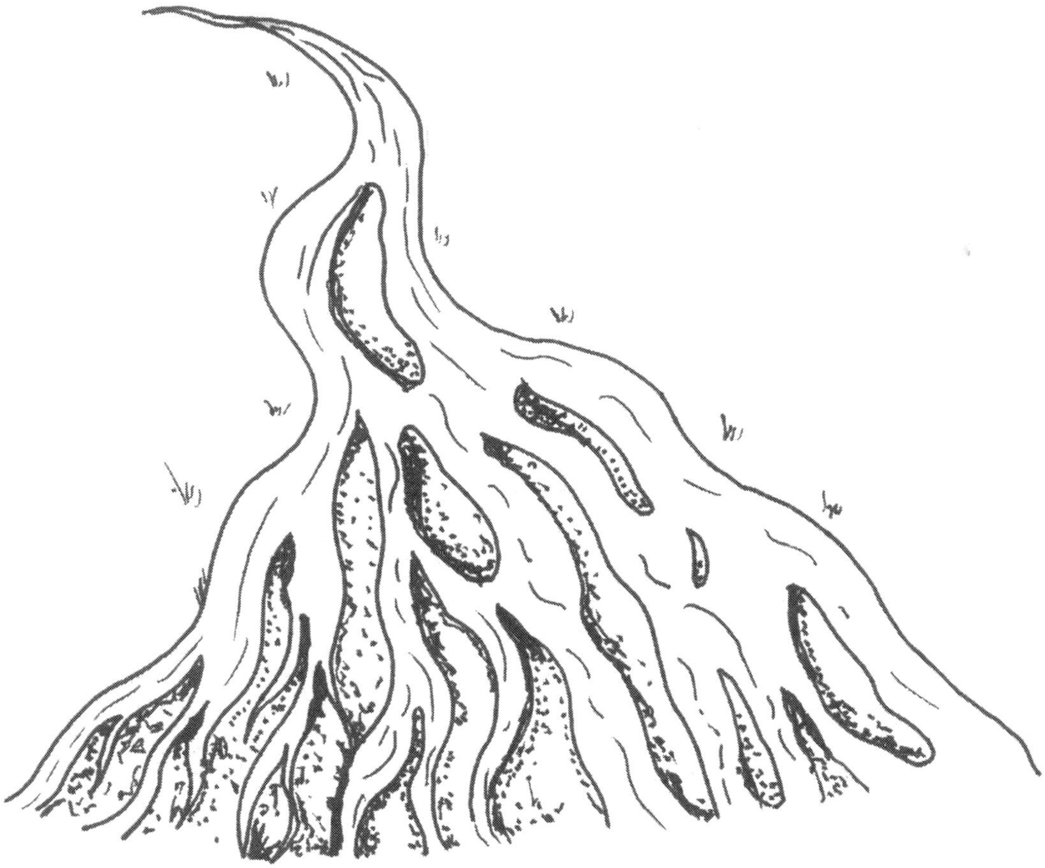

This shape is echoed through many natural forms. The Creative Way is one of nature's chosen forms: it is how the life force naturally expands, how energy diverges, how new land is made fertile, new ecosystems created. We see it in the form of seaweed, trees, blood vessels…

And brain cells… Our neurons look like dense networks of tree branches (dendrites) coming off a central round body (the nucleus), looking for another neuron to connect with. Each neuron has transmitters and receivers. The flow of information travels physically along the dendrites to a synapse. There it is transported chemically across the minute gap between the synapses via neurotransmitters, such as serotonin.

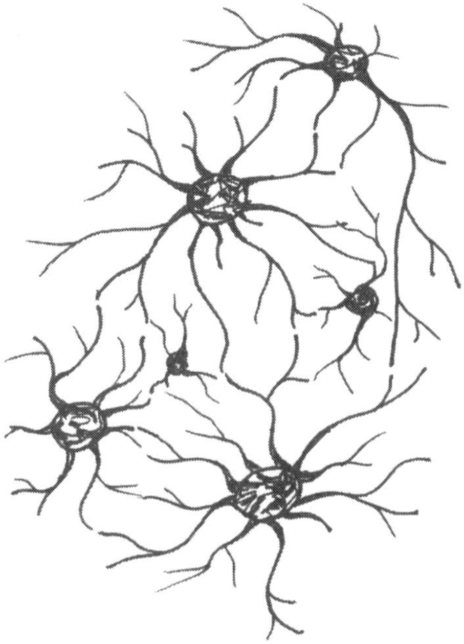

We are born with 100 billion brain cells, about as many as there are stars in the Milky Way.[xlii] But only 2,500 synapses (connection points) per neuron. However, by age three, we have about 15,000 synapses for every single neuron. As we approach maturity many of these unused synapses are pruned away.[xliii]

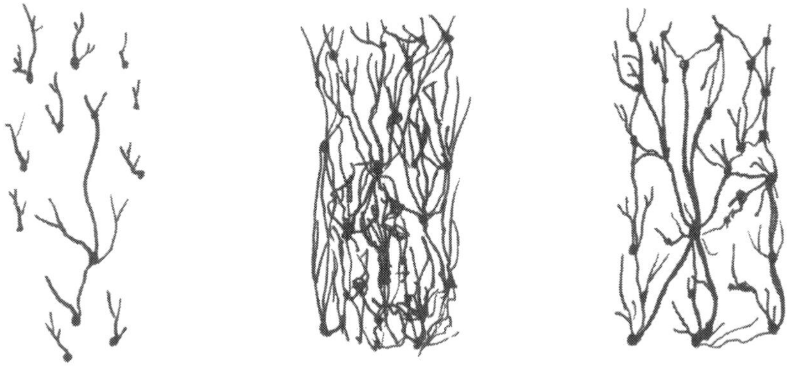

Previously creativity was explained in terms of left brain and right brain thinking. Newer research shows that whilst there are two hemispheres, it is far less clear cut: many regions of the brain interact.

By adulthood we have developed certain behaviours and thinking patterns that have become hardwired into us through repeated use and cultural and environmental rewards. These look like brightly lit highways. They are our default settings that we can follow with little awareness or energy, in part because they are the ones most rewarded by society, and mirrored by those around us.

Neuroscientists used to think that this meant that the behaviours themselves were hardwired and unchangeable once we reached maturity. But new understanding of brain plasticity shows that we are capable of developing novel connections between our brain cells over the course of our entire lifetimes. Fluidity and novelty are always possible: the possibility of creativity is hardwired within our brains.

The Creative Way is a neurological reality. Instead of following the super-highway, in whatever field we are functioning in, we are capable of going down the unused side paths: literally going off the beaten tracks of our brains, allowing our synapses to make new, original connections.

These new synaptic connections can take us in unforeseen directions.

But we may also find ourselves travelling down one and then another as we reach a dead end, finding a place where there is no feasible neural connection…or the information flow is too weak for us to understand. So we back up and try another one, and another. But we do this without really knowing we are doing it, and at high speed.

These new neural paths ways are literally dark, they have not been traversed before by conscious activity, maybe by you, or perhaps by no one in your culture, or even in the world…ever.

This is the reality of the term 'a light bulb moment': a new synaptic connection has been made and if your brain were scanned at that moment it would show the light literally coming on. Your brain cells have been connected in an original way, meaning that the flow of information is happening in a completely new pattern, illuminating new pathways of knowing.

In those of us with neurodiverse brains, our neural pathways are by definition more divergent, which means following the norm is much harder for us to do naturally, leading to regular overload. The flipside of this is that given the right conditions, this additional 'chaos' can lead to unfathomable and previously untapped creative potential as we make unique connections.

So how do we consciously travel The Creative Way within our brains?

First, we follow the thought, visual or aural spark mentally, through many of our senses as an internal experience. If we are paying attention, we are able to retrace our steps, discover how we got there, and are then able to use our expressive skills to articulate this realisation through our chosen medium. And then, if we are really brave, we can continue travelling forwards along the synaptic road publicly, creating as we go, witnessed as we travel towards an unknown destination. This is the shared creative experience that impacts all who witness it, rather than just a carbon copy performance that entertains.

In creating something new, your brain rewires itself: through your creativity you are literally making yourself anew. But this effect does not just stop in our own brains. Or even those of the people who witness our creativity directly. The morphic field – popularised by Rupert Sheldrake in the story of the hundred monkeys – shares the discovery that once one brain has been able to traverse new space and make new connections, this ability is passed on. Not only in the obvious ways of teaching or observation, or even genetically to our offspring. Rather it has been discovered that something happens in the quantum field of consciousness making this leap possible for many others who have had no direct exposure to it. Our ability to think a certain thought, or perform a new skill, enables this potential ability in our whole species. And so, creativity is not just an individual act but an act of human connection. In this sense, we are each a brain cell, reconfiguring our very ability to function as a species.

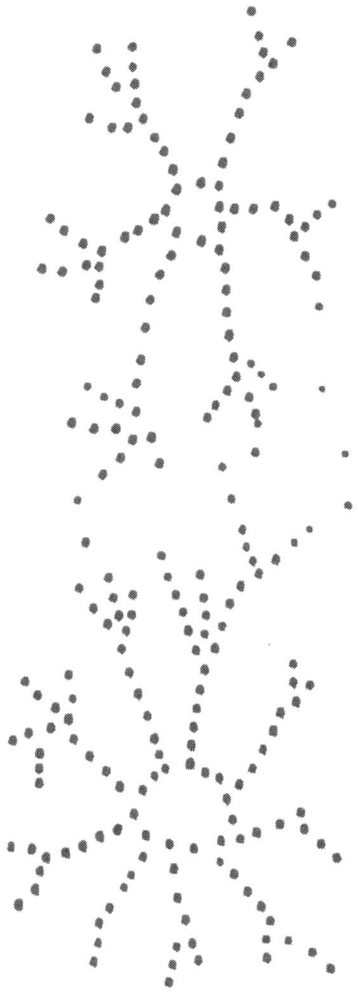

CHAOS

The Opposite of Flow

> Don't close down, don't seal your fate.
>
> Don't play small.
>
> You've got so much to create.
>
> Eleanor Brown, "What You're Looking For", from *Spirals*

We are entering murky waters. Not the clear flow of the pristine stream freshly born from the mountainous uplands, but the place where the river suddenly drops out of sight through a sinkhole into underground chasms. Or when the force of the watercourse causes whirlpools and rapids so fast and furious as to whisk our feet from under us, plunging our heads under the muddy waters. Chaos is everywhere. We cannot see. We are breathing water. The element that we trusted ourselves to has become the thing that might kill us.

These are the times where the winds rise, the rains pelt down on us, and life as we know it is washed away by the ferocity of the storm. These are the times when we are so disoriented by the events in our lives that we forget who we are or why we are here. Tragedy, loss, grief, depression and anxiety become tsunamis that take us down…

Far from the transcendence of flow, this is the territory of fear, when rather than a life bringer, water takes on the guise of death.

At times when it feels like the flow is too big, and we are too physically or emotionally vulnerable to feel the fullness of it, we shut down to it, keeping all our energy inside just to stay alive. At these times the river may go underground, into the depths of the unconscious mind. The flow may disappear for days, months or even years.

These are the times when creativity is often the only thing that can save us. And yet creating is the last thing we feel able to do.

Creatrix Speaks

At night, when my mind wouldn't settle, the paintings flooded out of me. Standing in my dead mother's kitchen, painting images of the grief that was only just beginning to make herself known to me. It is a companion I have grown to carry cloaked around my shoulders, and stuck between the fibre of my ribs.

For a year after, I didn't create any paintings.

Instead, my energy was spent forcing the grief to sit like a wolf at the door, foaming at the mouth.

I had to throw myself into the work.

Her legacy...me.

With the weight of my love and admiration for her – my need to be as good as her, my need to continue to make her proud...the work, it just found me.

Erin

> "The river does not flow in polluted, we manage that. The river does not dry up, we block it. If we want to allow it its freedom, we have to allow our ideational lives to be let loose, to stream, letting anything come, initially censoring nothing. [...] Then the river will flow, then we can stand in the stream of it raining down.
>
> Dr.– Clarissa Pinkola Estés, *Women Who Run With the Wolves*

Resistance is Futile

Though our natural state is that of flow: taking in the world around us and expressing it back out, for most of us this is not how we live. When times get tough, storms hit, when we are criticised or shamed we lose our ability to trust the flow. Things block the process or shock us out of it. And we shut down to the outer world. Or our inner world. Or both.

When we have learned that we are not safe in some way, the inner Witness relocates into an externalised hypervigilant Censor and Critic, whose one job is to keep us safe. We learn how to protect ourselves, how to stay small. We create masks or whole-body armour as defensive structures to keep ourselves safe from the world. We learn to disconnect – consciously or unconsciously – from ourselves. But these fear structures become, in the end, a defence against life itself.

The life force keeps coming at us, but we can't let it through our bodies, because it doesn't feel safe. In time we lose touch with our connection to source energy. We lose our flexibility and forget how we can enter the flow state. That big energy – our own and source energy – coming up against the immovable barrier of our frozen physical body and racing mind is, I think, what we describe as anxiety. It's coming to us, but not through us. We feel the endless knocking at the door, but we stay locked inside, shaking, too scared to open it, or unsure where the key is. We daren't let it in. The mind races faster. And we try to shut it down with food or starvation or alcohol or drugs or distractions. If we do this for long enough it can diminish. But so too does our life force. For many of us, this is the only way we can feel safe.

Many practices may soothe the bodymind and calm us superficially, but don't help to actively shift these physical and energetic blockages, and so we stay chronically stuck and frustrated, cut off from source energy and our own souls. From experience I have learned that sex, dance, yoga, body work, swimming, depth psychology, massage, singing and screaming can help shift these. As does creativity itself.

Through the creative process, if we allow ourselves to enter it, we learn to internalise the Witness once more, to align it with our intuitive wisdom, to become comfortable with the big energies flowing through us, and find ways that we can express them.

The act of creating serves to unknot us physically and emotionally and release the trapped energy so that we can experience more direct flow from Source. It does not matter where or how we start…only that we do. First we must stop resisting it. We must let our guard down, our need to control just enough for curiosity, play and wonder to be ignited in us. The creative process itself then has its own momentum which will unfurl and guide our steps.

Creatrix Speaks

Creativity is my medicine, my spiritual practice, my passion and my reason for being on the planet: it saves me.

My partner has recently been diagnosed with stage four cancer.

I am heartbroken and scared...

Standing at the canvas and my hands in the paint is the only place I can truly try to process our journey. I take my hand away, prise fingers from hidden lips, I close my eyes and open my mouth and when I look again there are flowers...flowers and stars...there is salt and sweetness, there is colour and glitter...and words everywhere...

We must wobble forwards always and when we can, grabbing hold of and squeezing the hands that surround us...and I must keep creating and remembering that however desperate life feels there is creative magic to be found in the mulch and the margins.

Clare

> "You feel heavy because you are too full of truth. Open your mouth more. Let the truth exist somewhere other than inside your body.
>
> Della Hicks-Wilson

Blockage

The majority of our biological existence is about taking things in at one end, processing them, and excreting what we don't need. The creative process is as natural and simple as this. But just as stress, muscle tension, extreme emotion and tiredness can interfere with our physical digestive process so our tight muscles, emotional blockages, rigid thoughts, held breath and traumas impede the flow of creative energy through our bodies.

A creative block is literally that: something blocking the natural flow of the life force. Sometimes we throw up our own blocks and sometimes there are cultural or systemic blocks to overcome.

And these dams are not just ours. Vast blockages go back down through families and cultures. Dams that have been built by generation after generation. Beliefs that were transmitted in our blood and the bread we broke together around the family table. Shame that was passed on from the day we were born, pacts of silence in exchange for safety.

We received these blockages like gifts, thinking that they must be for us, because they were given by our loved ones. And we accepted them as our own, believing that they would keep us safe. In time they became the reality that we inhabited, the thing we called life.

Since the creative flow is experienced on a subconscious level, so our blocks appear here too. We may be able to access and release blockage through movement, sound or bodywork. But oftentimes we need to consciously identify the block, inquire into its origins in order to shift it. Often just naming it, bringing it into consciousness is enough. We can do this by speaking it aloud or writing it in a journal, giving voice to what has previously been unspeakable. Visualisation helps. Painting, drawing, dramatization, expressive movement, stamping, crying, talking with a trusted friend or therapist...all these techniques help. One bit at a time, the stories, voices, feelings and beliefs that stand between us and our inner world, us and our outer world, crumble and fall back into the flow.

Experience

One way that our bodies manifest resistance and energetic blockage is through physical illness. I have been amazed to discover over the last few years that my migraines and autistic meltdowns are directly related to my creativity. This doesn't make them any more fun. Or any less real. But it does make me realise that they are part of the process – perhaps not forever, and certainly not to be aspired to – but they are part of my creative process for now.

This is not the same as saying that these sufferings are self-induced, imaginary or psychosomatic. They are not desired on any level. But they are necessary, until I am able to find other ways to release my physical and emotional tension and allow flow to come through me on a more continuous basis.

It might be because of fear and shame of what might emerge. Or it may be that what is trying to come through me is just too much for what my physical body can handle. Sometimes I do everything within my power to deny it and keep it in, to contain it, other times my resistance is unconscious, or because I do not have the time or space to release what is emerging.

I can feel it – pushing, bursting, trying to get through this invisible wall of tension. Looking to ground itself through me, but it hits my tight shoulders, my locked diaphragm and it starts to swirl inside, churning my stomach with anxiety, my brain whirring faster and faster as the energy gets trapped in the top half of my body.

It takes a meltdown, a panic attack, an orgasm, dance, a brisk walk to move it through – sometimes it takes hours, other times weeks or months before I can contact the energy and it can move freely within me – it can mix and mingle with my own energy that is no longer shut down, and find a way out into the world. When I am not using every ounce of my strength to bolster myself against the terrors of the world, this is when the magic happens.

Both migraines and meltdowns slow my bodymind right down to soul speed, they make me stop running around and rest, listen deep, they dis-able me so that I can hear beyond my own crazy mind. They are the build-up of soul, of sacred energy that has been unable to pour through my tension and the defences of my bodymind. Without fail, right before and right after a migraine, I receive revelation, a major creative insight, a flurry of creative expression, a deep knowing.

It is strange, but I know it to be true.

The Madness of Art

> The road to creativity passes so close to the madhouse and often detours or ends there.
>
> —Ernest Becker, *The Denial of Death*

Just as a literal river rises up from its source through strata of rocks formed in deep time, bringing up mineral elements and washing them down to the ocean, making it salty, so too the creative energy rises up through the layers of psyche, bringing up previously trapped ideas and feelings – both creative and destructive.

This is why creativity can feel so dangerous, because it threatens to bring forth the ancient that has laid buried, to wash away our carefully constructed psychological dams that we built to ensure our safety.

We may discover as we begin to unleash our creativity on the world, that our depression, our fear, our anger, our sadness and our traumas are also released. However much we wish to, we cannot undo our psychic control over only that which we choose for the world to see. It can be scary and challenging as our life force that we have managed to keep carefully controlled thus far, is unleashed on the world in all its colours and flavours.

We soon discover that raw creative energy is an undifferentiated stream of information – sounds, images, movements. And when it takes us over without filter or aesthetic editing, is perceived as madness. We become The Crazy Woman and the irrationality of this state of being terrifies our culture.

It is completely understandable, therefore, why we may choose to consciously resist our creative callings, afraid of what will emerge from the darkness. And so we choose what we perceive to be the safer option: keeping it all bottled up inside, away from the eyes of others.

But this energy does not disappear if it is not used. It is either channelled into other activities, or its current is reversed and it becomes negative and destructive. Brené Brown reflects from her years of research into shame that,

> *unused creativity is not benign [...] it metastasizes into resentment, grief, heartbreak. People sit on that creativity or they deny it and it festers.*[xliv]

I have noticed in myself that this unexpressed creative energy obeys the same flow dynamics as my creativity, but inverted – spiralling downwards rather than up, when it hits blockages and constrictions. It energises the

Storyteller within to weave dark and convincing tales of days gone by, the Visionary foretells impending doom, the Editor is transformed into a cruel, dictatorial Critic, the Hunter uses its pattern-tracking abilities to 'connect the dots' in a negative way. The desire to share and connect is flipped and we find ourselves isolated and alone.

This is how we enter the dark and get stuck there.

The Darkness

> When I cannot see words curling like rings of smoke round me I am in darkness – I am nothing.
>
> Virginia Woolf, *The Waves*

Darkness in many guises is common for the creatrix – from minor episodes after intense productivity, to major episodes related to deeper soul issues, traumas and life experiences.

Our journey through the darkness may take months or even years, and tends to happen at key points in our lives. It seems that it is only through the total breakdown of our old selves in the form of depression or psychic distress, that a new self can break through: bigger, more vibrant, more compassionate and wiser than we were before. In order for new connections to be made, old ones must be severed. It is a brutal process…and for some of us it is pathological. But I am convinced that it is a part of The Creative Way…the death side of the creative cycle. It is a dark initiation of the soul that breaks us open.

We can fight the darkness with all the energy we have, or we can pre-empt our passage by choosing voluntarily to lie fallow, to enter the void of our own volition. We can learn the rhythms and tripwires of our own journeys in the dark. Through experience and applied compassion we can learn to care for ourselves during them, activating the energies of Medicine Woman. But still we must live through them. There are no short cuts to the transformative process. Whilst the days of depression seem interminable and unnavigable from an internal perspective, from a more detached point of view they seem to be the human equivalent of a caterpillar going into a chrysalis.

It is at times like this our creative practices can become a life-raft to us, sustaining us with the colour, pattern and meaning they bring us into contact with when nothing else feels real or true. When our own faces look strange in the mirror and our hearts are broken, we might find a place to shelter from the storm by doing the simplest of crafts – knitting a scarf, doing a doodle each day, journalling, sorting buttons, taking a photograph.

But sometimes we are so overwhelmed by the experience, so exhausted by the emotional and physical deluge, that we cannot create anything at all. Colour is drained of its hue, words lose their meaning and dance out of place before our eyes. These are the times that the creativity of others can sustain us. We can receive the medicine of creativity, the healing and sanctuary that it can bring, the sense of communion and deep understanding that we can only experience through art. We breathe in life force through the creative work of others and are filled up once more.

> These places of possibility within ourselves are dark because they are ancient and hidden; they have survived and grown strong through darkness. Within these deep places, each one of us holds an incredible reserve of creativity and power, of unexamined and unrecorded emotion and feeling.
>
> Audre Lorde, *Sister Outsider*

Often learning to keep our bodies grounded and the mind as witness as the inner and outer storms roll through is all we can do. If we can jot down notes in the eye of the storm, their raw energy will be something we can harness later. But usually all we can do is to try to stay alive through it. And later, when it has subsided, we can beachcomb through all that has been thrown up from our unconscious minds, to see what treasures might have been exposed, how the landscape has been changed, and what from the depths has been revealed. From these unbidden treasures our most powerful offerings can be crafted and shared, which may in turn become life-rafts for others in their darkest days.

Creatrix Speaks

I go back to teaching arts and crafts, but my aspirations are elsewhere. I have been teaching sewing, knitting, sculpting in public school for more than a decade and it takes my energy. I am a volcano of emotions ready to erupt. I dream of creating what is bubbling inside me. I had closed my ceramic workshop to take care of my young sons. To show the father of my children, who does not understand my irrepressible need to create, that I put the family first. To stop dispersing my energy. In any case, I was no longer creating, I was only teaching others, and that was gradually wearing me out.

Closing the ceramic studio was necessary. Believing that it would save me was a mistake, of course.

My mind started to play the same song again and again: get up, wash, dress, feed the kids, fight daily to take them to school... There was no more time to feel, to smell the air, to ask myself: "How are you here and now, Zoé?"

No time to care for my inner self.

To paint, to carve or to draw the colours of my pain.

In November, my mind blows me a suicide scenario.

I'm courageous enough to call for help.

I enter the psychiatric hospital. I will not describe what looks like 'One Flew Over the Cuckoo's Nest'. In a lucid flash, between my underwear, I slip my notebooks, my pencils, glue, scissors, my pens and my knitting stuff in my suitcase. During admission they search my bag. My scissors are removed. I had not considered that!

In this place of care that is not one (but an emergency one, and thankfully they do exist), the patients spend their time waiting. Waiting for the right time to eat, to smoke, to sleep... We are trapped by grey walls and rare walks. There are few visits because there is no place to welcome visitors. No psychiatric interview, except at admission. Nobody to explain to my children what is happening to me.

I see we have to be alright to get out of here. I go out of the room quickly and go to draw at a table in the hallway. I draw mandalas, words and images, I draw the family, I draw who I am, where I am. I create a little book to explain to my sons what depression is. I water the pain down, I dilute it with colour, I do not want to hide the pain, pain-ting it with my brushes to see the gift. The gift of coming back to me, to my essence. I look at it, I transform it into art, I make it beautiful.

Between November and February, I will be interned three times. Three times at the time of my period. But I am the only one to have noticed that.

On leaving the hospital, my multiple art forms finally come together in an ode, a tribute to the feminine, ceramics, paintings, sanitary towels, songs, texts... The instinct I have to create *is what sustains me. I do not know how to live without it. It has allowed me to turn every traumatic episode I have lived through into something tangible. Into object-witnesses of my inner path. Creativity allows me to be in the world, and my great sensitivity has become my strength.*

Zoé

Burnout

> "There is a pervasive form of contemporary violence to which the idealist most easily succumbs: activism and overwork. The rush and pressure of modern life are a form, perhaps the most common form, of its innate violence.
>
> Thomas Merton, *Conjectures of a Guilty Bystander*

Creative flow is at the heart of our ability to create – yet we do not learn how to cultivate, protect and express it. We are led to believe that unless we are always performing at full capacity, doing all the time, we are worthless, in danger of being forgotten. Creative energy naturally expands and contracts, but instead we force it into the 'On' position and wonder why we experience inner drought.

Do not underestimate how much energy creativity takes. Sure, it fills us up on one level, but it requires lots from us too. We need to rest, to build our strength levels back up and take time out after every major creative project. If we have less energy, through burnout or illness, and still continue to create at the same pace, our own life force is poured into our creations, not leaving enough for us ourselves.

Many of us have not only the voice of The Work at our backs, but also the incessant voice of our own drive and all the potential critics past and future. So many of the creatrixes I know are fabulous overachievers, Type A personalities who push and push regardless of the resistance they face. What is one of our great strengths, becomes toxic for us. We don't allow ourselves to stop pushing, for fear of missing out, being too goddamn enthusiastic and excitable, trying to prove ourselves, all of which ends up with us damaging ourselves.

Burnout is a twenty-first century epidemic brought on by forced productivity, the deification of *work*, and the lack of respect for our physical and energetic cycles. It is a condition that we as Highly Creative People, with unreliable incomes and self-esteem, are especially susceptible to.

Burnout is energetic exhaustion. It's what happens when we believe that we are the source of our creativity, rather than the conduit to the flow. And it happens when fear drives us: we push ourselves against our natural rhythms, our creativity becomes work and any pleasure evaporates.

Being creative and an entrepreneur is a crash course in learning to trust the process. We must find a way to surrender to the constant flux, staying responsive and responsible, whilst knowing we are only partly in control. We have to trust the seasons of plenty and poverty, summer and winter. To be healthy creatrixes we must care for our physical bodies as well as our energetic selves during all phases of the process. We cannot deny the needs of one to serve the other.

But for many of us, existing in our physical bodies in this world is such a challenging experience, their needs too great or confusing, that we would prefer to live in the worlds we create for ourselves, than face the reality of this world, this life, this bodymind. This has certainly been true for me.

For many of us being creative is the only time we feel fully alive. Often the Highly Creative Person can begin to lose their own human self within the identity of Magician and Artist, fearing that without the super-human abilities and energy that their direct connection with Source allows, without the status or approval that our creativity garner us, we do not have worth, value or interest to others. We feel like shells, abandoned and discarded by our audience when we show our disappointing humanity, our weaknesses and foibles.

And so, we push harder, try to live our lives permanently afire with our creative connection – and find ourselves burning out in the process. We are, after all, human. Our bodies and minds are only able to stream so much of this high-level energy through them before they collapse. But that doesn't stop us wanting more: wanting to be these super-human versions of ourselves.

The drive to make more Great Work, to change the world faster is our greatest asset and our biggest downfall. Our impatience with the state of the world, the need to be getting on with the next thing, the frustration at how slowly things move – be it the editing of a book, or waiting for bureaucracy – drives us hard. When we hit empty and refuse to rest, we begin to run on adrenal energy which gives a rush and then a slump, depleting our immune systems, and often causing weight issues as well. Adrenaline is our friend to get us through extreme times when life suddenly demands our all. It gets us up on stages, out in front of audiences. It gets us to hit send on scary emails and take creative risks. It is our high-octane energy. But it is vital that we do not live or create from this place on a habitual basis. We need to learn to come down from this high and allow our bodies to rest and recharge.

We need to learn to create in a way that does not kill or even harm us. We need to dedicate ourselves to discovering how we can channel the work and embody it…and cherish our vulnerable human selves in the process. We do not need to sacrifice ourselves on the altar of our creativity – it can be a transformative mode of healing, rather than drawn-out self-destruction.

Creatrix Speaks

For me, it has always been creativity that has drawn me back from the precipice, back into life, in those moments when I have felt lost to myself. Whether it has been dance, song, painting, sculpting, it has always been the creative seed in my heart that has allowed the possibility to emerge of a new relationship to the sacred within myself, a deepening of my understanding of the world and my place within it. It is creativity, as an act of love, that re-immerses me in a meaningful dance with life.

I have been known to embark on journeys deep into the underworld of myself, prone to spells of relentless questioning as to the worth, purpose and meaning of my life. I have hoped for a revelation that might illuminate a clear, bold and courageous life path, one more socially sanctioned than this feminine, fluid, swimming in the within, as I move through subterraneous layers of shame and rage and self-loathing. From within these spaces there often lies a deep and painful procrastination around my creativity, a veiling over but also a seeding, of this devotional practice, sourced in the deep inbreath of the self, an expression of my love, with which I create new possibilities for enriching my relationship with the sacred.

My impulse to create has always been a crucial part of my own salvation. As a sensitive one prone to these spells in the darkness it has been my heart's deepest longing to express what it is that I find there, that brings me back from the underworld. Like the little girl leading the blind Minotaur, as though my words and image making were the translators of the ineffable, making decipherable to my bemused intellect the turbulent waters of my emotions, bridging the languages of my body and my mind, and giving a face to the divine, which my fumbling and finite self so longs to behold, so longs to be held by. The compulsion to bridge the dark and the light leads me home to a place where I can stand with a foot in both worlds.

When I create something it is like springtime after the long winter, this creative force within is my love for self and for life, flowing and furling itself outwards like a sprouting shoot. I fall in love with myself again, rejoicing in the way that falling in love has of dissolving your boundaries and brightening the eyes with which you see the world. It is a quickening and an entreaty to beauty and integration, to make bearable the times when I am lost and alone and at sea.

Lucy

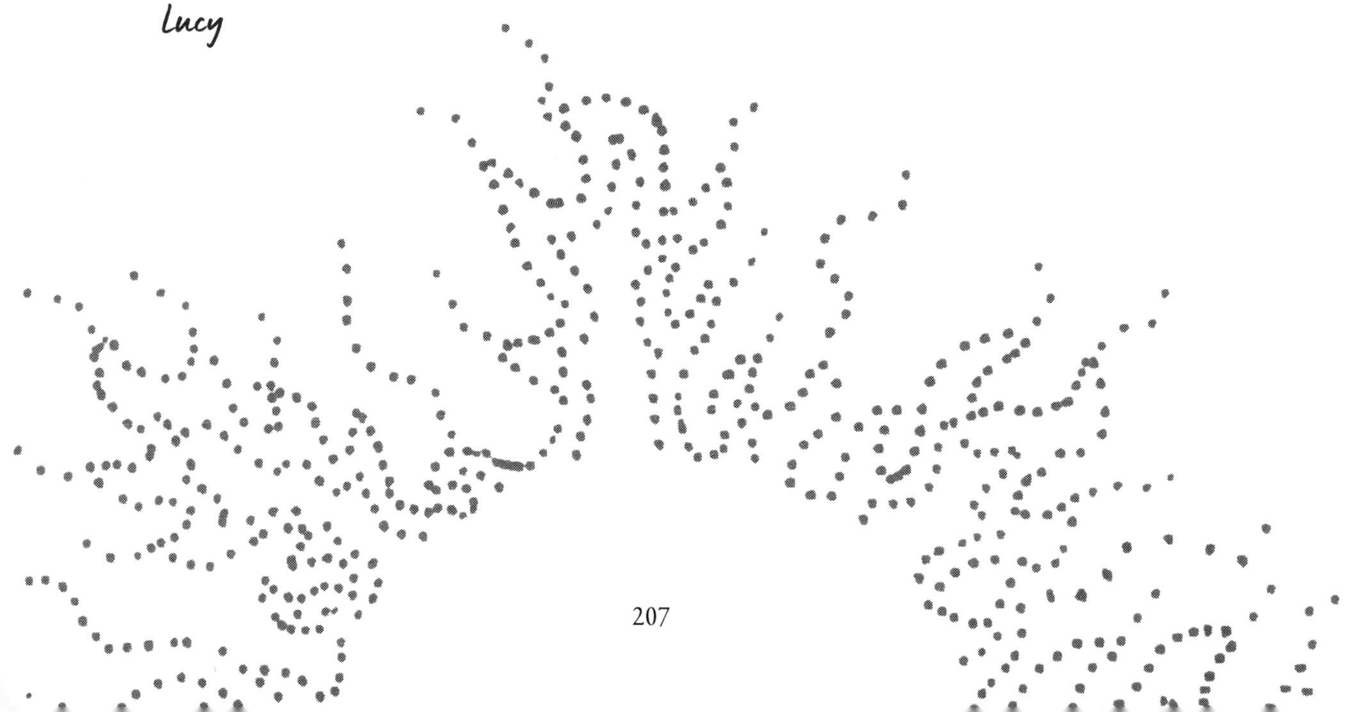

HEALING

“

Art is a wound turned into light.

Georges Braque

Art as Medicine

Our creativity is our companion to all parts of the journey, especially the most painful. Our ability to transform what in our culture is perceived as a curse into a blessing is a gift, not only to ourselves but to those around us too. Broken hearts have provided so much music. Countless paintings, films and books have been forged from pain. Creativity heals.

Since the mid-twentieth century, creating art has been considered a valid and useful part of the healing process by mainstream medicine, especially in mental health facilities. As Clare Hunter notes in her article for the Guardian,

> *After the First World War, doctors experimented with getting shell-shocked soldiers to embroider as a way of healing mental scars and it proved a surprisingly effective way of steadying their hands and settling their minds. [...] From the unlikely marriage of men of war and fine needlework, occupational therapy was born and has remained a mainstay of medical practice ever since. [...] There have been many studies exploring the relationship between creativity and well-being: the benefits, particularly for those suffering from mental illness, of the mesmeric immersion in crafts as a relief from inner turmoil.*[xlv]

Creativity is an incredible tool for self-expression. It helps us to work through trauma, tragedy, loneliness and grief, feelings our culture tends to provide no forum or space for. In processing and sharing them we give others the container for also travelling through these feelings. This in turn begins to connect us with a wider community.

However, the focus of creativity within medical contexts can often be superficial. The creative process itself, how healing occurs and why it is activated by creativity, are not given much consideration. In the UK this is beginning to change within the mainstream, with the advent of 'social prescribing' on the National Health Service, where family doctors will now be able to 'prescribe' dance, art, music and sporting activities to alleviate multiple health complaints.[xlvi]

It is also recognised by community centres in America, which are creating spaces for migrant women to gather and create together, as a way of slowly mending their shattered bodies and souls, and weaving new communities.

> *Embroidery is not just a way of weaving themselves together as individuals or even a community, but these threads weave them back to homelands forcibly abandoned, childhoods and family members long gone.*[xlvii]

Healing doesn't need to be the main focus of our creativity, and our art does not have to be *about* our struggles in order to heal us. Creativity may offer us a precious respite from the pain and suffering that have come to dominate our days. It gives us an opportunity to stop, and listen, not just with our ears but our whole beings. It allows us to drink the beauty and colour of the world through our senses: to experience the bodymind as a place of pleasure and connection once more. We begin to taste our tears, to see our love, to touch our pain and remember our belonging. Rather than keeping our inner worlds repressed to ensure our physical survival, we learn to express them through our medium of choice. Creativity turns us back on to the beauty of life that our experiences of pain and suffering have clouded.

Creativity that is most obviously healing is that which is repetitive and reasonably simple. Soothing physical activity, using colour and gentle movement, including centring or meditative elements and pleasurable sensory input: soft fibres, squishy clay. Creative activities that 'cross the midline' of the brain and body, such as knitting, woodwork, embroidery, playing an instrument or dancing have been found to be the most helpful in integrating full brain functioning and physical coordination.[xlviii] Activities done within a group setting such as knitting or improvisation, that integrate playful elements promoting social laughter and interaction, enable us to override the dominance of the inner Critic, improve the isolating symptoms of depression and anxiety and elevate our pain thresholds.[xlix, l]

The healing power of creativity fascinates me. In more ancient types of healing that have been lost or disregarded by our modern culture, objects were often made by a person requiring healing, incorporating symbolic materials considered to have healing properties. The act of creating a shawl, doll, shield, potion or piece of embroidery was as sacred and medicinal, as much as the materials and the resulting object.

In the passage below, Laura speaks beautifully to the healing that passes through her and into her dolls, to reach those that the dolls are made for. These small creatures of cloth made collaboratively with the vision and memories of the customer, interpreted by Laura's intuition, skill with fabrics and channelling ability, become medicine containers of profound healing.

Creatrix Speaks

I realised a year ago that if I did what I do now several centuries ago, I would have no doubt have been burnt as a witch for making 'poppets'. I make healing dolls. My doll-making just sort of evolved into this pretty soon after I discovered my calling to this craft. I have never identified myself as a witch or healer, but it seems that this is indeed what I am.

I have made custom order dolls for nearly ten years now. I make the doll in the image of the person it is for. They are made of completely natural materials and in the traditional Steiner fashion. I found very soon after I started this work, making custom dolls, that people were reaching out to me as part of a healing journey, either their own or to help someone else on theirs.

I have made healing dolls in many shapes and sizes. Tiny angels to represent a lost baby, a huge doll so the lady holding it would feel like a small child again, dolls with crystals inside their heart space blessed by a mother's hopes and love for a child about to undergo heart surgery. I have made dolls that are representative of inner children to be held and loved and I have made dolls that are to be buried in the ground.

As soon as I begin a dialogue about a healing doll, a special kind of magic happens. I need complete solitude and peace, as I allow myself to step out of the way and channel the doll: what it will look like, how it will feel to hold, its character, its essence. A clear picture comes into my head and I can describe very clearly what I see to the person seeking the doll. As yet, in ten years, this 'instinct' or insight or whatever it is called, has not been wrong once.

The doll is made in the same manner, in solitude and peace. It is a ritual: my hands do the work, a work that they know so well. My body is relaxed and my mind free of thoughts, my heart and soul are open.

The doll is created before my eyes, it is as if I am watching someone else make it. In a sense I am. I recently heard her described as 'She Who Makes'. While I am creating dolls, I am in her service, she works through me. I am her vehicle to create in this world, to create what is needed. This is my gift and I treasure being both a witness to this process and part of it. Often when I have finished a doll, I will come back into the room again and it is as if I have just seen it for the first time and I have little or no memory of making it. I am honoured and humbled to do this work, and glad that I don't live several centuries ago, when what I do would have been so dangerous.

Laura

Recalibration

> "To sew is to pray.
>
> Louise Erdrich, *Four Souls*

For the Highly Creative Person, creative expression is how we order, experience, process and calibrate our inner world. It is how we exist fully as ourselves. Creativity allows the organisation of inner chaos and confusion, and allows us to move through it, to retell it, to reimagine, to witness it, to put some order and interpretation on it. Making art is a way of acknowledging and processing the unconscious elements of our psyche, of mapping the internal journeys of our lives.

Without access to creative expression we quickly find ourselves out of kilter. Cut off from it for long enough we become physically and mentally ill. At some point in our lives most creatrixes have the experience that Tara Leaver expresses with such simplicity, "I finally, truly heard the voice within me saying I must create to be well." [li]

In a discussion with Jen, whose words you will read in a moment, we discovered that it is not just the process of creativity that is vital for our wellbeing, but also the fruits of it. Both of us had realised that physically and energetically having our creations around us is extremely important to us. It is as though we are able to witness a part of ourselves that we have no other way of accessing. We need to live with our artworks, to share physical space with them and witness them continually in order to continue our experience of learning and transformation, in order to fully embody their medicine.

This is interesting to me, as it seems that it is not just the process of creating, but the work itself, that is imbued in some sort of special energetic property – which the memory, or even a photograph of it, is not. We all know this on some level – as seeing a print or photograph of a painting is never the same as sharing physical space with the original. Just as watching a recording of a concert or play is never the same as being there in the room. This tangible, energetic exchange we experience from sharing space with creativity is why live events, despite their price, don't go out of favour. We know, instinctively, that resonant works of art contain an energetic charge within them that impacts us viscerally.

When that art is our own, when it has come up through our bodies, dredging up memories and feelings with it, when we know the story and process of how it came to be, when we know what it cost us, no wonder it is so valuable. Our creations are some of the most powerful medicine of all, an anti-venom of sorts, made by us, from the unique wounds that we carry.

Creatrix Speaks

As a child and a teenager, art was my thing. I loved to draw and paint. I would lie in front of the television every evening with a sketch book and colours. Oh, the endless possibilities of a blank page.

Art class made secondary school bearable and I was lucky to have an art teacher who saw a spark in me and gave free reign to my creativity.

I amassed a folder full of my work, a beautiful expensive folder that my mum bought for me on holiday. My friends would show my work to their parents. I wanted to go to art college.

But, it was not to be. I was clever, really clever and it was decided I should study for a proper job.

I don't remember fighting my case. I don't remember seeing that as an option.

I went to university, became totally overwhelmed there, had a breakdown and then followed many years of drifting. Every now and then I would paint a little bit, but there was a barrier there and I would quickly give up.

I kept the folder, though. For twenty-five years I carried that piece of me from place to place, stored it in attics, under beds, behind couches.

In my early forties I began some really deep personal work, which culminated in reading Lucy Pearce's powerful book, Medicine Woman, which in turn led to me getting a diagnosis of autism.

The process of assessment for diagnosis involved me giving a summary of my life to date and recounting my 'trauma' list. The diagnosis itself was a relief and a gateway to self-compassion but the process brought up quite a lot unresolved issues.

I began to draw. Every night. Animals, beautiful animals. And with each one I drew I saw them reflect my true self back to me. I

”

Without my strangenesses, I might not have become a writer, so as with many afflictions sometimes there are reasons to celebrate.

Siri Hustvedt

would flick through the sketch book during the day just to remind myself that I could do this, that this is who I am. So much emotion came up. There was a deep well of grief for the loss of my connection to my art and my creative self. There was the joy and gratitude of returning home to myself.

I felt like I had been carrying a big scab that had covered me for years and it had now fallen off leaving fresh new skin but with some raw patches that still needed tending.

Within a couple of months I was sketching family portraits, then painting canvases. The blockage had been released and there would be no stopping the flow now. And with this release came other releases in my life as after years of struggle and burnout things began to move again. A little bit of ease came into my life and suddenly there were more opportunities where there had been mostly difficulties.

I began to share my work with my partner and siblings first, then on Facebook. I needed people to know that this is who I am, that this is part of the soul of me. I needed to be witnessed in my completeness.

With the reclaiming of my creative self my way of seeing the world shifted. I can only describe it as I now looked with an artist's eye: shadows, lines, nuances of tone came alive everywhere. And I remembered that this is how I viewed the world as a teenager and I felt a deep connection with and love for my younger lost self. As I write this, I remember that during my breakdown, the overwhelming feeling was that the whole world had lost colour and texture for me. I can see now that it actually had.

Today, my new sense of wholeness and heightened awareness of who I am has given me a strength and a sense of power in my own life and is in the process of fundamentally shifting how I relate to the rest of the world.

I feel I am home at last in myself.

Jen

Follow Your Bliss

At the centre of creativity is playfulness and curiosity, out of which comes joy and pleasure. In play there are no mistakes, only unexplored avenues and fresh adventures.

As adults we are encouraged to be right, to be clever, to work hard, to strive to be taken seriously, to create the next Instagram-able moment. Creative play frees us from this and allows us to become fully open to experiencing the world as it unfolds...and to play with it once more. Whilst watching the Andy Goldsworthy documentary, *Leaning into the Wind*, I remarked to my husband that if it wasn't called art, what we were really watching was a grown man climbing trees and playing with mud and leaves. This is the truth of creativity – we are reclaiming our childlike delight in playing with materials, in seeing what happens, in wondering *what if...*

In many cultures, especially those with Judaeo-Christian roots, we have been taught to be suspicious of pleasure. We consider it to be indulgent, superfluous, dangerous even. Pleasure will lure us in...and ultimately do us in. And so we train ourselves to ignore pleasure, deny it, defer it. Hungrier and crazier we get. And all the while we feel further and further from ourselves.

The irony is the more it is denied, the more twisted, more damaging of self and others, more compulsive and controlling, our pleasure becomes. We become caught in a destructive spiral...the opposite of the life-affirming, pleasure-inducing, creative spiral which we long for.

Pleasure is an unfakeable mark of engagement of the full nervous system into a transformative, rich state of being. The outward signs of pleasure can be faked, the inner experience cannot. The experience of pleasure moves us out of functioning pre-dominantly from the sympathetic nervous system, from adrenaline, the realm of fear where most of us in the modern world spend most of our time. And moves us into the realm of oxytocin and endorphins – into the instinctual, mammalian body – engaging our connection systems.

I encourage you to follow your bliss and do what lights you up...

Climb a mountain, a hill or a tree.

Pick some flowers and really see and smell each one.

Swim in a pool, the sea or a river.

> I wish you a wrestling match with your Creative Muse that will last a lifetime. I wish craziness and foolishness and madness upon you. May you live with hysteria, and out of it make fine stories.
>
> Ray Bradbury

Walk barefoot in the mud.

Light a fire (in a responsible place).

Visit an exhibition or performance which inspires you.

Plan an adventure.

And then another…and another.

Play…alone or together…laugh like a lunatic.

Clear your inner and outer clutter until you feel you can breathe more freely.

Search out images and words that inspire you…and keep them where you can see them.

Pull out old work of yours that you're secretly proud of and put it somewhere you can enjoy it every day.

Listen to music you love, up loud…and sing at the top of your voice… maybe even shake your booty too!

Make sure you are surrounded by colours that you love…in your clothes, and your home.

Read an incredible book…and then another.

Take part in a ceremony or festival.

Paint your face.

Dress up.

Read a poem aloud.

Stroke an animal.

Watch the birds.

Cook some delicious food and eat it with someone who you love.

Connect…or reconnect…with at least three people who inspire and uplift you.

Have bliss-filled sessions of pleasure and passion…alone or together.

Do more of it than you think possible. Be greedy. And then some.

Be self-indulgent. Be joyous. Taste life on your tongue. Fill your belly full…

Have so much fun you think you might burst…

Allow your senses to be wide open. Feel your energy coursing through your veins.

Learn to trust yourself. Fully.

Wherever you are, in your life, in the world, allow yourself moments of freedom. And as you experience them, be fully aware of the sensations in your body, your feelings, the colours and sounds and smells…

Perhaps…just maybe…you feel called to record these experiences in some way: take a keepsake – a ticket, a petal, a photograph, make a sketch of how it was, record it in your journal… Shhhhh don't tell anyone but this is The Work.

You're doing it now. Right now. From your heart and soul. This is embodied, passionate, meaningful creativity.

It feels good, doesn't it?

So, keep doing it…as many times a day as you can… Let it keep drawing you deeper.

Follow your bliss, and it will lead you home…to yourself.

Experience

The creative act is about intimacy. It is about trawling our depths, playing with what we find and sharing this with others.

When I write a book, I get naked. I write things which even my husband doesn't know about me. I write thoughts which come to me from my depths, or from somewhere beyond.

When you read a book like that, you receive that intimacy. In that moment of reading it may connect deeply with you, with parts of yourself that you have considered too shameful to voice, too private, too precious, too raw: senses, emotions, thoughts that you haven't really been able to express before. Suddenly here is someone putting into words and images that which is most vulnerable to you. And in that moment, we connect, through the vehicle of art. Two souls connect, outside of time and space.

When you choose to live creatively in this world, you are choosing to enter vulnerability. You are choosing to enter into intimacy and not just with one lover but with unknown others.

Intimacy is powerful stuff: beautiful, empowering, transcend-

"

I began to realize how important it was to be an enthusiast in life. [...] If you are interested in something, no matter what it is, go at it full speed ahead. Embrace it with both arms, hug it, love it and above all become passionate about it. Lukewarm is no good. Hot is no good either. White hot and passionate is the only thing to be.

Roald Dahl

ent...and addictive. Our bodies and minds want to have more and more of it, again and again. This is when we may start trying to force things, to satisfy our longings, when really we need to approach ourselves and the creative Source as lovers. We need to woo, to be playful, to be loving, affectionate and open-hearted. We need gentle foreplay to open ourselves up, to allow ourselves to come into our fullness before we come into union with the transcendent.

Creative Inquiry

Flow

- What does flow feel like to you? Where in your body do you feel it?
- What does it look like in others?
- Are there certain times of year, times in your cycle, times in the creative process or times of day that you feel it more? Are there certain times when you find it impossible to access?
- Do you only experience it during creativity? In what other areas of your life do you experience it: sex, exercise, nature, prayer…?
- How does your experience of flow currently inform your creative process and how you schedule your creative time?
- Do you still create when you are not experiencing flow? What happens at those times?

Creative Practice

Creative flow

Grab a material that excites you – dough, clay, sand, acrylic paint, marbling inks, watercolour paints, raw wool, silk… It might be one that you've never used before that you've always wanted to try. Or something you haven't touched for years. And start experimentally. Really experience it through all your senses, explore its different properties. Play with it really slowly – slow down what you are doing, focus on every movement. Now do it fast, without any sort of thought, move instinctually and wildly. Don't try to make anything clever or intentional or recognisable – just play…and make some mess whilst you're at it.

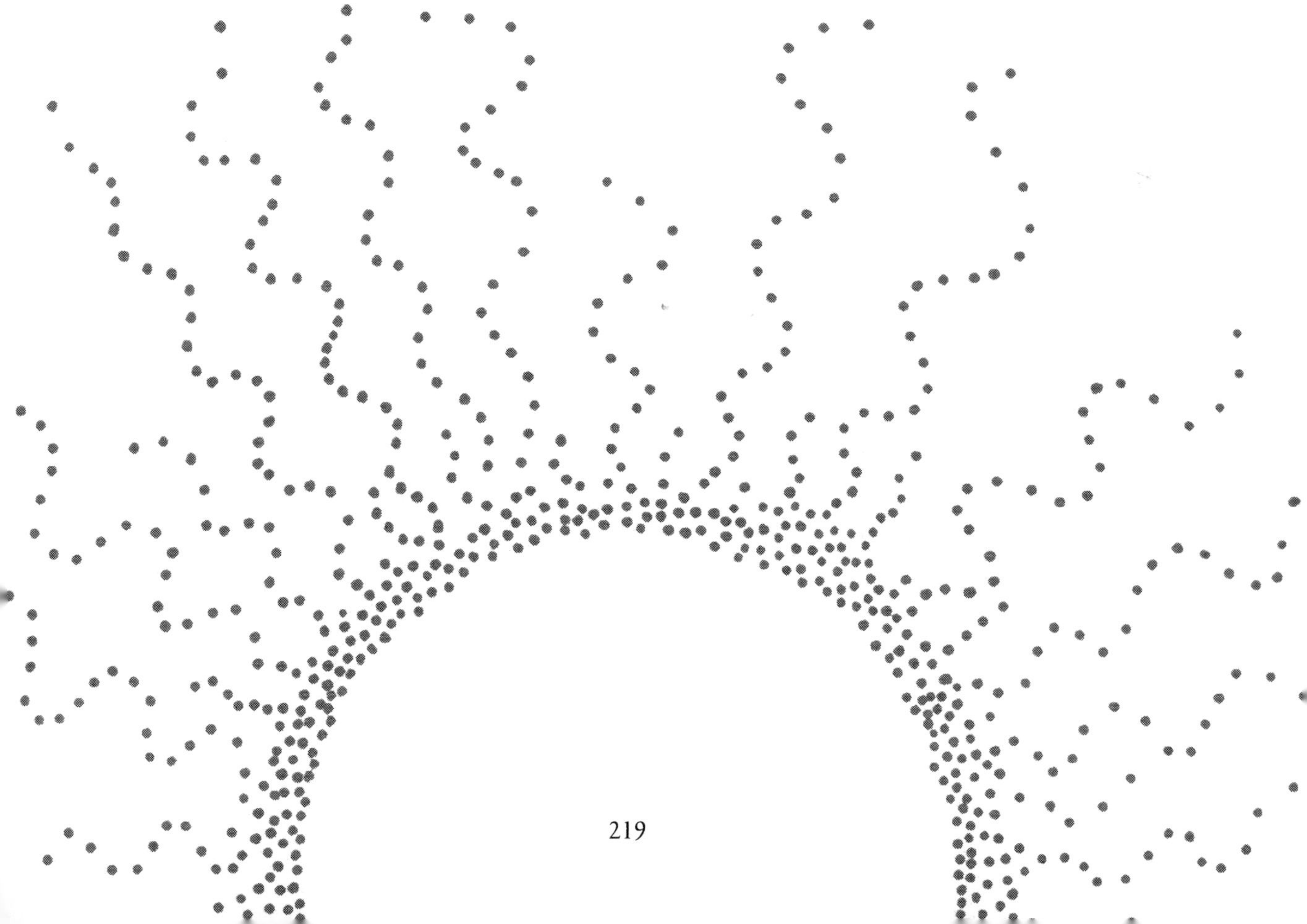

5

I am she

Who sees what cannot be seen,

Who knows what cannot be known,

Who speaks what cannot be said.

COURAGE

> Walk tall, kick ass and never forget that you come from a long line of truth seekers, lovers and warriors.
>
> Hunter S. Thompson

The Constant Companion

Committing to creativity is committing to a life of continual risk-taking, discomfort and ecstasy. The reason we do it, however, is that on some deep level we do not have a choice: for us living a normal life feels even more scary and impossible.

As Highly Creative People who are walking off the beaten track, we find ourselves having to face our fears on a regular basis.

- Fear of failure.
- Fear of success.
- Fear of being exposed.
- Fear of being seen for who we really are.
- Fear of not being acknowledged.
- Fear of not measuring up.
- Fear of judgement.
- Fear of not being good enough.
- Fear of looking stupid.

But perhaps what we most fear is "not that we are inadequate. Our deepest fear is that we are powerful beyond measure," as Marianne Williamson so memorably puts it, in her book *A Return to Love*, "It is our light, not our darkness, that most frightens us. We ask ourselves, who am I to be brilliant, gorgeous, talented and fabulous? Actually, who are you not to be? Your playing small does not serve the world."

Creativity, in a culture that engenders conformity, takes courage. To step up, speak out, to try something new, with no guarantees of success, to prioritise vision over certainty, beauty over economy, joy over efficiency, danger over safety is brave work. Never underestimate the courage it takes to go against the grain and dare to be more fully yourself.

Without courage we cannot be creative. Without feeling fear, at some point, we will not reach our creative potential. And so we have to find a way to live with fear, to tolerate it. From first putting paint on paper through to selling our work, there is plenty to be scared of. But this is where creativity lies – on the edge of our comfort zones.

> Don't worry about getting it right. Just get it started.
>
> Marie Forleo

Experience

Fear has been my constant creative companion. I remember the first time it really impacted my creativity, I was twelve years old and had been cast in a leading role in our school musical. I had genuinely never considered whether I was good at singing or acting or not, I just enjoyed doing them unselfconsciously. But then, in the final performance, one of my leading co-actors made a comment about me singing out of tune. Having a very literal mind and tender heart I believed what she said to be true. Not just for that moment, but for all time. I allowed my voice to be taken from me. I was never able to sing alone on a stage again.

I went on to a professional acting college for a year when I was eighteen, however when I discovered that at the beginning of my second year I would be required to sing a solo, I freaked out. I spent the summer as an anxious mess and two weeks before we were due to start back, I quit. My terror was real and crippling. For years since then I have suffered nightmares where I try to open my mouth, to speak, to sing or scream in danger, and nothing comes out.

I was a powerful member of many choirs in my latter school years. But never a soloist. But, and this is the ridiculous thing, I can sing. I've got a great voice, something many people remark on with surprise when they hear it. I never once stopped to question this twelve-year-old girl's authority on the matter. Never once thought that maybe her comment was rooted in jealousy or insecurity or teen tactlessness. Or maybe even that on that particular note, at that very moment, she was right. But that it did not define me as a singer. It did not invalidate me as a creative person.

"No one can paint, write, whatever, without being vulnerable. One has to be very strong to be vulnerable.

Joan Mitchell

Breaking Silence

We each have defining stories like this where our courageous expression of our authentic voices was cut dead. And from that moment we learned that to stay safe, we must stay silent, we must fear and disown that part of ourselves because of the shame and danger it may bring us.

I have spoken to so many people who have experienced this shutting down after critical comments from parents, teachers or siblings. It seems to usually happen in our late childhood or early teens, at a time when we are crossing from unconsciousness to self-consciousness. Where previously we have not really thought about our how we appeared to others, suddenly we are made painfully aware of our imperfections. We feel judged and shamed, and the magical freedom that we had previously enjoyed is cut off at the roots.

Brené Brown notes in an interview with Elizabeth Gilbert that,

> *When I started the research on shame, thirteen years ago, I found that 85% of the men and women who I interviewed remembered an event in school that was so shaming, it changed how they thought of themselves for the rest of their lives. […] Half of those people – those shame wounds – were around creativity. So, 50% of*

those people have creativity scars.[lii]

That's a lot of creatively damaged people in our world. So that's the first thing to know: you're not alone in this, and there is nothing to be ashamed of for feeling scared. Sadly fear and its associated emotion of shame are all too common amongst us Highly Sensitive, Highly Creative folk. They get unsettled, like the sediment in the bottom of a jar of pond water. These specks of mud make a fog that we cannot see through. The voices of doubt and panic, fear and shame shout so loud that they drown out our wise inner voice of intuition. They become the totality of our reality. Until we remember that they are not…and the inner Witness can emerge.

Our task as creatrixes is to return as quickly as possible to our inner, authentic voice and be guided by it, create from it. Not from the expectations of others, or even our logical self, not what we should write, or ought to do, but the deepest soul truth that longs to be expressed through us, which sounds like a clear bell in the dark night.

You may have noticed that fear and shame drain you of energy. This is because fear is your creative juices imprisoned behind the barricades of the bodymind. It is trapped there because of your experiences or knowings of the danger of expression. But is only through expression: through sharing words, images, sounds and movements that we can transform our fear back into our native creative power and the energy will flow once more.

> It's not your job to wonder if you're good enough. It's not your job to wonder if you're ready. It's not your job to look at other people and compare yourself to them. Your job is to do the thing that lights you up and that you love.
>
> Leonie Dawson

Fear in Context

It is easy to belittle our fears and tell ourselves that they are silly.

But let me share a secret with you: your fears, your creative blocks, your resistance are not just personal. They are part of a far bigger story. And once you realise that, it makes it a whole lot easier to manage your responses.

Sometimes we can get so stuck in our own small stories that we miss the broad sweeps of history that have shaped us and people like us.

Highly Creative People have tended to be adored and celebrated when they bide by cultural norms, or challenge them just enough to be exciting and inspiring rather than threatening. But when they get too weird, they

> The Fraud Police are the imaginary, terrifying force of 'real' grown-ups who you believe – at some subconscious level – are going to come knocking on your door in the middle of the night, saying:
>
> 'You are guilty of making shit up as you go along, you do not actually deserve your job, we are taking everything away and we are TELLING EVERYBODY.'
>
> Amanda Palmer, *The Art of Asking*

are perceived in some way as a danger to the status quo.

Because they are. *We are.*

We are powerful. We ask uncomfortable questions. We don't follow the rules. We have an enviable native ability to connect to the life force, to harness deeper levels of consciousness. We have an intimate experience of being able to navigate the inner darkness that our culture fears. We have charismatic abilities: our words and images speak deep to the souls of others. We tell others to look beyond the mundane world of drudgery and taxes to something bigger, braver, more beautiful, far more real – a reality beyond the control of politicians, civil servants, teachers and priests. We have a direct connection to soul that threatens the patriarchal gatekeepers. We possess uncontrollable spirits and a braveness which scares the rule-followers. We have a commitment to ourselves and to The Work that transcends our commitments to this world and its rules. Time and again our souls rebel, and they show others how to rebel too.

To live at odds with the dominant superficial forces of your culture requires courage, conviction, a certain fuck-you spirit and bloody-mindedness, vision, faith and a healthy dose of madness. And yet, as we have seen, creatrixes tend to be Highly Sensitive: we are aware of the potential cost of our creativity.

Throughout history, people like us have been imprisoned, beaten, shot, starved, dispossessed, disinherited, broken and medicated for what they expressed, and how. In many countries people like us still are. Look at the news on any given day and you will see a Russian journalist or singer jailed for using their words to creatively question the system; Chinese artists and authors exiled from their homeland; a hundred lashes for a woman dancing to secular music in Iran; the work of those who question Muslim ideology publicly burned.

We have a long global history of oppressing artists and their creative expression. It shaped the ancestors whose stories we have learned. It shaped the art that we were allowed to see. It shaped the families and teachers that brought us up. It has written the rules that we, as creatives, are trying to break. People like us have gone bankrupt, gotten divorced, gone mad and committed suicide, tired of trying to fit in a world which is so twisted and small in its vision.

In Western countries we prize freedom of expression, within wide parameters: you are rarely killed or imprisoned or beaten for creatively expressing yourself today. But only in the very recent past D.H. Lawrence's work was legally banned for public indecency. I remember clearly, as an aspiring writer, when author Salman Rushdie had to go into hiding in the UK because of a fatwa and his books were burned: I was nine and he was a writer who lived in the same country as me.

Fear oppresses creativity. On a personal and collective level. Many of us still feel as though we can and we will die or be killed for breaking the rules, for speaking up, for expressing ourselves. We think we might die if we fail. The remembering, the knowing, of how dangerous art can be, is still real for us.

Those of us who have the privilege to overcome these inner fears and create without threat must do so. For it will fill the world with more courage. And we must join in solidarity with those who face physical suffering or exile so that their voices may be heard.

> You can spend your time on stage pleasing the heckler in the back, or you can devote it to the audience that came to hear you perform.
>
> Seth Godin

Experience

This fear is old.

These are the words that hit me, after the sucker punch of anxiety which has almost floored me. Once again.

This wave of fear tells me of danger, of impending, life-threatening doom. The same fog of fears my body raises to successfully ground my creative self as she begins to take flight. Not the sort of grounding you do in yoga, where your roots reach into a beneficent Mother Earth. But the sort air traffic controllers do when they realize the plane has been overrun by terrorists.

My anxiety is a city of worries the shape and size of high-rise tower blocks that shut out the sun. It combines the hot fire of fear with the cold, dark, clammy, formless terror of despair.

It is as familiar as my own face. And yet it presents nothing new – no new insights, no new concerns. Just terror.

Fear seems to be creativity's conjoined twin. But I forget. And so I only lay a place setting for creativity, when fear barges in and starts shitting on the table.

Each time I dare to share my work, to step further into my own creative power, fear emerges from the shadows. This wild beast I thought I had escaped. This terror I thought I had tamed. Here it is, holding me hostage once more.

I thought, at some point, perhaps my second book, or fifth, perhaps after my second birth, my third art exhibition that it would dissolve in the light of experience and evidence to the contrary, that the world will not end because I have opened my mouth. That I will not be killed for my words or my images.

But it doesn't. It hasn't.

This fear is old. It reaches back to the first time I was silenced. The first time I was shamed. I have worked through these, I will the fear to leave.

But still it remains.

It is older than me. Tens of generations its roots go back. Oh, what this fear has witnessed, what it has heard over the millennia. It knows the dangers, and warns me of them.

Beware. Stay small. Stay safe. Shut up, don't draw attention to yourself.

Stay alive. Stay alive.

Here it is, once more, ripping my guts to shreds. I hold my mauled innards in my hands. The shame of it burns me.

None of it is real, I tell myself. It's all in your mind.

Except it is real. My body tells me this fear is as real as me. Perhaps more so.

This fear is as old as the world.

I am tired of it. Not just tired to my bones of being woken up at first light with a pounding heart. Of lying awake at night, willing darkness to wash over me, rather than another night of nightmares.

But tired of this fear.

This feeling of wanting to vomit my own guts. The feeling that my knees are going to crumple beneath me. The dry mouth. The clenched jaw, solar plexus on fire. The paranoid thoughts. The tight chest. I am sick and tired.

This fear is old.

And not just old for me. Nor those in my life whose hearts must sink as I announce once more the arrival of this unwanted guest.

But this fear that awakens within me is not just mine. It is yours too. And theirs. Personal. Collective.

Fear is humanity's shadow. It is ours. And it is old. And it is casting its shadow over us all right now.

We are sick of fear. Sick from fear.

Some of us avoid it by playing it safe, by setting up camp well within the bounds of our comfort zones. Others will fight fear with fear and use it to throw flames at others – attacking and shaming and trolling.

However we respond, still it is there. That fear which sets off our bodies like a fire alarm. That makes our hearts pound and we reach for the vodka, the cigarette, the Valium, the cake, the candy...anything to dial down the terror and let us breathe.

This fear is old.

Primal.

Primitive.

But it is ruling the game here today. Not just in our own private lives and careers – but in the world. Fear rules.

Old fear. Ancient fear. The wild animal within awakened by the swirling threats without. The terrorists and trolls outside have replaced the threat of lions and tigers for most of us. We live on constant red alert.

How can we negotiate a truce? How can we make a peace treaty with it? How can we tap into its power and transform it into something that fuels us positively, something that energises rather than paralysing and constricting us?

We are entering a new era.

Or rather, we can, we will, if we can find a way to transmute its energy into creating change. If we can step through the portal that fear offers us, and into the chaos of creative potential.

Shhhh, listen in to the void, beyond the old voice of fear is a voice even more ancient. Can you hear it? The voice that calls your soul.

Let your body know that it is safe. In this moment. It is safe to be you. To be here. Now. Allow yourself to come, gently, gently back into it.

The fear is old.
Its time has come.
It has tried to keep us safe. But instead has caged us.
It is time to fly free of it,
At last, at last.
Trusting ourselves to our bodies, and the silent voice that echoes beyond.

> East of Ordinary there exists the landscape where you take yourself by the hand. Where you walk forward trembling with tears running down your face.
>
> Jennifer Louden, *The Life Organizer*

Getting Naked

My experience of living creatively is that most of the time I feel like I'm walking around naked, where most of the world is walking around fully clothed. Pictures of my childhood summers show me almost always literally naked. I thought that was just normal being a kid in the eighties. Then I looked again at the photos: in every one it is just me. I guess I have always felt more comfortable in my own skin. The only thing that changed was my self-consciousness, my awareness of being observed, being different, being weird.

We have been taught that nakedness is wrong. Bad. Threatening. Obscene. Shameful. In many places it is illegal and will make others worry for your sanity. How far we have come from an acceptance of our own natural state, to being so threatened by it. The same is true of our emotional selves – our culture makes us scared of what we are. In Western culture, once again, this goes back to the creation story of the Bible, where Eve, having taken a bite of the fruit of the Tree of Knowledge, suddenly sees her nakedness and experiences shame, quickly covering her body.

At no point did the Creator God tell her that her nakedness, her body, his supposed pinnacle of creation, was not shameful.

So for creatrixes the challenge is how to be naked in a world filled with fully dressed people wearing armour and masks, that have been taught that nakedness is shameful, and their place is to judge others. We must learn how to keep ourselves psychologically and physically safe, whilst pushing our own and our culture's limits. In the wise words of Neil Gaiman,

> *The moment that you feel that, just possibly, you're walking down the street naked, exposing too much of your heart and your mind and what exists on the inside, showing too much of yourself. That's the moment you may be starting to get it right.*

> The parts that embarrass you the most are usually the most interesting poetically, are usually the most naked of all, the rawest, the goofiest, the strangest and most eccentric and at the same time, most representative, most universal.
>
> Allen Ginsberg

Creatrix Speaks

After months of crippling anxiety and absolute terror, I began painting giant self-portraits...ten big paintings emerged which helped me reclaim parts of myself I had had stolen or given away...it was the only thing I could focus on. And slowly I painted myself back to life.

Before I knew it there were forty women and girls painting portraits in my tiny house every week, all reclaiming parts of themselves and their stories... We hit the news and got ourselves an exhibition at Tate Liverpool. I collected a hundred more paintings and we were on Woman's Hour. We had seven thousand visitors who all had their own stories to share.

I was still recovering from the breakdown but my muse and the Universe had other ideas. Soon we were receiving funding from the National Health Service, local councils, prisons, schools, probation services to expand the project. In all, I worked with over one and a half thousand people, creating life-size self-portraits. The exhibition was incredible – a testament to everyone's deep creative potential and magic, vulnerability and juiciness.

Every single person I have worked with over the years has wobbled to the canvas, unsure of their ability to create and scared of being not good enough, not creative, not able to tell their story... from politicians to business leaders, directors of the Tate Liverpool to children in schools... Every one of those people I have been in awe of as I watch them bravely make marks on the page.

Clare

"

Literature is strewn with the wreckage of those who have minded beyond reason the opinion of others.

Virginia Woolf, *A Room of One's Own*

Seeking Approval

Very often people assume that if you are creative you must therefore be very self-confident. The reality of many artists couldn't be further from the truth. Instead the words that play on loop internally are:

Is this good enough? Am I okay? What about this?

We find ourselves trying to read the signs of who we are, what we should do, where we belong. We look for an authentic reflection of ourselves in myriad places and faces. And in this brave new world of being creative on social media we have more witnesses to hand than any human has ever had in history. We can receive the approval of strangers at the click of a Like button.

We are wired for approval. Like wasps to warm beer we are motivated to seek it. Our bodies light up from the inside when we receive it. Endorphins flood our systems. We crave more and more.

And this second-hand approval may be as good as it's ever got for us. Because somewhere early on we learned to distrust our own intuition and look for the judgement of others over our own.

It is time to change this.

To seek our own approval as our yardstick.

To trust our own intuition.

At last.

Creatrix Speaks

I find that the permission for my creativity to flow freely is reliant on the approval of others, and that when my art gains the approval of others I allow it to flow freely, and I'm propelled forward. But when that external reaffirmation isn't there I feel shame, doubt, embarrassment, and I go back into my shell and cease to create.

It's as if some child within seeks constant approval. Is my art okay? Is it beautiful? And if it's not, is that some sort of negative reflection of me as a person?

It's such a vulnerable thing, sharing these honest unique expressions of ourselves, and sometimes I find myself feeling like a rabbit in the headlights, absolutely terrified.

It's ironic really, this desire to be fully seen, in full vulnerability and truth, while at the same time the total terror at the idea of not being approved of.

Mirin

> When you no longer need approval from others like the air you breathe, the possibilities in life are endless.
>
> What an interesting little prison we build from the invisible bricks of other people's opinions.
>
> Jacob Nordby

We Step Up...Shaking

Each day I step up, shaking, to my work.

I face my fears of being judged as less than perfect, of hearing my inner critic writ large in others, every time I sit to create.

Before my fifth book, *Burning Woman*, came out I was consumed by my terror of the critics – psychologically and physically. I thought I was literally going to be killed for it. That took a heavy toll on me.

And yet, when I did send it out into the world, it was not death threats that I received but breathtaking endorsements, from heroines of mine... and one accusation of plagiarism. It has since been shared by many more heroines, including the singer Pink, who shared it on her Instagram. It has won awards and speaking invitations and has sold over 10,000 copies.

But still the fear remains almost paralysing each time I share my work.

Each time I dare to unleash what lies hidden within I feel my own smallness. My own faults and failings. I feel embarrassed.

“

Where your fear is, there is your task.

C.G Jung

And then once the smallness has passed, the bigness of what I am doing hits me. For a moment I see how deeply threatening my work is for our culture and the status quo: it unequivocally names the fact that women have been actively oppressed for millennia. That women have a right to their power. It claims that women's voices matter. Women's sexuality is powerful and good. Through my own contribution, I am giving permission for, making space for, supporting, fomenting that which has been actively, viciously, surreptitiously denied and controlled for generations. I am doing it without any authority or permission but my own, without an organisation or spiritual tradition at my back. And I am sharing my personal story with strangers.

No wonder I feel vulnerable, shaky and doubtful as to whether I can do it.

But I carry on.

Because some part of me knows it matters.

And the women who experience my work confirm this again and again.

And so now I realise that when my body starts to shake, it is not that I am weak, but rather that I have touched the invisible walls of power that have kept me silent thus far. I walk into fear, and do my best to feel it and let it flow through me and out. It makes me shake, makes me sick, but ultimately makes me stronger as I confront, consciously, time and again the patriarchal power structures that I have unconsciously internalised. I practice, shakily, standing in my own power.

It helped me hugely hearing a woman interviewed who ran the Omega Institute, an elite retreat centre that hosts speakers like Pema Chodron, Vandana Shiva, Byron Katie and Deepak Chopra. She said that in her experience, even the most well-recognised and respected speakers of our era experience what is described as 'imposter syndrome' – the fear of being found out.

Fear is normal. It is human to worry that we are not enough. The problem is when we believe it as fact and allow it to limit us.

In the wise words of Anna Lovind,

Fear is not a roadblock. It's a road sign, showing you where your current borders are. It's an invitation. A point of entry.

You move softly through the fear and into that vast, new landscape. After a while you face another border, and the fear that comes with it. Every time you face it, the zone in which you can move freely grows. You need to learn this language, this rhythm of moving and pausing, because fear will be a constant companion on the journey.[liii]

We have been told that we shake because there is something wrong with us.

This is a lie.

We are shaking with the life force that is longing to be released, that is trying to break through in order to be witnessed.

So I encourage you to step up when you feel small. Building your courage every time you do. Step up. Again and again. Some days you may be able to push through the fear and shame, other days you may not. But step up. Show up. And speak truth. And bear witness to your creativity.

Keep walking.

Keep feeling.

Keep breathing.

One step at a time.

Stopping and resting.

Each time you need to.

But keep stepping up. Shaking.

And do The Work.

"

There is no greater threat to the critics, cynics, and fearmongers than a woman who is willing to fall because she has learned how to rise.

Brené Brown

SUCCESS

The Spotlight and the Shadows

> There's a difference between wanting to be looked at and wanting to be seen.
>
> Not everybody wants to be looked at.
>
> Everybody wants to be seen.
>
> Amanda Palmer, *The Art of Asking*

Being in the spotlight – literally and metaphorically – is a part of creativity that many creatrixes struggle with. The spotlight can give us a sense of being seen, accepted and loved by so many. It can be thrilling, glorious and addictive. But not always, and not for all of us. Many of us are deeply uncomfortable being looked at. For as well as showing our glory, being in the spotlight can reveal or amplify the shadows that we try to hide, exacerbating our vulnerabilities as we navigate the strange sensation of being watched and judged by dozens or millions.

This is the paradox of the creatrix. The spotlight can energise us. When The Work is flowing through us we, who may get nervous speaking to folks one-to-one, are able to stand up and perform in front of 1,000 people. We, who may often find ourselves unable to write an email, are able to organise 100,000 words to create a whole new world in book form. But it can also make us freeze. We may crave witnesses on a deep psychological level, but dread an audience. And yet, our work needs exposure if we are to make a living from it and maintain our motivation to create.

As creatrixes we have to have a constant, reflective and dynamic relationship with the spotlight: considering what attention we are courting and why. Whether it is ourselves that we want to be the focus of the public gaze or The Work.

And it is for us to decide. Because there is a sense that those in the spotlight are fair game, and there is no such thing as bad publicity. The cult of celebrity means people living in the public eye become considered public property. It is a vulnerable place to be. If we are not in charge of the spotlight, or when we stand in it, it can be extremely dangerous for us psychologically. We must learn how much of ourselves we can safely gift to the world, without giving ourselves away. We need to discover how much of ourselves we are willing to share before our lives become a performance in themselves.

Glamour

Those who aspire to create and don't have real life mentors are often wooed by the glamour of being an artist. Hear the word actor and you probably think of Hollywood, launch parties, designer dresses on red carpets and glitzy award ceremonies – versus the reality of thousands of wannabe actors waiting tables, being turned down at endless auditions, perhaps developing a drug habit or being sexually exploited.

The creative person, especially the creative woman, is required to perform the fantasy of glamour for our culture. Glamoury is one of the oldest forms of magic,

> *an illusion based on a projection of one's magical energy altering the awareness of a physical form in order to trigger certain emotion(s). It makes objects and/or living things appear different from what they really are.*[liv]

The lighting, costumes, make up, glitter, music and perspectives we use as creatives all help to create and sell an enticing illusion, allowing audiences to suspend their disbelief, shift states of consciousness and enter other worlds with us.

We find ourselves drawn to charismatic cultural magicians, to absorb a little of their glamour through autographs, touch, selfies, events and even sex. It is as though by getting close to the artist, we get closer to the magic that all human souls long to touch, taste and dissolve into. And wannabe creatives yearn to learn the magic behind how to transform energy into thought, word and visions…and how to draw fame and fortune towards themselves.

However, the reality of the artist when unillumined by the creative pow-

> The bridge between the words glamour and grammar is magic. According to the OED, glamour evolved through an ancient association between learning and enchantment.
>
> Roy Peter Clark, *The Glamour of Grammar*

er, may be rude, impatient, messy, unkind, forgetful, tired or simply disappointingly mundane. Rather than magical, they are just an ordinary human, except without much of the polish we expect from a person in our society.

This can also feel hurtful or shaming for the artist. They know how they use glamour to enchant. They know, and often try to run from having to be, the real human full of paradox and frailty that lies underneath. Some part of them knows that the magic is not of them, but comes through them.

This is why it takes such courage to show up to the spotlight as our human selves and set the stage for the magic to come through us and surrender ourselves to it. At that moment we become witnesses, with the audience, of the process of magic too. It makes us all more fully alive.

This is the blessing and majesty of accepting the role of creatrix: being both magic-maker and front row seat to the magic.

Creatrix Speaks

My life seems to be a continuous series of leaps of faith, jumping into the unknown, exploring in the darkness.

It's both terrifying and exhilarating at the same time.

Often it's the idea of doing the jump and taking that leap of faith that is far more terrifying than the reality of doing it. It's the ideas and speculations...the going into the unknown that can seem so daunting, yet, more often than not, when we do it, after the first few moments, it feels totally normal.

Mirin

Critics, Trolls and Other Nasty Arseholes

I have made a choice not to court celebrity, and therefore media can be done on my own terms. I choose to keep well out of mainstream media which upholds different values than I do, where pulling creatives limb from limb, otherwise known as serious-minded reviews and interviews, are blood sports perfected over centuries. I only work with media outlets and journalists that are genuinely interested in the work that I am doing, rather than looking for someone wacky to ridicule.

I am forever grateful to be born when I was: to have the option to harness the powers of social media and deal directly with the people who support my work. For most of history mainstream media and critics have been the gatekeepers to the marketplace and public attention for creatives. In order to succeed you would have to take your chances with them, and do it on their terms.

In the digital world both good and bad publicity can happen at warp speed. 'Going viral' is what creatives today both long for and dread. In a realm where Likes lead to Follows, and clicks lead to income, the tides of social media can also turn in a moment. Disapproval can lead to full-scale personal attack and the destruction of a reputation in a matter of hours.

I, like most creatrixes have had my fair share of criticism. I have defended my values, my work, my reputation online. I have lost sleep, health and probably income to keyboard warriors. They have nearly broken me and stopped me from sharing my work.

And why? Because I believed that these people were the authorities on my work, rather than me. I believed that the power lay with them.

Somewhere early on we learn to accept that we can never be all things to all people, and what we have to offer will always be a disappointment or waste of time or money to some. There will always be folks who don't like or get your work, that is a given. But then there is the person who wants to let you – and the world – know just how much you suck, and what a fraud you are. It seems to usually come from people who cannot focus their own creative energy constructively, and are frustrated with their own achievements, and so with the time and energy they have on their hands, and the

> I have spent a good many years being ashamed about what I write. I think I was forty before I realised that almost every writer of fiction or poetry who has ever published a line has been accused by someone of wasting his or her God-given talent. If you write (or paint or dance or sculpt or sing, I suppose), someone will try to make you feel lousy about it, that's all.
>
> Stephen King

power of the internet, they project their own destructive energy onto you.

If you're thin-skinned and Highly Sensitive, which is what makes you a great creative rather than an egotistical critic or troll in the first place, you're going to struggle with this aspect of creativity. So, if – or rather when – this happens, you need to know that it will probably come out of the blue, blindsiding you. It stings like hell and can be disorienting. The energy from the attack often gets lodged in your bodymind.

Handling criticism is most challenging because it brings public scrutiny to our (alleged) failures. The shame that this evokes can be crippling: we feel scared, alone, exposed and found lacking. This is why having our work publicly ridiculed or even slightly criticised is a hard blow to our Highly Sensitive selves: we receive it as a communication that our Work, as an extension of our deepest souls, is not okay.

> "May you never be the reason why someone who loved to sing, doesn't anymore. Or why someone who always spoke of their dreams so wildly is now silent about them. May you never be the reason of someone giving up on a part of themselves.
>
> Sharouk Mustafa Ibrahim

The truth is that no critic, however much they might feel the authority on me and my work, even if they have read every one of my books and blogposts and listened to every interview, truly knows me. They know the parts of me I make public, but they do not know the whole human that is me. And more importantly, they don't get a say in that.

We must remember that in art, perhaps more than anything else, there are no right answers, there is no ultimate world authority. Art is, by its very nature, subjective. And therefore criticism – or praise – can only ever be representative of one person's opinion. It is not The Truth. It is for this reason, I'm sure, why most artists learn not to read their reviews, good or bad. For when we learn to look at our art through the eyes of others, when we mistake the projections of others as our own reality, we lose sight of our own values and sense of self-worth.

After years of being deeply hurt by criticism, what I have finally come to realise is that 90% of the time it is not about me. The 10% that is about me, I can use to learn, develop, adapt, improve and grow from. I heed feedback given with this intention. But for those who seek to attack, it is always about them.

In time you will learn which criticism is worth heeding, which requires no response, and which deserves to be read out in a snooty voice whilst imagining their small bug eyes and green slimy skin before ritually burning it. Whatever it takes to get the poison through you and out of your system.

The bigger you get, the more folks you are exposed to, the more criticism you will naturally get. But also, hopefully, the more appreciation too. It is vital to keep it in perspective. For every nasty criticism I get, I receive maybe four hundred times the amount of gratitude. Deep, heartfelt thanks, tearful sharings of how my work has touched them. It is up to me as a creative to hold this close, and let this truth, this reality, be the one that reflects what I do and why. Be sure to collate the most treasured responses you receive and keep them somewhere close to hand. Come back to these each time you need a reminder of what you are doing and the effect it has on the world.

”

You Making Cool Shit also makes the Worst People mad. Good. Fuck 'em. Make stuff that makes those monsters mad.

Chuck Wendig

The Inner Critic

If, most of the time, the outer critic doesn't have the power to actually destroy us, then why are their words so painful?

Because criticism tends to reignite all our own inner critical voices and re-open our wounded places. Our first clue that the inner critic is active is thoughts like...

- *You're too...*
- *You're not...enough*
- *No one will ever...*
- *It's not as good as...*
- *It's not important!*
- *You suck!*

Do you recognise these? I know I do. Critical voices – inner and outer – tend to shout loudest when we are at our most vulnerable: when confronted with the blank page, the shaky start or as we prepare to reveal our work to others. These voices have kept me company through the writing

> "A lot of our unique weirdness is exactly what we were shamed the most for in our childhood. [...] In order to express your inner genius that is your weirdness, you have to be willing to risk uncertainty and vulnerability. It has to be a challenge to be expressed. It has to be a challenge to find it, or it won't have meaning.
>
> J.P. Sears at Wired for Wonder

and publishing of all my books, my drawing and painting, my interviews. They are my devoted companions. One of the most tiring jobs as a creatrix is engaging with these inner critics almost every time I sit to create. Often it seems like it would be much easier not to go there.

The inner critic is built up of voices that we have internalised over the course of our lives each time we were vulnerable: from things that parents, teachers and other children said to us, things we heard them say to themselves and plenty of special ones we have created just for ourselves. It can be hard to catch them without a lot of practice because some part of us believes that what they say is true.

And so instead of tuning the voices out, we turn up the volume and listen, and they begin to take over the show. Rarely do we take a moment to stop, and listen, to question them, or just leave them to chatter away.

Talking to many creatrixes, I have come to understand that the Critic often takes the guise of a formidable inner patriarch. This twisted masculine presence has an enormous fear of Feminine flow, chaos and its potential destruction and fallibility. It becomes our internalised Gatekeeper of what we get to express and how it must be done in order to be acceptable.

Our job as creatrixes is to reclaim the keys to the gate of our Feminine flow.

The best time to do this is when the Critic is least energised – after sleep, orgasm, exercise or when carried away with passion or excitement. We do not need to kill off the Critic (which in the end is their biggest fear), for the healthy inner Masculine is a strong guardian, clear seer and rational adviser. But when this energy is twisted, the Critic summons up the destructive powers of the creative force, throwing up blocks, destroying ideas and sneering at vulnerability.

Know that you always have a choice – you can listen to the Critic, swallow their poison, hand them your power, stop sharing your work and stay safe from potential future criticism. Or you can put on your big girl pants, go out and make more of your stuff. Make it bigger and bolder and brighter and wilder and messier. Make the art you've been longing to see.

You are a magic-maker...so go make magic.

Creatrix Speaks

I admired my big brother, Charles Marquis. He was an amazing soul and a gifted artist who could render just about anything. In my youth I told myself a story that I could never be as good an artist as he was. I made the dreadful mistake of comparing my art to his. This 'story' weakened me so much that I not only lacked confidence around drawing, but I became paralyzed and too scared to even try. The fear of failure was excruciating.

At fifteen, I thought to challenge this fear and took an art class in high school. There I created a number of portraits and felt disappointed by them all! Even the ones my teacher applauded and entered into a statewide student exhibition. My brother, seven years my senior, heard about this and asked to see my work. I reluctantly showed him. He looked at each drawing and expressed how much he liked them. Not really hearing him, I pointed out the flaws in each one and how the faces were flat and unrealistic and different from the way he and others I knew, drew them. He interrupted my criticisms and said these words that I will never forget, "Be your own kind of artist, Shuron."

That changed everything for me. It set me free from the chains I had imposed upon myself and I never again compared my art to anyone else's. My dear brother has long been gone from this physical plane but he left me with a life lesson that I am truly grateful for. I did not believe in myself then, and it took many years of practice before growing that confidence in my work. But I now know who I am, and it is through appreciating and having a greater understanding of the creative process, that I am able to stand here and say, "My name is Marsia Shuron Harris, and I am an Artist."

Marsia

"

The inner critic in some form is universal and has nothing to do with art or creativity as such. The critic really arises from the fact that creative activities wake us up and lead us to knowing. [...] Knowing is dangerous because it leads to change.

Pat B. Allen, *Art is a Way of Knowing*

Perfectionism

> Perfectionism is just fear in fancy shoes and a mink coat.
>
> Elizabeth Gilbert, *Big Magic*

Meet Perfectionism. She is another loyal companion of most creatives.

Most of us spend our lives questing after making Great Art and being constantly disappointed in our ability to make it. We are used to being surrounded by the perfected products of others' best ideas, and we do not see the flops, the failures, the scribbles and sketches that it took to get there. We compare our messy process to the carefully edited final products of others, and feel the sting of failure.

To create we have to not only be prepared for the possibility of failure, but make it our greatest teacher. We need to become its most avidly curious and grateful students.

It is completely normal that not all or even many of our creative ideas will turn out to be successful in the world's terms. The authors of *Wired to Create* offer the examples of Beethoven, Shakespeare and Thomas Edison as creative geniuses who are revered by our culture for their successes, but who, within their body of work, produced far more duds.

So we're in good company. We get to follow our passions without any guarantees of success. We have permission to try lots of things and to fail at many of them.

Failure is an option. It has to be. Failure shows you have walked beyond the pale, and are now traversing the domain of the unknown and the untested. This is where the magic lies: new solutions and new horizons. You will not find them if you stay safe.

These are not just nice words to soothe your ego. Mistakes are simply neural pathways that do not currently connect. Materials that do not yet hold. They are the chaos before the coherence. They are not shameful.

The more we learn to dance to the tune of our own innate creativity, rather than following the missives of others, the more we can discover. As we learn to release our attachments to our creative products as being definitive reflections of our own egos, the more fun we will have and the easier creating will become.

When we are creating, we can't be precious. We have to be bold and brave. We have to try the crazy, the untested, the non-viable, in order to track down the impossible and make it possible. We need to commit to trying and trying and trying – throw all options into the pot and see which ones taste delicious. If you are doing something that has never been done before, what are the chances of getting it 'right' first time? What even is 'right'? Maybe there are myriad possible answers, infinite iterations of beauty or possibility. Stop searching for the mythical One and Only, it's a lie propagated by our cultural myths and authorities to control us.

Letting go of perfection and control gives room for our creations to surprise us by morphing in front of our very eyes, taking radical departures from what we had planned, and showing us new possibilities. But only if we are open to following their lead. 'Mistakes' can become exciting new ways forward, and 'failures' can open our eyes to previously unconsidered possibilities. A failure, after all, is just another set of marks we have made. It is only the meaning that the Storyteller weaves around them that defines them.

This is why understanding the intention of our work is crucial to establish early on. Otherwise we can waste so much of our energy chasing other people's dreams, measuring ourselves by other people's yardsticks, listening to the wrong people, becoming upset and frustrated, or feeling our talents are being abused or wasted.

If our sense of success is only defined from the outside – by the acknowledgement of our peers, the cultural establishment, fame and money – then we are more vulnerable to the criticism of others. Whereas if we know that our values and intentions are different from those of the critic, it is far easier to disregard them.

I share with you words attributed to Ralph Waldo Emerson, which helped me to recalibrate my own sense of success,

To laugh often and much;

To win the respect of intelligent people and the affection of children;

To earn the appreciation of honest critics and endure the betrayal of false friends;

To appreciate beauty;

"

Don't aim at success – the more you aim at it and make it a target, the more you are going to miss it. For success, like happiness, cannot be pursued; it must ensue…as the unintended side-effect of one's personal dedication to a cause greater than oneself.

Viktor Frankl, *Man's Search for Meaning*

To find the best in others;

To leave the world a bit better, whether by a healthy child, a garden patch, or a redeemed social condition;

To know even one life has breathed easier because you have lived. This is to have succeeded.

So how might you define success?

> Mistakes are almost always of a sacred nature. Never try to correct them.
>
> Salvador Dali

- It might be that your work touches others as deeply as you have been touched by the works of others.
- To recreate sensations, memories and experiences not just accurately but with deep emotional and spiritual resonance.
- To feel the deep soul satisfaction of expressing what lies untouchable just beyond your grasp and vision.
- To actualise the transformation you long for in yourself and the world.
- To share your vision with the world.
- To have your creations deemed valuable or worthy of artistic merit.
- To finally be able to rest easy, knowing that you have done what you are here for.
- To feel yourself fully seen and heard.
- To achieve a certain standard of living.
- Seeing your work shared in certain places or by certain people that matter to you.

Realistic views of what success looks and feels like to us can help immunise us to not only criticism, but also the pernicious virus of perfectionism.

We don't have to be the best...or the only. We simply have to be an authentic expression of ourselves and our visions.

Whatever we aim at, we are always unique, because there is only one us in the whole world with this body and these life experiences. And that is our gift to the world.

We just have to accept it ourselves first.

Stop Waiting... Start Now

Tell me, how long have you been waiting for success...for the time when your talent is finally recognised? How long have you been hoping that today is the day that you finally make it?

Have you waited until the moment that your Facebook page hit 100K? For the day your blog went viral? For the record company or the publisher to come along, contract in hand, to sign you up? Because this means you are worthy, are good enough, to share your work with the world. At last.

Please, stop waiting for someone else's approval, for someone else's version of success. Stop trying to be perfect. And start getting your hands messy.

Make and share, make and share. Creativity was made to be shared, so stop waiting for the perfect time or place.

Stop adding terms and conditions.

Just share your work.

It doesn't need to be big or nothing. Take a chance on what you have. Start small. With someone you know. Then a few more people. And a few more. Keep widening those circles, making bigger ripples. You can reach more people next month or next year. But not unless you start somewhere.

Please don't be precious about it, waiting for far off perfection.

Put your work out there now.

As it is.

Risk that it's good enough. Risk that it's terrible. Call it a work in progress. Know that you will make better. Let your old stuff go out into the world so you are free to make new stuff. The old stuff might not make you

> "Don't think about making art, get it done. Let everyone else decide if it's good or bad, whether they love or hate it. While they're deciding, make even more art!
>
> Andy Warhol

as rich or as famous as you secretly hoped, but it will free you up to move forward. And it will go out there, doing its thing, reaching new folk – collaborators, customers, supporters. It will start to seed you a community who will help you and your work to grow.

Remember…

You get to make the rules.

You get to make the art.

You get to put it out there.

You get to make, and make, and make.

> Do what you can, with what you have, where you are.
>
> Theodore Roosevelt

Put your mind on creating a body of work. Not a magnum opus. Be brave. Be generous. Stop waiting for happily-ever-after. Stop yearning for the glamour.

Start now.

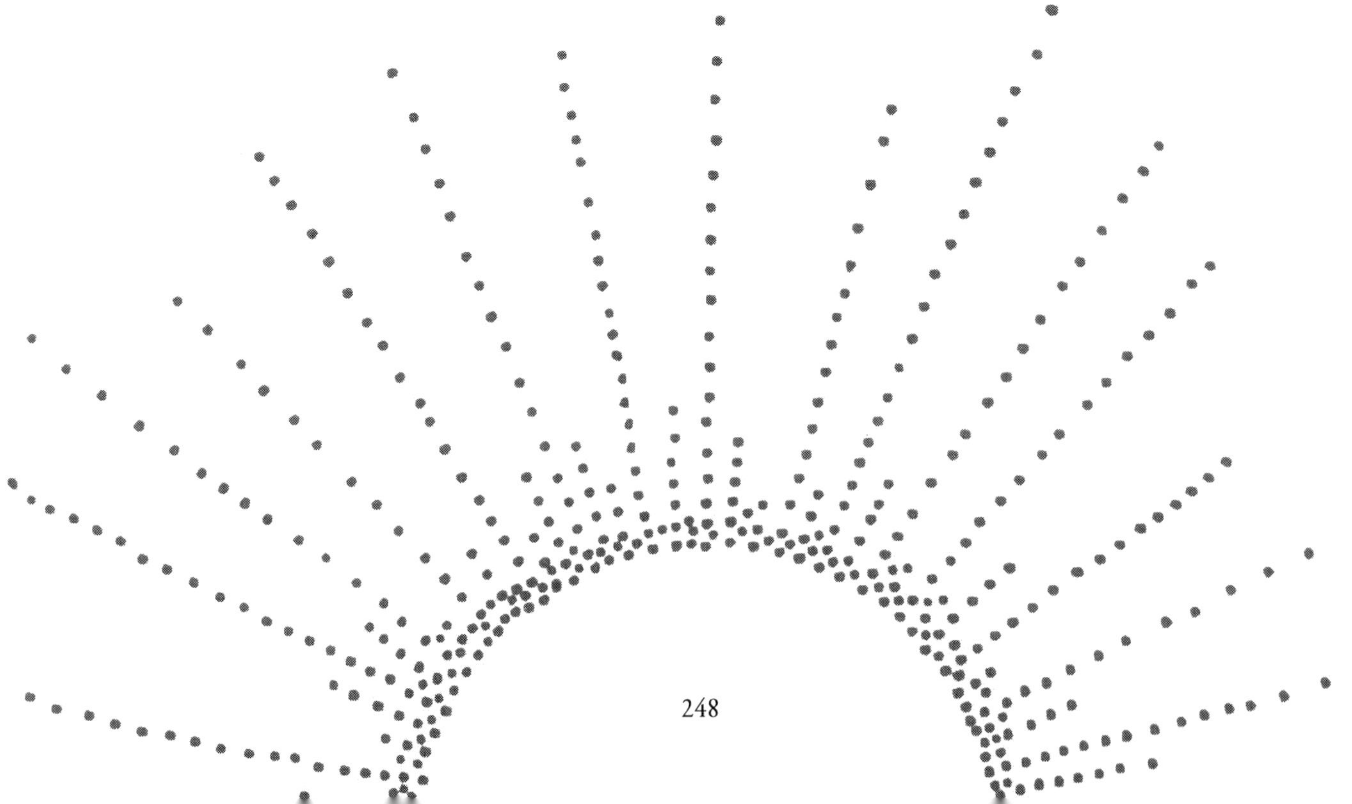

MULTIPLICITY

Too Many Passions

I don't know where to start – not because I don't have any ideas, but I have too many!

I seem to be writing seven books at once. How do I know which to focus on first? Or do I write them all at once?

I love to paint and dance and write...how do I know which to choose? I'm interested in everything...I don't know how to possibly make it work.

These are some of the questions I am regularly faced with from women who are wanting to create but don't know where to focus. They are all asking the same thing: *my creativity is endless and multi-faceted, but I am a human being, limited by time and energy. How do I focus that energy so that I can actually create just some of the things that my mind can imagine, without driving myself bat-shit crazy in the process?*

I totally get it...because I experience this too. Often I feel like a 4D person in a world that wants one dimensionality.

In the modern world of social media marketing we are expected to find our niche within a niche. And stay there forever. If you want to hit the big time the main advice is: focus on one thing. If you want Instagram followers by the tens of thousands you need to just do books. Or monochrome. Or gluten-free baking. Or dresses made of flowers. Or #coloursorganisedneatly.

Stardom requires specialism. A little box with your very own unique label. You must be original...but not *too* different to everyone else. You need to stay in your lane on the superhighway, so that people know where to find you, how to classify you and what to expect.

> I would ask you to write all kinds of books, hesitating at no subject however trivial or however vast.
>
> Virginia Woolf, *A Room of One's Own*

This box feels like a coffin to me: a place to contain lifeless bones. And I know I'm not alone in this.

Chances are you know me as a writer. But writing is only a small part of my creative expression. My life is filled with many different art forms. Each has a special role for me and for my soul's expression, in that sense they are not interchangeable, each is vital:

> "You can waste a perfectly good life trying to meet the standards of someone who thinks you're not good enough because they can't understand who you are.
>
> Barbara Sher, *Refuse to Choose!*

- Painting lets me interact directly with colour and energy.
- Drawing helps me to slow down, look carefully, be precise and give form to thoughts.
- Sand sculpture helps me find physical form.
- Playing guitar and piano help me to find my rhythm.
- Spiral-making helps me to channel the abundance of a season into a calming and centring symbol that I already know the form of by heart.
- Writing allows me to hear my own inner voices, unravel my feelings and share them.
- Knitting and crochet help me to slow down, follow a pattern, feel colour in form, make patterns and physically experience the untangling required in my head and the patience that goes with it.
- Collage allows me to practice recreating a new image from existing images, and to listen to my intuition to make new discoveries.
- Rock balancing helps me with patience and finding a still point.
- Dance helps me to move into my body and all the energies latent within, enabling me to embody and release them.
- Clay work helps me to merge with materials and find a way to enter into fluidity of consciousness.

- Singing helps me to find my voice and express my emotion through it.
- Cooking helps me to nourish and celebrate those I love.

These have all become central parts of my existence. But it has taken years to allow myself a life full of these expressions. They felt greedy, trivial, unnecessary, indulgent, pointless. I felt the pressure to choose just one, and become a master at it. After all, that's what everyone else seems to do.

It has taken even longer to allow myself to weave them together, under and over and through each other in my own weird way. It was only when finishing this book that I saw that music was a key thread that weaves from my father, who used to manage rock and roll bands, through me and my siblings on that side of the family. Music flows through me: in the songs I have written, the dances I choreograph, the playlists I make to move and write to. I now share each of my playlists with my readers so that they can experience that part of my creative self. Wool, too, is not my living, but it weaves insistently through from my maternal side. I have spent more of my time knitting and listening than writing in the past year, because I have learned that if there is not wool and music, the words and images dry up too.

> I like messy people; people who don't fit in a box or stay between the lines, but whose integrity is greater than any rule book and whose loyalty is stronger than blood.
>
> Jim Wern

The Polyamorous Creatrix

The sexual sphere is in many ways several steps ahead of the rest of Western culture right now. With the emergence into the mainstream of gender nonconformity, multiple forms of sexual orientation and ways of being in relationship, we are beginning to realise and accept the fluidity of sexuality and gender expression as vibrant and enriching to our culture, rather than threatening. The braver folks amongst us are daring to play in these waters. The same stands for creative expression. I believe that creative polyamorists are vital for cultural transformation and the shifting of paradigms, as we excel in transferring ideas and methods from one field of knowledge and applying them to others. Our culture has demanded heteronormativity for too long. As in all areas of life, diversity rocks, and is far richer than monoculture.

I think that we polyamorous creatives are wonderful. We are lovers of many things in a world so full of magic you'd have to be crazy not to want to explore it all. We are beautifully imperfect complex beings in a world that wants us to keep our broad-ranging passions as dirty little secrets in private. We are what Barbara Sher, in her book *Refuse to Choose*, calls 'Scanners' – folks who are "genetically wired to be interested in many things."

The issue is not our multiple passions, contrary to what teachers, parents, partners and bosses might have made us feel. The problem is that this is not the norm in our monotheistic, monochrome monoculture. So, odd-ball actor – excellent. Odd-ball actor that also takes the occasional straight part (stay in your lane Miranda Hart and Melissa McCarthy). Odd-ball actor that takes the occasional straight part, and also likes to paint (cringe, Jim Carrey)…who does all this as well as playing in their own band (double cringe, Johnny Depp).

"Historically, specialisation is a recent convention. Most of us are born natural polymaths.

Nuno Roque

But it hasn't always been this way. Throughout history there have been a subset of polymaths: renaissance men and women, who refused to be boxed in. These folks spoke six languages, painted watercolour landscapes and wrote philosophical treatises. They may also have had a home laboratory where they discovered one of the laws of nature that had evaded humanity thus far. They were celebrated by their cultures. And still are by ours. Just as prophets and saints and gurus are much easier to appreciate at arm's length, with some cultural whitewashing of their genius and editing of the foibles of their humanity rather than when having to live amongst their messy contradictions.

As women we are naturally and culturally good at having many balls in the air. Since time immemorial women have been healing and birthing and growing things and keeping the finances straight and protesting injustice whilst caring for the animals and weaving community and sewing clothes. Our multiplicitous creativity has been vital for human existence. Our species would have been fucked if all women were niche experts in only one thing. It's time to celebrate rather than denigrate this superpower…and joyfully allow it to exist within our creative lives.

And so I counsel you to nurture *all* your parts: your quirky, contradictory, don't-fit-into-any-neat-box bits. They are your keys to your unique genius. And they matter. They might not get you the world's biggest Instagram following. But they will bring you something richer and deeper, more substantial and sustainable – your own satisfaction and self-understanding and authentic connection with those who resonate with your work. They will bring you the ultimate gift of your work and purpose of your life: you fully expressed.

Creatrix Speaks

Until the episode of illness that I went through two years ago, I could not find my artistic way. Working in one medium has never seemed to be my way. It is rather by what I didn't do that I defined myself. In other words, I felt lost. I was constantly judging my work and that of others. I was wondering, "What is the point of creating, when there are so many objects on earth?" For many reasons, depression hit. I watched her approach and slammed the door in her face.

Three years passed. She came back. I opened the door wide. She entered. I embraced her. It was her or death. We danced a few months. I knew there was a hidden gift. Even though I was terrorized. I took up my pens, my brushes, my pencils, my notebooks. And I took time for myself. Time to create. Time to be something other than a wife or a mother or a teacher.

I drew mandalas in vulva shapes. I wrote all my questions in there. Then I modelled them. I continued the exploration of the wild feminine, reading Women Who Run with The Wolves. I found it so dense that I came up with the idea of illustrating it to better assimilate it. I carved tales out of porcelain, one after the other, as witnesses of my evolution to recover my health.

For my forty-second birthday, I invited my friends to come and create with me. I wanted to make zero-waste crafts together: waxed fabric wraps, DIY lipsticks... I had even planned for us to sew washable cloth pads. From there came the idea of creating a range of organic cloth pads in a variety of fabrics.

> Doing what you love isn't a privilege; it's an obligation.
>
> Barbara Sher, *Refuse to Choose!*

I gifted some, and then I started selling them. The day before an exhibition in which I was showing the creations of the last months, I suddenly saw that what came out of my hands formed a coherent whole. A journey through Womanhood. Without any fixed intention it had simply come and met me through my work.

A couple of months later, I was invited to attend a painting workshop. During that time, the journey through Womanhood went on, deepening and taking on colours.

On New Year's Eve, I was looking for a technical solution to cut the cloth pads out of the fabric without pinning the pattern. I needed to simplify this uncreative step. Suddenly an image flashed across my mind. I have the vision of my paintings and illustrations, printed on fabric. They are already cut off on the printed fabric. I see art on an object that will end in the bottom of someone's panties and I burst out laughing! And so I started my tests and discover that creating artistic sanitary towels fills me with joy!

I no longer wonder about the usefulness of my art. It keeps me healthy and that's essential. If it can bring a little poetry to the lives of others, then that is good too.

Zoé

Choices, Choices

So having just encouraged you to follow your passions, I'm now going to counsel you that you can't necessarily do them all at the same time. Most Highly Creative People have books full of ideas…but even the wellest of us have only so much energy and time to actually make them happen.

I often joke that I need at least three lifetimes to fulfil at least some of the big creative ideas that I've had so far. My dear friend Laura (whose voice you have read in this book) suggested employing a body snatcher to provide me with a second body as a solution to the 'problem' of too many ideas and not enough time!

The buzz of new ideas is so exciting, believe me I know that. But often we forget that just because we have ideas, it doesn't mean we have a moral obligation to make them happen.

Read that again.

It's true! Often we feel some sort of obligation to The Work…or ourselves…or to our communities that we *have* to act on every idea that comes our way… Otherwise we have failed them, failed ourselves. Otherwise The Work might go away forever.

But leaping with two feet into every new idea can leave us zigzagging here and there, getting knocked off centre, never getting anything done, whilst getting burned out in the process.

I see so many multi-passionate creatives become crippled by doing too much. I have been in this situation myself, countless times: having too much energy going in too many directions; not being able to focus; not knowing how or where to start; not being able to bring projects to completion.

For optimal health, we as multi-passionate creatives require a large degree of fluidity, flow and self-direction in our lives. We need the flexibility and courage to voice when we have reached overwhelm and the permission – inner and outer – to cut back that which we can no longer sustain.

I now have a checklist which I go through when a hot idea strikes:

1 – **How much does this excite me?** What is my intuitive response to it?

2 – **What will it cost me?** Both in terms of finances and energy.

3 – **Where might it take me and what could it make me?** What doors might it open for me? What people might it connect me with? What skills might I learn from it? What is the potential financial income from it?

4 – **How far will my excitement carry me?** And how much more energy will it require after that to see it through to completion?

5 – **What else do I have on now?** How much energy do I currently have

> If you're a person with no one passion but many interests, it may help to think about them enriching each other, rather than distracting from each other.
>
> Mari Andrew

committed to other things? To what extent will they suffer? What can I drop if I want to commit to this? (Be aware that we tend to underestimate the cost of creating by at least 100% as we are only aware of how it will be in a perfect world – not taking into consideration illness, disruptions, materials not working, delays outside our control…)

6 – **Is this *my* idea?** (Often others try to get creative people to collaborate or do their ideas for them. If it is not your idea or it doesn't have your whole heart be extra cautious about committing energy. Beware of taking on projects just to be nice to others, for fear of upsetting them.)

"Creative success means balancing your love of starting things with a habit of finishing them.

Marie Forleo

7 – **How does it fit with my current intentions, ambitions and commitments?** Does it build on what I have been doing? Does it add variety or contrast? (An important reminder for the multi-passionate creative is to remember your body of work – it is not just about this project. You are not expected to create a body of work in a day or a year but over a lifetime.)

8 – **What will it give to others?** How will it contribute to my community?

9 – **What can be shared?** How much of this needs to be done by just me? How much can be delegated?

10 – **How will I feel next month…and in ten years if I don't do this?** Or…how about if I do this in a month or a year…or ten years? Why not let it sit and see if the enthusiasm is still there?

Do not get out of the habit of noting down ideas when they come. It's really important to keep taking notes. Just remember: writing them down is not a commitment to *doing* them in all their technicolor glory. There are so many more responses possible to our multiple creative urges than just following each one to fruition…here are just a few.

- Maybe you can do it on a different scale? Perhaps a mini version is all that is required – a sketch rather than a painting; a poem, journal entry, blog post or short essay rather than a book/album/exhibition.
- Maybe it was meant for you in another stage of your life? Perhaps it is an echo from the past or future which you picked up on your inner radar… A seed may be being planted that will gestate for many years until you have the space to tend it.
- You could just admire it as an idea. Enjoy the burst of adrenaline you had as it came through. Bless it. Thank it. And leave it there. Just as it is.
- Or maybe it was meant for someone else? Share it with some people. They might have had the same calling and have the energy and desire to bring it to life. And if they do, you can support them in sharing it with the world.

”

Creativity is a natural extension of enthusiasm.

Earl Nightingale

Creatrix Speaks

I feel like a madwoman sometimes. My creative process is far from linear, especially having so many outlets for my creativity: paint, words, dance, singing, pottery, clothing… I dip in and out of these different outlets…but having so many outlets can mean progress moves slowly. And then on occasion come those moments, that can last for days, weeks, sometimes months, where my creative juices seem to have dried up.

Mirin

Self-Care

You have finite time – the same twenty-four hours as everyone else – so you do have to prioritise, and leave a lot of ideas as dreams, rather than burn yourself out. Not doing everything now isn't the same as not following your dreams ever: it's respecting your grounded human reality… We need to learn that saying *no* is as sacred, important and as good as saying *yes*.

Some of the ways we can take care of our multi-passionate selves include:

> "There is a fine line between genius and crazy…I like to use that line as a jump rope.
>
> Unknown

- Creating boundaries on how, when and where people can contact you, and how you will respond.
- Respecting your limits – I love Kate Northrup's suggestion of treating your to-do-list as sacred space rather than a dumping ground.[lv]
- Make fallow time a core part of your creative practice – on a daily, weekly, monthly and annual basis. Build retreat into your schedule. Rest, take breaks, take holidays, prioritise self-care.
- Admit when passion has morphed into crazy and off-load.
- Learn to 'ground' your energy in healthy ways.
- Remember you can't do *all* of it, all at the same time. Have different timelines and time frames for each passion. Some projects may have to go on the back burner, or the long finger. Dedicate time to different projects – schedule each project. And when you're doing one project, leave the others be.
- Close some browsers – internal and external!
- Find a way to curate your passions and talents that works for you. You may choose to have separate blogs or businesses for each creative passion, so that certain worlds don't necessarily cross over for your customers – some might be private/hobby/side ventures and others

your 'main thing'. You can indulge multi-passions in Pinterest with a different board for each – each a little dreamworld, vision board and research folder. Same with Facebook – you can have multiple pages with different identities and communities.

- Find ways to weave each project into a coherent body of work.

- Rebrand when your public persona no longer fits your private one. If your focus changes or your passion evolves, it can be hard for the people who loved who you were and what you used to do to adapt – they want the old you. You will lose some folks as you evolve, it can feel uncomfortable…but you cannot sustain what is no longer true for you. You will keep many with you…and will attract new folks who resonate with who you are and what you love now. You don't owe anyone the gift of who you were before.

- Prioritise creative play.

- Interweave little bits of creative expression throughout the day – doing a photo for Instagram, a Facebook post, a jot in your journal, a doodle whilst you are talking, singing when you are in the car…

> "It is not the artist's job to please anyone, but to bravely do the work that they are most compelled to do.
>
> Steve Peters

Own your right to be a multi-passionate creative. Wear it as a badge of honour. Learn more about it. Redefine it as being dynamic, exciting, authentic and more attuned to the ever-changing source of creativity and your own multi-dimensional nature.

Practical Organisation for Multi-Passionate Creatives

A myth of the creative is someone who is dishevelled, surrounded by dirty coffee cups, with paint on their hands and a slightly wild look in their eyes, not knowing what day it is, turning up for appointments a month late, drifting into solipsistic reverie mid-conversation and not being able to handle money. Okay, so maybe they're kind of true. But as a multi-passionate creatrix in the modern world you need to find ways to organise your time, resources, ideas...and if you are making money, how to handle that too.

In the past more creatives handed over their organisational affairs to agents or personal assistants (often partners, sisters or daughters). Technology has enabled us to do much of it ourselves. There are incredible tech tools to support every part of the creative process – most of them have a free version to try.

Some useful working practices that have been invaluable to me over the years are:

> You can't use up creativity. The more the you use, the more you have.
>
> Maya Angelou

- Break down projects and processes into manageable chunks using a list or diagram, so that you can do them step by step rather than becoming overwhelmed by the vast scope of what you are trying to achieve.

- Set yourself deadlines and schedule these into your calendar or online planner so that you can see the upcoming due dates for each.

- Compartmentalise – if you have lots of projects on the go, you can't do them all at once. Set aside distinct times each week for each project where you focus all your energy and attention on just that. If you get any ideas related to your other projects, as you undoubtedly will (you've got to love the scatter-gun/hyper-focus contrariness of the creative brain!) write down the idea, park it and come back to it in your time slot for that project.

- Whatever your creative work, be sure to save your offcuts: your scraps of fabric, small bits of wool, cut paragraphs, not-quite-right images. Keep them both from your original collecting and collating phase, and from your crafting and editing phase. You will often find that these hold within them magic not needed for the project they were culled from, but the seeds of a new project. Or something to patch a hole you inadvertently made in your work by cutting too much! Treasure these offcuts. Within them you will find the physical material to try something else out without risk or cost. Use them to make patchwork quilts, compilations, collages… Display them in your workspace. Sort through them as you begin work on a new project.

- Keep your space and tools organised…and from time to time declutter!

Creative Inquiry

Fear and courage

- What does being in the spotlight mean to you?
- How can you centre your creativity rather than yourself?
- Where do your personal fears come from and how do they influence your creative process? At what parts in it are your fears most active?
- How honest are you about sharing your own fears with others?
- Who gives you permission to live your life fully as a creative person–either by living an inspired life, by sharing their wisdom or by simply talking about the challenges they face? Have you considered that you may be one of these people for others?

Recognition

- Who do you want to see and hear you?
- Do you long for fame, celebrity or recognition? What do you believe they will bring you?
- Who do you want to take you seriously? What would change if they did?

- What award would feel like a worthy reward of your work?
- Who have been your biggest critics thus far? What do you think motivated them? How did you respond?
- Does something have to be perfect, otherwise you won't even try? Do you need to be in control at all stages (have you ever wondered what would *really* happen if you weren't?) How good is perfect? What are you basing your standards on?
- What is it you are most scared of when it comes to living The Creative Way? Dare you write these things down now…all of them…the inner fears, the outer fears?
- What do you believe might be the consequences of walking The Creative Way?
- What has been the reality of walking The Creative Way thus far? How many of your fears have been proven true? How did you deal with this reality? How has it shaped who you are and how you do your work now?

Multi-passionate creative

- Do you identify as a multi-passionate creative? What are the upsides and downsides?
- Do you have a system for keeping track of your ideas?
- Do you have a system for planning your time and organising your energy?
- What do you need to unlearn about the negatives of being multi-passionate, from folks who have told you it was wrong or unacceptable?

Creative Practice

Success

What does success look like to you? Create a collage, sketch or other visual representation of what success is to remind you when you falter.

Burning the rulebook

Write out a list of creative rules that you currently follow – consciously or unconsciously. Write out the rules you learned about what art – Great Art, women's art, your art – was and wasn't. What you shouldn't do – be it starting a sentence with 'And' or using black in a painting. Consider as you write them out: who set these rules, when and why? Have you ever experienced punishment, failure or humiliation for breaking them? What did this teach you?

Create a burning ceremony. Burn this rulebook.

Now, write your own…based on your values, skills and ideas. Fill it with ideas and possibilities that are totally inclusive of you. Share these with others you teach and speak to, so that they in turn have permission to burn the old, unconscious rulebook about what creativity is and who gets to do it.

I am she who…

Rather than define yourself by each individual project, which might feel overwhelming and exhausting, dive deeper into the threads and energy that you are weaving together in each one. Create a mind map, WORD+ image piece or collage collating these different threads with the prompt, *I am she who…*

6

Only you can be you

Only you can create what you will create

That is worth something

That is worth everything.

WORK

The Creative Entrepreneur

> Draw the art you want to see, start the business you want to run, play the music you want to hear, write the books you want to read, build the products you want to use – do the work you want to see done.
>
> Austin Kleon, *Steal Like an Artist*

What if…

You could find a way to make a living doing what you loved?

You didn't have to choose between your work and your Work?

You could create a working life that actually worked for you?

That was as dynamic, exciting and passionate as you are.

Which actually fulfilled you on more than just a financial level.

Where you called the shots.

There is more than one way.

More than one way to earn a living. More than one way to live creatively. It's not reserved for movie stars and pop idols. And whilst there is no guaranteed success…nor is it dangerous or irresponsible as you may have been told.

It requires courage, sure. And work…lots. But most of all it requires thinking outside the box. Something we are ill-equipped to do by our education system.

I have done it. In fact, three generations of my family have done it. On both sides. So, it's second nature to me. But I know to a lot of people it's not. It's scary, alien and unknown. It's something they might risk for a summer when they're twenty. But not with kids in tow. Or a mortgage.

Let's get really clear here, whilst I'm talking about following your dreams, I don't mean quitting your full-time job today hoping that a vague idea you have will be able to support you right now. But I am talking about constructing a life according to your own priorities, values, skills and needs. Bit by bit, strand by strand, weaving the life you want to live.

It's also important to acknowledge that earning a living from our creativity is not necessarily a choice for all of us, at certain points of our lives…or ever. At times we will need more financial or emotional security than earning creatively would allow. At other times our audience is not big enough to make a living. Or our mental or physical health is not strong enough. Or our caring responsibilities are too onerous.

At times earning a living puts too much strain on our creativity – pressuring us to make deeply personal work public, or make our creativity more palatable or populist, which then blocks us creatively. Earning a living through creative entrepreneurship is not a superior moral choice, and we have not failed if we choose not to, or cannot, right now…or ever.

But if we do choose to make a living from our creativity, unlike the vast majority of professions, artists are expected to just know how to do it, and are judged harshly when they don't or can't. We don't expect this of our lawyers, architects, engineers, teachers or scientists. But we do of creatives.

For many creatrixes, and perhaps for you, The Creative Way includes not just our leisure and pleasure, but our work too.

Have you ever dared to ask yourself: *what if…?*

"

Work is love made visible.

Kahlil Gibran

Creatrix Speaks

I've had times of being very public with my creative work and times of being intensely private. I am in a constant tussle with this and figuring out how to be with my own changing nature whilst sustaining a public artistic presence in the world with integrity.

The question I am living is – is there a healthy space to reside in between the compulsion to create, the therapeutic nature of creative expression, the desire to share it and let it find people who will connect with it and dwelling within the music market?

I have certainly stumbled many times with how to manage all this. For me, a red herring was believing the rhetoric of 'if you do what you love you will manifest success/make a living from your art'. That hasn't been the reality and it has been an unhelpful destination to aim for and has actually spoilt the journey. When creativity is a life force, for me to rely on that to be my means of survival in the world has ironically ended up almost killing off the life force itself. I certainly got lost in trying to push my work 'further out there' into avenues and through ways that might garner more visibility but felt at odds with my intuition and boundaries. I got lost in how to value and believe in my work based on the external rather than internal. I got lost in the wilderness of recording studios and self-promotion and social media and how exposing it was to share songs that came from my most vulnerable places.

> If you're feeling a call to share your voice, help others heal and make a difference, running a business from the heart is the next stage of evolution being asked.
>
> Mirror Living

The truth is, I believe I lack many of the components required to be a working artist! People have said to me that I need to grow a thicker skin if I am to be 'in the music industry' – but I know that if I did that, I wouldn't be able to write the songs I write. They come from the thinness of my skin, from perceiving and feeling the world in a certain way, of journeying and residing in places that don't easily equate to any form of 'industry'. At heart, I am simply a songwriter, and then a recording artist. The other roles that go with it: marketing, promoting, performing are things I can do, but come with much challenge. And I'd rather not play into an 'industrial growth society' with its relentless push for progress and success meaning bigger and better. I'd rather not play the game of it all and stay independent and do as much as I can do within my specific circumstances and in a way that's healthy and balanced to me. And trust that my work connects to who it connects with – knowing that you never really know where it flows out to.

Eleanor

The Big Bang Myth

First we need to bust the myth that goes something like this: you create your masterpiece and put it out there. It gets discovered. You become an overnight success. You earn six figures…win the awards…and will never be under pressure to work again.

Wannabe creatives try to find the formula that will let them cut the dark nights of the soul and get straight to the pot of gold at the end of the rainbow. They may spend large sums of money on coaches who promise that if they follow their simple five-step process they'll be earning six figures a month in the first month.

Some folks I know have spent years writing their BOOK, making it (in their eyes) perfect. They might pay big money to an ex-major publishing house editor.

And then, they try to sell it to the hottest literary agent or the biggest publishing company.

But it doesn't sell.

Or maybe it is taken up by a smaller publisher, who wants it completely re-written.

Or perhaps they pay a fancy self-publishing company who once again is full of shiny promises of success.

Then maybe it sells ten copies.

Or a hundred.

Perhaps even a thousand.

They feel rather disillusioned: *where's the big bang?*

They have no twelve-city book tour, or Best First Novel Award. No New York Times best-seller or six-figure contract. They've set up their crystal altar, said their affirmations, cut the nay-sayers out of their lives. But they're scraping around for money. Their book only has three Amazon reviews and two are from their friends. And it's only been featured in one special interest magazine – and that's because they paid for the ad.

They believe that they have failed. And feel the burn of shame. So they fold up their creative dreams and hide them at the back of the desk drawer and lock it up. They shamefacedly start applying for office jobs. And vow never to be so stupid again.

”

I worked half my life to be an overnight success, and still it took me by surprise.

Jessica Savitch

And it's not just writers. I know artists and musicians who are holding out until they're perfect enough to launch their big work. They are waiting patiently to be plucked from obscurity. They don't share anything. Because if they can't get the famous gallery or the big producer or the massive festival…then they won't put their work out there. Not until there's some sort of guarantee of success, some recognition of their innate genius. Not for them the starting small and working their way up approach. They need to start where they belong: at the top. They want a gold-plated guarantee that they won't fail. Failure being rated equally as lack of recognition…and lack of money. And so they stay locked in their turret, waiting for their prince to come and rescue them, so they can gallop off into the sunset and live happily-ever-after. As they deserve.

The media likes to focus on the fairytale story of overnight success: the supermodel talent-spotted in the shopping mall, the platinum-selling singer that won a TV talent show. They sell the role of artist as celebrity story to hungry wannabes so starved of soul and life by the drudgery of Western capitalism, who are longing for a life of colour and freedom, being seen and heard. Which is interpreted as 'fame'. Our egos long for this. We have been taught that we are both nothing…and immensely special. We have learned that we have one shot. At love. At success. At creativity. So we have to pick well. It's all or nothing.

And when it comes to creativity, that usually means nothing. Because chances are, we do not have the contacts, the agent, the confidence, the massive fan-base starting out.

We haven't internalised the understanding that, like any other line of work, making a living as a creative is a step-by-step, magical but mundane and completely unpredictable process, woven from multiple successes… and failures. You work your way up. You take your chances, perhaps get a lucky break here or there. Privilege may get you higher, faster, and prejudices against people like you will hold you back. But it's a long and winding road.

Instead we're conditioned to shoot for wealthy retirement before we've even started, rather than focusing on building a creative life – a life that is a messy but real expression of our art, which can, little by little, support and sustain us.

This is what I want to speak to. Because I'm passionate about busting the myths about what it means to be a working creative.

Becoming a millionaire from one artwork is not synonymous with making your soul work and having the freedom to create. It's a dream you need to let go of right now. It's like winning the lottery. Unlikely…and pretty undesirable.

Do not drop your idea about making a living from your creativity. Just be careful when starting out that you're not resting your self-worth, your family's livelihood, your right to create on the first creative work you sell to the world… Or the second. Or even the tenth.

> Do what you love and you'll ~~never work a day in your life~~ work super fucking hard all the time with no separation or any boundaries and also take everything extremely personally.
>
> Adam J K

A New Way of Working

None of the featured creatrixes have taken the traditional route of: find an agent, music label, publisher or gallery, sign a contract, get a juicy advance, be tied down and beholden to mainstream media and the celebrity culture in order to make a living. Instead we have produced and self-published our own music, books, clothing and art, or moved between many independent producers, or organisations. We have found ways to live and work outside of the mainstream for the most part, creating another way combining ancient and modern technologies of connection: women's circles, storytelling, market stalls and crowd funding, Etsy, Mailchimp and Facebook.

We are creative entrepreneurs – and it is fair to say that we have mixed feelings about this. We love the benefits: independence, flexibility and creative control but struggle with the costs: financial stress and seasonal shifts in income; a pervading sense of insecurity in an economy and culture where a regular monthly wage and sick pay are the norm; overwhelm at the scale of things that need doing to make a living from art. We know what it's like finding new ways to make ourselves visible, whilst balancing our family's and personal needs for privacy and rest. We collaborate on fun projects that might not make a penny but enrich us in other ways, and do paid jobs that do not set our hearts aflutter, but keep the lights on.

It's a constant mix and muddle of lots of different things and more besides. As well as all the priceless things like being there to pick up your kids from school, working from bed in your PJs, not having to commute, having sex in the morning when everyone else is at work, or heading to the beach just because it's sunny. It's also doing a midnight author interview via Skype with a journalist on the other side of the world. It's the grateful emails from readers who say your words have changed their lives and sending newsletters that no one responds to. It's belonging to a creative circle of folks on social media who get you. It's getting asked to speak alongside heroes at conferences…and doing readings in bookshops to audiences of three. It's all this and more. The glory is right here in the everyday magical mundane.

> The artist who sells his own creations must develop a more subjective feel for the two economies [the gift economy and the economic marketplace] and his own rituals for both keeping them apart and bringing them together.
>
> Lewis Hyde, *The Gift*

Nowadays our culture divides life neatly into two distinct and disparate spheres – work and life – and recommends a 'healthy work-life balance'. This is a very modern (and warped) version of how to live. As though our human selves are different to our economic selves.

Those of us who walk The Creative Way are reclaiming an intertwined way of living, where what we do is not separate from who we are.

A creatrix is by her very nature a box-refuser. She is committed to weaving a web of many strands – so that work is pleasure-driven, family time and art co-exist, healing and creativity go hand in hand. Work partners might also be romantic partners, and friends our creative collaborators. We aim for a life where work isn't just one thing, but different things on different days, or even different times in an hour. Our lives are built up of passions, duties, obligations, some paid, some not, some hobbies which become work…or work which becomes hobbies.

Our creativity spills out into everything we do. When we mourn our loved ones we create work. When we travel we are drinking in influences that will later emerge in our body of work. We cannot separate out the threads of work and life. They all make up the fabric of The Creative Way.

Creating a Work Day that Works

When our creativity becomes our work we can bring bad habits and assumptions and old stories with us from the old patriarchal paradigm about what work means or what it should look like.

We need to regularly remind ourselves of the difference between The

Work – our soul's mission – and the physical and mental work required to materialise it. Our work can so easily become workworkwork, a late stage capitalist disease that most of us have caught, which slave-drives us past our healthy, natural abilities and requires that we labour like machines, ignoring all our human and soul needs.

Grab your pen and list what you think of when you hear the word 'work'.

First of all it's probably hard. Often forced or not enjoyed. Chances are there's a desk involved, and lots of other people. There are probably set hours and a salary. There's also a sense of foreboding on Monday mornings and a looking forward to weekends and getting home in the evening. There are pay days and pretending to the boss you're working. There are paid holidays, health care and the year's schedule given to you. As well as a place to show up to work.

When you become a creative entrepreneur many of these things fall away – you decide when you work, where you do it and how much. You get to decide what is important. You determine when and how much you need to earn, what rest days and holidays are. Well, the weather, your collaborators, clients, galleries, publishers and print deadlines don't just disappear but you have much more control over your own time and energy and how they are used. You are empowered to find new ways of showing up that are healthy and supportive of you on every level – so that your bodymind and soul are getting what they need.

When we are creative as a living we have to schedule in fallow time – naps, creative playtime, movement breaks, café sitting, reading – as integral parts of our creative working schedule. They're so easy to skip over, when we get sucked into the values of the 'Real World' – but they are vital practices to reconnect ourselves to our bodies, our souls and our art.

In a fascinating article, Alex Soojung-Kim Pang explores work and rest as partners,

> *Research in psychology and neuroscience explains why layering periods of intensive work and active rest optimize both productivity and creativity. First, [we] can operate at a high level for about four hours a day; after that, productivity drops off substantially, so it's most effective to organize one's time around those focused hours. Second, our brains don't switch off when we do something mental-*

> ”
>
> The greatest geniuses sometimes accomplish more when they work less.
>
> Leonardo da Vinci

ly undemanding; the brain's 'default mode network,' which takes over in moments when we relax our attention, is actually as active and complex as the working brain. After periods of intensive focus, the default mode continues working on unfinished problems and exploring new ideas, even as our conscious minds are diverted or at play. Rest provides time for the creative subconscious to explore new ideas, work on unsolved problems, and come up with novel solutions. Third, activities that most effectively stimulate unconscious creative thinking – regular exercise, serious hobbies, and vacations – are also correlated with longer lifespans, higher levels of success and job satisfaction, and greater happiness. [...]

People who balance focused work and deliberate rest – rest that is scheduled, active and stimulates creative thinking – also have long, fruitful creative lives. They don't burn out or peak early. Regular rest restores and maintains their energy, provides a buffer against overwork, and encourages them to lead more balanced lives.[lvi]

I have spent most of my professional creative life not following this advice. Instead I tried to work intensely during office hours – because that's when my kids were at school, and other people were 'in office'. In the early days when I started out and couldn't afford help, everything fell on my shoulders: childcare, filing taxes, cleaning, emails, design, social media... However this eventually becomes a habit – trying to fit too much into not enough time...leaving no time, ironically, to be creative!

I have, through bitter experience, learned that living creatively doesn't work like that...but burnout does. So below I share some hard-won tips for healthier creative living.

- Never get too busy with business that you don't have time to create.

- Never get too busy doing stuff for other people that you don't have the energy left to do what matters to you.

- Build recharging into your business and creative models.

- Rest lots. Being busy is a fool's game. Make sustainability – from ecological to energetic – your watchword.

- Always have a plan A and B…but remember to leave space for magic.

- Be organised…and get support in this. Keep records and chart numbers…learn from them and the trends that they show, the patterns they reveal, but don't get distracted by them. Never let them run the show.

- Never, ever, ever lose track of the fact that you, your customers and your employees are all just human. Be compassionate if people are having a bad day…but don't put up with long term bullshit.

- Remember that trust is at the root of every positive interaction – financial or emotional – build trust, be trustworthy. Be as good as your word. Be honest if you can't do something and apologise if you mess up.

- Communicate clearly – follow up verbal discussions with written agreements. Use contracts where necessary.

- Keep to deadlines – and insist that the folks you work with do so.

- Be grateful…express your gratitude regularly and fully.

- Show up, be brave.

- Be generous. Charge fairly.

- Be approachable. But have clear boundaries.

- Dream big, work hard…but always allow yourself to be human.

- Remember you are not in it alone…nor are you the source of it all. Seek out the support you need.

- Remember to play.

As a creative entrepreneur what you will learn, sooner or later, is that you cannot do it all and still create. You will have to find ways to streamline work, delegate tasks to others and eventually grow a team. The accounts must be done, orders must be packed and emails written. But most of all, you need to find a way to ensure that your creativity keeps flowing…and along with it an income to sustain you through the dark times, the lean times, the creative times, the holiday times and the times when the river goes underground.

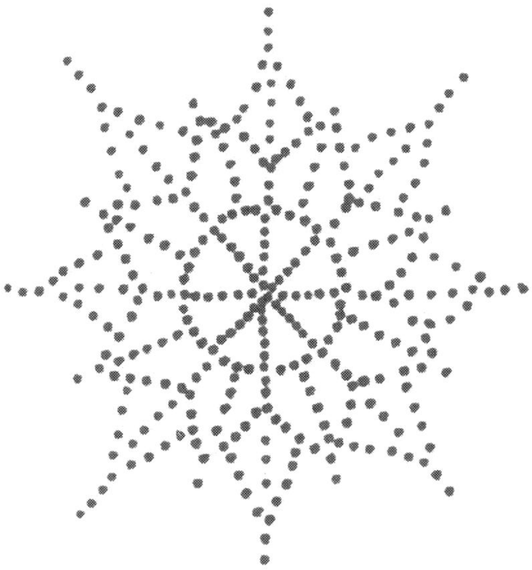

NETWORK

Sharing

> It takes a lot of courage to show your dreams to someone else.
>
> Erma Bombeck

When I started out trying to sell my work the thing that always most scared me was marketing myself. I thought that it meant I had to shout about how great I was, as I had seen in all the television and magazine ads around me. But I soon learned from other female entrepreneurs that the key to marketing within the Feminine paradigm is,

- Making and maintaining connections with an engaged community.
- Being generous.
- Creating and sharing great resources.
- Showing up authentically.

The primary focus of my creative work is not writing books, but building a community of like-minded people, and sharing resources with them which may be of interest and benefit to them. Some will be in exchange for money, most will not. I give generously of myself and in return I am the recipient of so much generosity, materially and spiritually. We are all nourished by our connections through this type of creative community. This is very different to the relationship that most businesses have with their customers.

As creatrixes we live with a spirit of deep generosity. We tell the story of our art, our process, of why we do what we do…and how we do it. Where traditional marketing requires vast amounts of capital for marketing teams and their clever campaigns and advertising slots on mainstream media outlets, as a creatrix you can use whatever you have to connect: a mailing list, social media, open studio times, signings, workshops, stalls to share what you make and who you are with others. Remember it is not just a product that people buy, but the *why* and the *how* – the story behind it and the connection that they feel with the maker and the craft. Share that with them. Not because it makes slick marketing, but because it matters – because this is another way of getting The Work out into the world. This is how you make ripples: sharing what it is you are called to do. Like in the children's game of Pass the Parcel, we keep passing on the gift, rather than hogging it for ourselves.

> Making money is art and working is art and good business is the best art.
>
> Andy Warhol

Once I realised that I did not have to sell at everyone in general, as in traditional capitalism, I felt much more at ease. I do not feel obligated to fight tooth and claw for my space in a crowded marketplace, trying to shout above the noise. There are enough folks with much bigger budgets doing that. And to be honest, most of us just tune it out nowadays, we are so immersed in and immune to traditional marketing.

The skills required to make a living from our work within this new paradigm are the same as those we have already honed and harnessed through our travels on The Creative Way. This is why creative folks can make such good entrepreneurs. We already have what it takes. We can…

Tell good stories.
Share a compelling vision.
Engage a community.
See from other perspectives.
Follow an unseen process.
Spot patterns.
Think outside the box.
Be resourceful.
Understand the dynamics of flow.
Be brave and put ourselves out there.
Work hard.
Research well.
Know our field…and do things differently!

But in order to share our work, we have to *be on our own side.* If part of ourselves is seeking to sabotage our work, our voice or visibility through fear, we are only half there. Take it from one who knows. It's exhausting to have to do battle with yourself before you even get past your front door. You cannot simultaneously hide and show up as yourself.

Showing up in your fullness, in your reality, has real costs and requires supports. Each of us has different things we need to be able to show up as ourselves. And it's not just a bowl of M&Ms with the blue ones taken out.

Creatrix Speaks

The desire for art to be my career leads to a whole collection of mind-fucks. A primary one being that I am pushed to present my art to the world. When it gets the world's approval, I make money, and life is good. In so doing, my sense of self-worth can sometimes get tangled up in what other people think about my art. I know I shouldn't attach my self-worth to the approval of others, yet, trying to make a living from these vulnerable creative expressions of mine, can leave me sometimes not knowing where the boundary is between me and my art.

Mirin

> It's so easy to get distracted by what we don't know or don't have, that we forget what we do know and do have.
>
> Tara Gentile

Public/Private

In order to be able to make a living from our work it must be visible to others. And usually, but not always, we must also be visible. Whilst our artefacts are containers of the work, we have to accept that we as creatrixes often need to be the gateway to persuading others to take a look.

Many creatrixes struggle with creating a brand as an artist which is authentic to them, integral to their work, whilst maintaining space for themselves as a human untouched by this persona. Developing a creative identity requires having a strong grasp of our own symbolic language and voice and an understanding of who will be drawn to this – what turns them on and off. We must also be open to adapting this brand to best reflect The Work as it evolves. Think Prince or David Bowie – they reinvented how we saw them, what they were called, again and again. They recreated their sound and their wardrobe to reflect where they were creatively at any point. They chose what they wanted to reveal of themselves, what facets of their personality to embellish and share, and the rest was kept more private.

For those of us who are neurodiverse, or who have tried to hide our sexuality, gender, mental or physical health issues, the idea of creating an external persona is probably one we're familiar with. But it might also be something we're tired of having to do.

> The place where I feel the most resistance is the same place that holds the greatest reward.
>
> Gina Gomez

Branding can be one of the most daunting...and exciting parts of our work. Because we get to make ourselves up: we get to chose our name and our professional appearance. We get to edit our energy to create the public face we want others to see and connect to. Bear in mind, however, that we only have so much leeway: the further from our authentic selves our public persona is, the further we have to fall if this divide becomes visible. I've lost count of the amount of times I have seen a great actor or writer interviewed – award-winning artists who fill stages, screens and books with their presence – who are...well, underwhelming, in person: shy, understated, quiet, self-doubting, depressing even.

We need to create boundaries around our public selves, however rooted in authenticity they are, because the human self is not made to be in direct relationship with tens of thousands and certainly not millions of people at any one time. We each must have times and places where we get to take off our costumes, our big selves, and be our small, vulnerable, messy selves, our unperformed selves. Even Madonna doesn't sleep in her trademark conical bra.

Experience

Over the years, I have built up my public persona as authentically as I can, whilst keeping myself safe. First a mummy blogger and editor of a parenting magazine. And then, as my children got older, I let go of my mother-first identity and my desire to be more adult in my themes came through, thrilling some, gravely disappointing others. An unexpected extra transformation happened when I received my diagnosis of Aspergers, and needed to weave this identity into my creative persona.

I found this hard, having spent a lifetime trying to be acceptable to others.

But it also gave some part of myself the permission to step further forward.

Over several years I have created Lucy H. Pearce – a braver, bolder version of myself. She who had the courage to write the books and make the art I longed to see in the world. It just required that I step into her.

Through her I get a chance to be the self I sense inside: my best me. My creativity gives me a vehicle for my larger potential self that is crippled by the way my brain functions under stress in social situations. In my books I get to be closer to her, to learn from her...just as much as my readers do.

But I worry that when they see me that they expect me to be Burning Woman – I am not. I can channel her wisdom, read her patterns, but I am an apprentice of her, just as I am of Creatrix, of Medicine Woman and The Crazy Woman. They are archetypes I am aware of in my psyche – but I am not them.

It was one of our Womancraft authors, who has become a dear friend, Amy Bammel Wilding, who pointed out that my issue was in lining up Lucy H. Pearce and lucy.

Both are me. Both are totally real, authentic channelings of my own energy and being. Yet one is a creative persona, a larger-than-life self that enables me to reach beyond my own personal fears and limitations and step into the world.

I love being Lucy H. Pearce, there is much she brings me. But the amount of energy she requires is more than lucy can manage for more than short bursts. And so I have learned to focus my energy on taking care of lucy when Lucy H. Pearce is in town: setting *energetic limits, caring and nourishing myself, resting more.*

I also fear Lucy H. Pearce. I fear what she requires me to bring through, and the potential repercussions there could be for my vulnerable human self and life, when I share her creations under our name.

It was in preparing for the biggest event of my career, two workshops and a keynote in a week, I realised another angle: I don't have to 'put on' Lucy H. Pearce. I am already her, she is me, my soul. When I embody her I am fully alive, fully switched on with the Source power pulsing through. She is always with me, in me. Her energy, vision, colour and courage are always there, imprisoned, disguised, repressed by the fear of what others will think. Sometimes she pulses strongly, at other times her quieter visionary and reflective qualities are more apparent. She is deeply cyclical, she must weave and gestate, as well as present and perform. But she is always there. In order to live, and live fully, she must live fully. She both has her own unique energy as well as being embodied by me. We are in a mutually reciprocal relationship – each must flourish so that the other may flourish.

Over the years I have learned to embody her more consistently in my private life. Through my work I am being called to embody her publicly. However dangerous this may feel to me.

> A great company is a conspiracy to change the world; when you share your secret, the recipient becomes a fellow conspirator.
>
> Peter Thiel, *Zero to One*

Brave New Worlds

Social media allows us to create a global community around our creativity. Thanks to the internet we are able to build our own platforms and find our own audiences without needing the approval or acceptance of the traditional cultural gatekeepers. We have the tools to do this for ourselves.

In the past creatives had to win the support of a patron – either a wealthy individual or organisation – in order to succeed. They had to find trusted go-betweens – people who would handle the money, the administration, the contracts, the business…for a cut of the profits. But with the democratisation of publishing tools and the wide reach of social media, many of us are choosing to go it alone. We are able to cut out the middle-men and become entrepreneurial women on our own terms, keeping far more of our own earnings.

You have all the technology you need at your fingertips to share whatever it is you make with the world right now. You can upload your images, an MP3, a video, a talk, run a teleconference call, self-publish your book right now. Stop playing by the rules of last century. You don't need anyone else's permission, anyone else's access, anyone else's money to start.

> Art is a glorious mutator. It evolves you. It evolves us. And eventually, the world.
>
> Chuck Wendig

All the world is literally now your stage, and you can make direct connections with those you are creating for, wherever in the world you are. You are able to be more responsive to their needs and desires. You can be quicker to respond with a new product than a large traditional industry, and get to keep more of the profit than if you were working for a label or patron. You can get direct feedback, make last-minute tweaks thanks to print on demand and short runs. You can ship easily thanks to drop shipping and internet shopping. You can have real nourishing conversations with those who love what you do and strike up lasting friendships with your best customers.

What an incredible blessing it is to live now as a creatrix, with every mind and soul just a connection away. Be sure to harness the magic of this brave new world to spread creative wonder far and wide. Use this world wide web to the fullest of its potential to unleash the fullness of your own.

Experience

I want to share something with you that more than perhaps anything else I have done in my life, certainly anything I have done collaboratively, is a proof of a greater mystery at play behind The Work, and the way in which social media supports powerful creative collaboration and fosters real life community.

Several years ago, when I was birthing Womancraft Publish-

ing, itself an online-based publishing company, I was drawn to a women's teleconference. The music for this conference – "A Call to Stand" – was played at the beginning of every session. That music, I was to discover later, was written by a musician called Eleanor Brown, who lived in south Wales, not far from where my grandmother, Lucy H. Crocker Pearce grew up, just miles from where my soul sister lives now.

On the Facebook group for this event I introduced myself and Womancraft, and received a message from a woman in the group who had just finished a book and was looking for a publisher. The woman was Nicole Schwab, the book was The Heart of the Labyrinth, Womancraft Publishing's first title.

A couple of years pass, I discover Eleanor Brown via Alisa Starkweather. Alisa is a soul-mother to me, I discovered her when I was researching my first book, Moon Time. She is the founder of the Red Tent Temple movement and has been a massive champion of my work. I have spoken to her in some of my darkest times.

It turned out that Eleanor had too. In fact, the next time I came across Eleanor it was because Alisa was sharing a song that Eleanor had written, based on a conversation: "Alisa's Song: In the Roots We Are Together" – I listened to it on loop for months as I wrote Burning Woman... and discovered the rest of Eleanor's music via Bandcamp.

When I had finished Burning Woman Alisa made contact. She knew how soul-defining a process it had been for me. She wanted to make it possible for me to go to America to attend her Daughters of the Earth event, and to help share my work with her community. A few weeks later she was to do the same for Eleanor. She believed in us, in our work, and wanted to help the next generation of creatrixes who were coming through over here in Europe.

Not long after, Eleanor put out a crowdfunder call for her next album, Meet You There. I supported it in a breath. Several months later it arrived, and it is no exaggeration to say that that album got me through the hardest, deepest, darkest winter of my life as I was living and writing Medicine Woman. I put on track seven "Meet You There" and literally breathed through it.

Breathe, breathe into silence...

in the minutes before first my daughter's and then my Aspergers diagnosis, when I couldn't keep my anxiety under any sort of control. Her words kept me alive moment by moment when I couldn't function, when I couldn't hold onto life anymore.

I believe it is important to acknowledge and thank those who have shaped our souls, so I reached out and let her know how important her music had been that winter. She shared that she too had had a hard, dark winter, and that she was called to share a song with me: "We Will Not Be Lost To These Times."

I listened, and cried.

I've been living in the wasteland
I've been clinging in the dark

I've been hearing all these voices
and losing hope and heart.

From a lineage of silence,
I break the biggest vow

So I'm rising from the ashes
and speaking truth to power.

I sent her back a doodle from my journal – an acknowledgement that I too had been travelling this journey. I wrote "Just please know that as much as one person who has never met you can, I feel I get where you are at and honour it, and know just how fucking hard this 'staying alive to create' thing is. And that I am here for you if and when you want or need, because I am so grateful for you."

The story behind her song is of one who didn't make it through. A man who was found at the foot of an oak tree. On the land of the woman (Joey) whose teleseminar I had first discovered Eleanor's work on all that time ago. He had died the weekend that Eleanor and Joey and a circle of other women had gathered in that place.

She asked me if I would consider doing the artwork for the cover, and my soul said a loud resounding yes, even though I was busily finishing off Medicine Woman. It was a short timeframe, she wanted to release the single on the anniversary of the man's death in mid-August.

I saw a man amongst the forest,
when we crossed across the fire

He laid his life down by the oak tree,
as we breathed his final prayer

We intertwine in our estrangement,
we parallel in tender time

So I choose a different story,
I choose to face what's mine.

I sent her the artwork. The image of the oak tree, with a figure curled up in its roots. An image full of spirals and the Celtic landscape which imbues both of our work.

There was silence for a few days after. Then she tells me that the day after she received it one of her dear friends had taken an overdose, gone into the woods and curled up at the foot of a tree and died. The image took on an even deeper, almost eerily psychic meaning.

It turned out the man was cremated on the exact same day as her friend, on the Thursday. Eleanor went to the tree where her friend had died that Friday whilst his family went to scatter his ashes at his tree in Scotland. They played this song up there at the same time Eleanor played it for her friend.

Says Eleanor, "It is a lot to process, the grief, the trauma, the triggers and how best to tell the story and honour both their lives."

So come back from these edges,
in this wilderness of mind.

On a bruised and broken planet
that renews without our kind

This is more than just my story,
this is written in the land

In the roots amongst the fir trees,
yes we rise to overcome.

The story continued in that I sent a copy of *Medicine Woman* to Eleanor when it launched, which happened to be the time when she most needed to read it. And just as her words had kept me here through my darkness, this time it was my words that held a light for her.

It seems we are connected in the roots, at this soul level, we feel it and what it is to be keeping alive right now. We have never met in real life, and yet our creative paths are deeply woven together.

And so, we come full circle once more. In the process of writing this book we had a long and beautiful conversation about our own experiences of creativity, and you will read some of her powerful reflections on these pages.

We will not be lost to these tides
No, we will not be lost to these tides.

Building a Social Media Platform

You may be an old hand at social media. Or perhaps you don't know your 'tweets' from your 'pins'. Wherever on that spectrum you might be, I want to share what I have learned about harnessing the power of social media as a creatrix.

Whether you are looking to be picked up by a publisher or agent or intend to go it alone, your social media platform is vital in this brave, new interconnected world. A social media platform sounds a very intimidating thing, but really it is exactly what it says: something which lifts you up so that you can be seen and heard.

> Risk being seen in all of your glory.
>
> Jim Carrey

Your platform helps you to communicate:

- who you are
- what you do
- what you stand for
- and that you can be trusted.

Think of your platform as an actual physical platform for a moment... You get to be the carpenter. You get to design it. You get to decide how it looks. And then you create and curate the content that is shared from it, and how it is presented.

It's a very exciting process!

Your platform needs to be sturdy. You need at least four solid supports to spread the weight evenly. And so if one breaks, or is weaker, the whole thing won't come tumbling down.

- A blog or website should be one pillar of your platform – both as your own broadcasting channel, but also as a way for people to make contact with you. It should be easily searchable on Google and other key search engines.

- A major social media outlet (or preferably 2-3) should be your next pillar. Depending on where your tribe hangs out these currently include: Facebook, Twitter, Instagram, Pinterest, YouTube…

- The next pillar should be in shared space: guest posting on other blogs, reviews, interviews or features in magazines, podcasts, newspapers or radio with online links.

- And finally, one pillar should be in real life, either through teaching, coaching, your business or services, speaking engagements, stalls or other ways of being seen and known.

It is crucial that you do not put 100% of your time and attention into platform-building online. Whilst it seems like the world and his mother are on Facebook and Twitter, the popularity of platforms change. And there is still a substantial demographic that limits their social media engagement for all sorts of reasons, or who do not go online at all. Plus, life's more fun if you're not on the computer all the time: connecting with people, sharing stories, getting tipsy on champagne at a book launch, overhearing a conversation in a café and realizing you've found a potential customer, meeting like-minded folks whilst speaking at a conference… Human psychology goes: know…like…trust.[lvii] If you want to attract folks towards your work, this has to be your continual focus. If people don't know about you, if they don't regularly see or hear from you, they can't possibly begin to trust you, feel curious, loyal or excited.

Wherever you are in terms of having creative offerings to share, you need to start building your platform now…if you haven't already. And build it up bit by bit. Start before you start writing your first book. Continue whilst you are creating your first exhibition. Share the story as you write the story.

Whilst numbers are not the be all and end all, when folks are choosing whether to host, collaborate with, publish or even buy from you, the first thing they will do is Google you, or pop your name into the Facebook search bar and judge your success and popularity by how many followers you have. Then they'll get a sense of how active you are, what your style is and if you are their sort of person.

So make sure they can find you…and that what you put out there represents you well.

The Springboard Philosophy

> The world has a you-shaped hole in it.
>
> It is missing what you see.
>
> It lacks what you know.
>
> And so you were called into being.
>
> To see the gap, to feel the pain of it, and to fill it.
>
> Tara Sophia Mohr, *Your Other Names*

If you are starting from scratch building up your public persona can seem very daunting. How to get your name out there? Where to start? How to let people know you exist?

Those of us who are introverts can often focus exclusively on doing everything ourselves – because it feels safer, less stressful, or so that we can retain control. But let me share a revolutionary thought with you: co-operation with people you might otherwise consider to be competitors is a great way for you to put yourself out there.

I have found that the best possible way to start building your platform is by appearing on other people's platforms whilst you grow your own. (This also gives you the training in connecting with an audience…and selling yourself and your work!)

It works both ways too: the creator and host of these platforms have free…or affordable…content provided for them. You become a familiar face in many places (remember: know, like, trust). They get your people coming their way. And they get to contribute to the up-and-coming career of someone whose work they find exciting. And you both have a new creatrix colleague to call on to collaborate on exciting projects.

Collaborating means that you share resources, ideas and costs: you are not going it alone, which can often feel so scary and daunting. Someone else has your back…and you have theirs. Plus you get the endorsement for you and your work from someone that you and your potential future tribe respect. You are instantly widening your reach to include not just your existing tribe, but everyone in theirs too.

Collaboration in all forms is a great way to take your focus off yourself and onto the shared vision that unites you with others. You get to share something which is not personally yours, which is often easier, whilst they will do the same for you. As long as you chose collaborators carefully and have clear agreements, it's a win-win situation.

Great ways to use other's platforms as your own springboard include:

- Contributing art or writing to magazines, newspapers and anthologies.
- Writing guest posts for bigger blogs and websites.
- Speaking at a teleseminar or conference.
- Being interviewed on a podcast...or interviewing someone for your own.
- Being part of a group promotion or giveaway.
- Exchanging promotions.

And most importantly, be sure to offer these opportunities to others as you grow – give back and be generous.

> To sell is above all to master the art and science of listening.
>
> Tom Peters

Marketing with Soul

Be sure to apply what you have learned through your creativity to your marketing, and harness it to support your work and The Work. That is why it has chosen you, because it trusts you to use your skills to get The Work out in the world.

Harness the power of WORD+image:

- Remember the power of naming is one of the biggest forms of magic we have. Choose great titles for your books, events, albums...that evoke the sort of energetic response you want.
- Pick or create a branding image which connects well with the title, and again harnesses the energy of it.
- Do your research – see what's popular, what sells right now...
- Whatever medium you work in, find the place where the magic en-

tered the work – the words, part of an image, section of the performance when magic took over…and share that. That is what will engage your audience.

- Use memes: a powerful image and a short quote that speak truth direct to the soul. Share the memes of others that amplify your own message, and create your own using snippets of your work. Be sure to share links to your work along with them, watermark the image with your details, and attribute the art or words of others when you share. As with all sharing, imagine it was your work someone else was using, what would feel exciting to discover?

- Video is another use of WORD+image but as a living, moving way of engaging your audience – keep them short and entertaining.

Other 'magic' to harness:

- The power of Artificial Intelligence – Google, Amazon, Facebook, YouTube and Instagram all have algorithms, coded instructions built in that say: if this happens, do that. So lots of shares or responses in a short time to a post or page automatically engage the algorithms to increase the visibility of a popular post to more people. This is how things go viral – the more people share, the more people are enabled to see the content.

- The power, energy and engagement of *communitas* by sharing the work of others generously…and asking your community to share your work. Provide links, images and blurb, make sure it's good quality and engaging, something they'd feel comfortable sharing…and don't ask too often.

- The power of the launch, when the energy is fresh and the excitement palpable to spread ripples and get folks excited. Ask your audience to share pictures of your opening night, with hashtags and tagging you. Ask them to share the arrival of your creations on social media. Other folks will pick up on this genuine enthusiasm.

- The power of love – ask folks who tell you how much they love your work to share that love onwards on social media, or as a review…or ask their permission to share it yourself.

- The power of your audience. When performing engage your audience and allow their energy to amplify your own. You can see how comedians, musicians, sports players and theatre actors do this – the audience's energy can enhance your own abilities and make you all experience the transcendent. A great show is the best marketing in the world, as each of these people will go home and tell their friends and family, and your circle of engagement will expand exponentially.

> The rare pleasure of being seen for what one is, compensates for the misery of being it.
>
> Margaret Drabble

Creative Networking

For those who are energised by interacting with other people, creativity offers the most incredible opportunities for meeting and networking with exciting folks. For those of us who struggle with the social requirements of creative networking, today's online world is on your side: social media was created for (and by) introverts. For most of us there is an added feeling of safety from connecting via a computer screen. With a modicum of tech-savviness, screens take a big sting out of social anxiety, allowing us to connect more quickly with large numbers of people, with much less stress. We can log on…and off…within our own comfort limits, without having to make justifications about why we need to disappear.

With blogs and websites we are able to control our environments to a large degree, creating spaces which feel safe and supportive. For the Highly Sensitive amongst us (putting my hand up here), focusing the majority of your platform-building online means that you're no longer having to tolerate the overwhelming noise, smell and visual stimuli of a traditional face-to-face networking event. You can be social and visible…and still feel in control. Online interactions also tend to lead to more immediate emotional intimacy – but lack the deep energetic connection of face to face interaction. So try to strike a balance and connect with people on the ground: customers, stockists, gallery owners, audiences, journalists…

If you're an entrepreneur, artist or writer, people often expect you to be comfortable with talking about yourself, networking and selling your stuff. It's an important part of your work. But instead many of us feel really uncomfortable doing so, especially early on, when any exposure brings the inner critic to the surface. And so, you can get stuck in no-man's land, needing to spread the word, to make a living doing what you love, but completely paralyzed with fear and anxiety.

Since I've started being honest about how hard I find sharing my work publicly I have discovered just how many other people struggle with it too. People started coming my way looking for advice, having seen me do my thing. So I want to share what I've learnt. Please know that I am a work in progress too – some days I can do it, other days I can't even leave the house. And that, too, has to be okay.

Know that you are not alone

So the first thing to know is that you are not alone in this. There is nothing wrong with you. Most people experience some degree of nervousness when sharing what is meaningful to them. That's why so few people do it.

Social anxiety is one of the most common anxieties. We fear the rejection of others on a primal level. Most people want others to like and accept them. Most feel vulnerable in an unknown social situation. So, please stop beating yourself up. The number one tip for social success is to put your inner critic back in their box and ease up on yourself. Show yourself the compassion you would offer a dear friend. And remember, chances are the people you're about to meet have no interest in eating you for dinner. They might even be nice!

Remember, the reason that your body is feeling anxious is because it's trying to keep you safe. It's just adrenalin priming your system for what your brain and body are interpreting as imminent danger. Your body's trying to be your friend, because you believe on some level that you are under threat. You need to find ways of out-smarting the inner critic so that you can bring your wonderful personality and important work out into the world to shine and connect.

Remember you're a sponge

Networking events sort the extroverts from the introverts pretty fast. If you're an extroverted-introvert – like I am – half of you is wanting to connect, the other half finds it exhausting and longs to run and hide.

If you're an empath remember that you're going to be picking up on the feelings of all the people in the room. You are a sponge…and there's a lot to take in. As a Highly Sensitive you're going to be feeling overwhelmed by the stimulation – the noise, the lights, different perfumes and aftershaves, the amount of people. Find ways to self-regulate and use them.

> "Fear and action can exist in parallel. In fact they should. Fear and discomfort typically mean I'm moving in the right direction and that I need to keep going.
>
> Paul Jarvis

Only connect

The initial walking into a mass of people freaks me out. I don't know where to go or how to start a conversation, and am sure that they all instantly hate me. Whilst social chit chat without an aim brings me out in hives, if I have a script and a purpose I can talk to most people one-to-one. It's all about focusing on connection…not your perceived lack of connection.

Be honest…or paint a convincing persona

With anxiety there are basically two approaches you can use…or a combination of them. The first is to be straight-up and honest, saying something like: "I find it really hard at places like this". Either the person will empathise and open up more honestly to you, telling you they feel the same and Bam! you immediately have a connection. Or if they don't experience it themselves or have overcome it, they will reassure you that you are doing a good job or offer some friendly advice. Either way, they will respect you for your honesty.

Or you can put a big smile on, have your script at the ready, and fake it till you make it. This approach is usually pretty exhausting but avoids emotional vulnerability and authenticity in a situation where you might not feel safe or comfortable being so open.

Strut your stuff

Wearing something eye-catching or outrageous is one of the easiest ways for other people to start conversations with you and to establish your creative brand. This might be distinctive make up or hair, an interesting scarf, unique earrings, a fab bag. Develop a signature style, so that you're easily recognisable. Incorporate your creative flair and the creativity of others you love into your appearance.

Body wisdom

Keep your awareness in your body and focus on a slow out-breath to calm the vagus nerve. Learn to stay aware of what is happening in your body, but then to move your awareness beyond it.

If you are a menstrual woman, know where you are in your cycle. If you are pre-menstrual or in your first couple of bleeding days, don't do any networking events unless they are totally unmissable. (For more on planning your creativity and work life round your cycle, see *Full Circle Health* and *Moon Time*.)

Some of us physically close up to protect ourselves when we are feeling anxious: we may cross our arms over our chests, our voices go quieter so people have to lean in further. Or we stutter, slur or race our words, making us harder to understand. Try to root yourself in your body, and ground yourself and commit to being as physically and vocally open with each person you meet as you can. Focus on the energy between you – can you feel it flowing? Are you shutting down? Are they?

Try to smile each time you catch someone's eye. It is a great way of breaking the ice. This tiny act of kindness spreads good feeling around the room. It also starts positive internal feedback, communicating to your own body that you are safe and can relax.

Names and faces

Names are one of my big struggles – people tell me their name, and thirty seconds later my mind is a blank. I also have something called face-blindness. There are a number of ways to get around this. Firstly, admit it at the beginning of the conversation, so they don't take it personally. Second, if they have a badge or have given you a business card, take a sneaky look to remind yourself. Third, when they tell you their name, use it in conversation a few times. And my personal favourite, make a little mnemonic or memory device in your head to help – something funny or rude usually helps! And find a way to get your name to stay with others too!

> "There are way too many caring, intelligent, talented, extraordinary people of the heart not doing what they love, not being seen because they haven't yet found a creative and conscious way of being in business and marketing.
>
> Mirror Living

Give a card

Be sure to have some business cards on you, it makes it easy to exchange details without scrabbling for a pen and writing names on the back of your hand. Why not make your cards a talking point? Make them breathtakingly beautiful, not just boring and businessy. I have my book covers and paintings on mine. They're beautiful and glossy, and come in a range of designs, so people can choose their favourites – they give us something to talk about and something to hold in my shaky hands.

Have your elevator pitch ready

I'm world-class at blathering incomprehensibly when someone asks what I do. My convoluted job title of author-editor-publisher-artist-teacher in niche women's work is not the sort of work that fits on the back of a postage stamp. So I craft a standard response for each of my 'hats' depending on who I'm talking to.

There's nothing worse than getting into labyrinthine explanations of what exactly you mean by your job, with the person looking bemused as you get more and more uncomfortable. Or feeling like you're being cross-examined, rather than getting the opportunity to share your services or products with the person you're talking with. I used to say I was an author of women's non-fiction. Which led to the question – *what kind of non-fiction?* To which my response was: *creativity and the menstrual cycle…* by which stage the person was looking for their excuses to leave!

Set yourself a challenge

> To live a creative life we must lose our fear of being wrong.
>
> Joseph Chilton Pearce

Set yourself challenging but realistic goals. And then acknowledge that you've achieved them when you leave. Maybe it's to simply walk in the door. Maybe it's to stay for half an hour. Maybe to talk to three people. Or hand out five business cards. Something with a clearly defined aim that you can feel proud that you have achieved. Otherwise, for us perfectionist Type A personalities, what happens is we leave and beat ourselves up if we haven't wooed every person in the room and signed every single soul up for our new program. Let yourself know that you are proud of yourself, that what you did may not be a big deal for other people, but it was for you.

Afterwards

Take some time to yourself afterwards to decompress. And be sure in the next day or so to write down the names of the folks you met, store their contact details somewhere you'll find them again. Do check out their website, follow their social media accounts and drop them an email to say you enjoyed meeting them. Networking events are only the beginning of potential relationships. Be sure to put energy into developing and nurturing them afterwards.

MONEY

Money and Soul

Art – to be considered Great Art – has always been kept at arm's length from money. The cliché of the starving artist has been promulgated. The same has been traditionally required of other conduits of soul – priests, monks and nuns have made vows of poverty, in order to enrich their souls. And yet their churches and bishops have always managed to square their spirituality with the immense material wealth they have accrued. And there has never been a cliché of the starving gallery owner or the impoverished art collector.

> When it comes to art, money is an unimportant detail. It just happens to be a huge unimportant detail.
>
> Iggy Pop

To thrive as creatrixes we reclaim our right to share our work with the world, and to be paid fairly for it. Receiving financial energy in return for our work is an important way of keeping The Work – and us – alive. Earning from our creativity gives us power, income, and shares our work with a wider audience. It rebalances the scales on so many levels.

And so, we have to learn how to bring our art – the language of soul – out into a culture based on a materialist, capitalist model. We have to enter the marketplace, and put a price on the priceless. To do so we must reframe how we relate to money and worth.

We live as energetic beings in a world of form. To be fully healthy and balanced we cannot deny either part of ourselves. And yet we do! Often those of us who walk the path of creativity and spirituality can feel really uncomfortable about the world of form. We feel, or are told, that it is a 'lower' realm, of 'base' interests, which can trap and defile us.

Physics tells us everything exists in wave and particle form.

Money is no different. It is a thing and an energy. Both.

As with anything in the world of forms, it exists in duality. It can be a blessing or a curse. As creatrixes we are learning firsthand how to interact with soulful awareness with the world of forms.

And this is where our system has gone wrong. It is not money itself that is bad, it is that it is not used as a blessing for the majority.

How we think of money directly impacts our relationship with it. Many of us have money blocks – often inherited from our family or culture, about what money is or what it means. Applying our creative understanding of flow to it helps immensely. It is our responsibility to keep the energy, the money, flowing. We keep the gifts moving, blessing everyone we can. We acknowledge our needs and the costs of doing business, but we do not hoard what we do not need. So often we are blocked both ways – in allowing the soul energy to come out through us into the world through our creativity (because we are scared, feel small or worthless) and also allowing the soul and material things to come back to us in return.

Money is our current form of exchange. But by all means find other more meaningful forms of energy exchange with others who are wanting to build a new paradigm such as barter, skill swapping, exchange, paying it forward or gifting…

This unofficial gift economy is strong amongst my family, friends and like-minded people. We all get a real buzz out of the real interaction, the genuine giving of our gifts and receiving of others. It is a powerful and empowering form of interaction and frees us from a sense of not having enough, towards an experience of shared abundance – a common-wealth.

However, the outer world revolves around money: last time I checked the electricity company didn't accept paintings in lieu of payment! So if we cut ourselves off from financial income, we cut ourselves off from the wider world and the possibilities it offers.

In order to give fully of ourselves, we need to practice receiving, something which we womenfolk are particularly poor at: payment, compliments, offers of support, gifts of love…how are you at receiving, dear creatrix?

Creatrix Speaks

Lots of business people and advisors told me that my dream about my wearable art clothes wouldn't work... well, also that anything

I've ever created in the world wouldn't work. I've had plenty of doomed advice. I couldn't get a government business bank loan even after going through the whole enterprise hub palaver… I am not in the in-crowd of 'I'll scratch your back if you scratch mine' and I also don't play the 'women in business' game: I don't fit the mould or bite my lip and dress the part.

Often it can feel like you're on the outside looking in and it's the same old faces all the time shining but listen to your intuition and your own gut feeling and your creative dreams and make your own party where you can… We are a motley crew on the outside but that's where I have found the most magic, the most juice is.

Here's an idea for all of us: if, by chance, you have been invited to give five speeches this year or have won ten awards or have a place at an important meeting or conference or you find yourself around people who can make things happen… how about we all take the opportunity to use any power and privilege to leverage power for others? Others who might be outsiders, others who might not look like or act like others in the room, who might stir things up and say things that haven't been said before… How about once we are in the room, we open the fucking doors for new faces, old and young, diverse new energy and give up our seats for people who would never be invited to the party?

Clare

The Value of Your Work

> An artist is not paid for his labour, but for his vision.
>
> James Whistler

Valuing your work, starts with valuing yourself and valuing The Work. Both are notoriously hard to do, as neither has an official price tag – both require you to name and claim the value of them.

It is important to remember that it is not just the physical object you are selling, but all the work it took to get there too. The object is just the visible representation of the work. When pricing work and considering the question: *What is my work worth?* the underlying question we often answer is: *What am I worth?* Because as women we have been taught to undervalue this hugely.

I love this story that the musician Sia tells about valuing her work, and the challenges she comes up against when doing so, as both an artist and woman. Because she is much in demand, having written over a hundred pop songs, including ones for artists like Beyoncé, Katy Perry, Christina Aguilera, Britney Spears and Rihanna, she insists on receiving fifty percent of the publishing profits for any song she writes, rather than the more common equal split between all the songwriters and producers,

A producer once asked why she deserved that kind of deal. 'Because I don't think I should have to pay for the fact that you need two people to do your job,' Sia said.

The producer replied, 'But it takes you, like, twenty minutes to write and sing the song. Then I have to go away and spend two or three weeks producing it.'

'Yeah,' Sia said, 'but it took me fifteen years to take twenty minutes.' [lviii]

As time goes on, our work finds its own value – a Picasso painting which the artist would have sold for hundreds of dollars at the time, now sells for tens of millions. It is just paper and paint. The value of it is not in its materials, or the time that it took to paint it, but in the value that we put on his body of work, his skill as an artist and his reputation.

As creatrix, you have it within your power to consciously tell the story of your art and yourself as artist, to create a body of work, a brand of you, to set prices that honour marketplace norms, your financial needs and aspirations. And then it is down to luck, fate, history and fashion.

But always remember that whilst the price of your work and the demand for it may rise and fall many times within your lifetime and beyond, your value as a human being never changes however much, or little, others are willing to pay for your gifts.

Creatrix Speaks

I'm working on how to find a balance between creativity being a defining force in my world and it being all-consuming. On achieving a balance between creating the amount of art that I feel capable of and that is flowing constantly, and how to earn a living whether it is through selling, performing or through other ways. I'm working on how to value my work and have it valued. I'm also working on how to find a balance between creating art myself, and how to work with or support other artists, how to build more healthy models of creative community together. I'm interested in finding ways to share our creativity like we are inviting each other into our souls to dwell there for a while, to listen and be present, rather than to critique, compete or consume.

Eleanor

Creative Income Streams

If you think about the various successful creatives you know of, chances are they have fingers in lots of pies. Some you may be aware of, others you may not. They might paint for their own exhibitions. Receive grants. Do commissions. As well as have a couple of books. And be paid to speak at events. And teach classes. And license products.

The reality is that most successful creative people have what Charles Handy calls a 'portfolio life'. Rather than having one 'job' which they rely on for all of their income, they have a variety of income streams.

The idea of income streams was so helpful to me as a creative starting out, trying to make a living creatively. The benefits of income streams are that they are: flexible, adaptable and great for creatives.

Some streams of work require you to be there to earn your money (such as teaching in a classroom) whereas others, such as selling your work online or collecting royalties, can tick away quietly by themselves. So do not limit your vision of how you can earn a decent living doing what you love.

Streams might include:

> "In today's uncertain economy, the safest solution to be in total control and enjoy freedom for you and your family is to have multiple streams of income.
>
> Robert G. Allen

- A full time job – salary.
- A part time job – paid per hour – either set hours or with reliable consistency, for a boss.
- Freelance or consultancy work – paid per hour or per contract with any number of employers.
- Self-employment.
- Running a bricks-and-mortar business.
- Online business.
- Live performances – theatre, speaking events…
- Teaching/coaching/tutoring/mentoring.
- Lecturing/leading workshops in your field – both in the skill itself, or teaching others how to appreciate it, use it, develop their skills or teach others.
- Selling services/skills – editing, healing, cleaning, consulting, repairing…

- Producing others' creative work – directing, film producing, publishing, agency.
- Selling individual physical products – in your own shop, at conferences, art fairs, events, festivals, farmers' markets, on the side of the street, car boot sale, back of your van…
- Selling reproductions of products (art prints) or do-it-yourself creative kits.
- Wholesale to other shops, selling others' products, distributing others' work.
- Selling e-versions of products.
- Bundling gift sets or premium packages of products or services.
- Commissions and bespoke pieces.
- Writing about your craft for newspapers, magazines or books.
- Presenting for TV or radio – paid or to promote your work.
- Creating a podcast or YouTube video content – which either links to saleable products or is monetised by advertising.
- Selling patterns or recipes.
- Affiliates, endorsements, advertising…
- Grants and scholarships.
- Government support and benefits as you transition from one type of work to another.

You might use some of the above in the early days of your adventures and transition into others as your time becomes more valuable.

Furthermore, just because you may not be able to make *all* your money doing what you love now, doesn't mean you can't earn *some* of your income doing that. Many of the most famous authors wrote their first book or two whilst working a full-time job.

To make a living from your creativity you have to be creative about it. There are infinite ways to make money living the life you want to live – you just have to apply your creative mindset!

Instead of thinking of making money as just one thing, instead you learn to think in terms of multiple income streams – some of which will support you when you're sick and uninspired, some which you can take more of a risk on, others which will be steady and reliable. Some which require you in person and others which pay you a small royalty over lots of units.

> "Proactively bring passion to everything you touch, to everything you do. No matter what task is in front of you, bring as much enthusiasm and energy to it as you possibly can. Bring your full attention, your full presence to every task in your day.
>
> Marie Forleo

So take another look at that list and ask yourself: *What income streams have I tried before? Which worked, which didn't? Which offerings do I currently have? How do they link up? Do they naturally flow from one to another? Are existing customers finding out about them?*

And then when thinking about monetising your creative offerings, ask yourself: *Am I making regular new content or products available? Do I have ways of trading up – for example offering: a cheap priced postcard, an affordable range set of greetings cards, a mid-range limited edition print, and the full price original artwork? In what ways can I add value without adding costs – can I sign my work, do an online Meet the Artist, gift a digital product?*

Practical tips for creating successful income streams:

- Don't be reliant on one employer/contractor/retailer.
- Have a balance of online/offline, local/global, products/services.
- Have both passive and active income streams.
- Have a balance of seasonal income streams.
- Use all your skills – brainstorm what you can do.

- Price fairly but well.
- Tell people you're in business.
- Accept money!

So, what does this look like in reality?

The following is what my own income looked like at the beginning of my creative career:

- 60% fixed income or reliable per-hour work.
- 20% online income from e-products, books, licensing.
- 15% paintings and cards sold at a shop.
- 5% affiliates.

Seven years later, my income has quadrupled, and the streams look more like this:

- 80% royalties and licensing.
- 5% speaking and teaching.
- 5% fixed income or reliable per-hour work.
- 5% affiliates.
- 5% paintings and cards at events.

As you can see, having nine paperback and e-books, plus multiple translations of my own titles, as well as publishing the books of others, royalties are now my main income. On one hand it means I don't need to take on regular paid work for others, but on another our income is extremely reliant on the seasons (folks buy lots of books in November and December, but not many in February or August). Furthermore, each title we launch is a risk: there is no guarantee of success with any book, but the same amount of work goes into each.

This leads me onto another reminder: remember, that unlike in a paid job, you will not be earning money for every hour you work. You need to build in behind-the-scenes time into your costs…and therefore your prices to allow for the time when you are:

- Planning
- Making
- Researching
- Designing
- Marketing
- Shipping
- Accounting
- Recovering

It is a rookie mistake not to, as only about 50% of your work hours are going to make you actual income. But they are going to support your work that does make money.

Be sure to take time at the end of each year to review your income for the year gone by, see which income streams are most productive, and which require the most energy from you. Take action on these findings as you project your entrepreneurial vision forward for the year ahead.

A New Economy

The old economy is not working for creatives: the collapse in traditional publishing and marketing models and the fast development of internet technology has left many artists with work more visible but incomes diminished. I fully believe that we creatrixes need to find ways to move beyond capitalism, because it's holding us back. As Daniel Lord Smail argues,

> *Capitalism generates stress through its unpredictability and hierarchical power structures, but it also alleviates stress by producing an economy organized around the production and circulation of addictive substances and practices.* [lix]

As creatrixes our work, The Work, can be a viable way of moving beyond both of these aspects of the System.

But instead many creatrixes find themselves stuck in and stressed by the System. Especially when it comes to money. Shame that we should be earning more. Shame that we're not. Shame that we're trying too hard and not succeeding in financial terms. Shame that we don't have enough to meet our outgoings or aspirations.

We believe that *we* are the problem. That we are the only ones with the problem. It's all our fault. Which is just the way the System wants it – make enough individual pain and the collective will be so focused on survival that they won't notice the bigger picture.

Shame freezes creativity and shuts us down, turning our energy against ourselves and making us reliant on the System for our sense of power and worth. By creating a healthy framework within which to live and work, we are less reliant on the structures of capitalism, and more reliant on our communities.

Our cultural story tells us that financial independence is the corner stone of individual maturity. It insists that financial wealth is a marker of hard work and well-earned success. But fails to tell us how different the playing field is today, to that inhabited by those who created that myth. Nor how assets create assets and capital creates more capital.

The focus is always on the individual…not the System we inhabit.

Programs like Jacques Peretti's *The Super Rich and Us* on the BBC and

> ”
>
> The planet doesn't need more 'successful people'. The planet desperately needs more peacemakers, healers, restorers, storytellers and lovers of all kinds.
>
> The Dalai Lama

Channel Four's *Low Pay Britain* examine this very real, very current issue. Watching them has really brought home to me the scale of this.

We are all, unless you are one of the 1%, seeing our economic value diminish. Right before our eyes. As money drains out and costs go up, we feel powerless. We feel ashamed that we are scrabbling for the money we need to get by. We are, in the words of the Occupy movement, the 99%.

Most of us are in a very similar situation. The thing that's keeping us trapped is trying to keep up the appearance that everything's okay on the outside…rather than being open and honest.

Once we see most people around us are in the same boat, we realise it is not our individual fault but a systemic issue that is affecting the majority, then we can choose to put our energy elsewhere. Not in attacking ourselves…but in changing how we live.

By following The Creative Way out into the world, we are hacking the System and overthrowing its assumptions. We are creating new communities that are doing things differently. We are discovering a richer life, one based on the sharing of gifts and beauty, rather than dominance and arrogance. We are creating a life that is worth living.

"

The present convergence of crises—in money, energy, education, health, water, soil, climate, politics, the environment, and more—is a birth crisis, expelling us from the old world into a new.

Charles Eisenstein, *Sacred Economics*

Creative Inquiry

Sharing

- What do you want to project into the world and why?
- What do you want to be known for?
- Who do you want to know you?
- Where do you want to be known?
- How much of yourself do you want to make public – and how much do you want to keep private?

- Who do you admire? What do you love about what they do and what would you do differently?

- What place do your audience play in your work? Are they just the people who financially sustain it? Or do you have a deeper human connection to them? Are they there with you in your mind when you create? In what ways does playing to the audience bring up fear in you?

Money

- In what ways have you taken a vow of poverty for your art? Has this been conscious or unconscious?

- Do you believe that art has to be separate from money in order to be pure?

- In what ways do you cultivate and take part in the gift economy?

- How hard is it to know the value of your work?

- How are you at receiving? Do you give too much away?

Social Media

- What are your loves and hates about social media?

- What are you scared of? What do you feel unsure about?

- What does 'going viral' mean to you?

- Which social media accounts do you currently have?

- Do you have separate 'business' and personal accounts?

- Is your social media persona and voice consistent across your various platforms? Make sure your profile pictures and biographical details are: high quality, clear, consistent, up-to-date and truly reflect who you are and what you do.

- How many followers do you have on each social account? How many new folks have followed your page in the last week? Month? Year? Keep track of how your pages are growing. Set yourself targets. Look at the statistics and see which posts are popular.

- How regularly do you post? What makes you post…and what makes you stay away?

- Do you post a variety of content: words, images, links to articles, events, work for sale? If not, why not?

- How are you generous on social media? Do you share the work of others with attribution? Have you run a giveaway? Choose something desirable (and not too expensive to ship) and get folks to tag their friends or share the post and follow your page to enter.

- Keep yourself accountable: make targets of where you would like your work to appear, numbers of social media followers you would like to add…and then take action to make this happen.

Creative Practice

Your Platform

Create a visual representation of your platform. Be sure to represent the four pillars. Make it beautiful, inspiring, exciting and strong. Consider what you look like on it, and why you are building it. Consider what you are trying to share. What the terrain and environment around you looks like. Consider the people you are using it to communicate with – your audience, tribe, customers...

Networking

Set yourself a real-world challenge, be it going to a creative group and sharing your work, going to a business networking event, speaking at an event, taking part in an exhibition or performance...and show up as your creative self. Be sure to take or wear something of your creative work, and a few business cards too!

Income Streams

Create a visual representation of your creative income streams including where they come from and how abundant each is. Consider the terrain and environment that they run through, and what these streams are feeding and nourishing. Add in possible new streams, consider what would happen if you combined a couple, or cut one off. Make it beautiful, colourful, inspiring and exciting.

CENTRE

We are not alone

Though we may create alone

We are each just one neuron in a magnificent consciousness

Making connections

Leaps of faith

Dancing in the dark

Apart but always together.

This is what we are for

Never forget.

I CREATE MY WORLD

"

One thing's for sure...if any one of us unleashes our creativity, our world will split open. We'll find unprecedented ways of solving problems and expressing our souls, and our lives will be forever changed.

Martha Beck

To follow The Creative Way in private is powerful. To follow it publicly and create as a way of life is a revolutionary act. When we dare to live The Creative Way, we refuse to live divided lives anymore.

To create is to say:

I am willing to give the gift of myself to the world.

Not because I am perfect,

But because my existence is precious.

I contain myriad beauty and wild possibilities

And I dare to be here as fully as I can.

I dedicate myself to this life.

To create is to commit wholeheartedly to being fully alive. In a world that is sleepwalking its way to conformist destruction, to create is to say *no* to this consensual reality that so many of us can no longer inhabit. And *yes* to co-creating new cultures. To create is to own the power of transformation, to fully embody our co-creative role in this world.

The ultimate achievement of any creatrix is to see our life as our greatest work of art, and rather than follow the second-hand script given to us, to make our life in our own image. Our courage to be seen doing this inspires others to live into their own transformation.

Our creations make doorways in the dark for others for others to slip out of the status quo and into the magic of greater possibility.

This is the crux of being creative. It is more than having an exhibition in a fancy gallery, or a thousand five-star reviews on Amazon. It's about saying *yes* to life, every part of your life, and *no* to fear on a daily basis. It is a spiritual practice, a living practice of turning our scaredness into sacredness.

As creatrixes, at this time in history, I see that we are sorting the tangled threads of the old world, turning them over in our hands, deciding which are too worn, and which we want to weave forwards into our new creation. We are adding the voices and visions that have been withheld from the collective. We are weaving them all together, each working on our own.

We need the full spectrum of humanity to show up and share our experiences: to make space for ourselves in our culture. Each new voice, each new body adds to the possibility of transformation for our species. This is why it is a priority to create space and time for this right here, right now.

The time is coming when we will stitch these visions and expressions together to make a beautiful new patchwork, a new community and culture that combines the best of us all, and our vision for the future. We will catch the next generation in it as they are born, wrap it around all of us, and know, finally, the power that is ours as human beings when we combine our creative brains, our agile hands, our feeling hearts…and the skills of every person, with the wisdom and wonder of the Mystery.

We have never, as a species, tried living this way before, with the creativity of a large percentage of our diverse populations harnessed for the greater good. Take a moment and just imagine what might happen.

> Human salvation lies in the hands of the creatively maladjusted.
>
> Martin Luther King Jr.

We ask ourselves when…

When will we be enough?

When will we make a difference?

When we have the courage to claim space for ourselves.

When we risk creativity.

When we relish our sensuality.

When we honour our lives and their experiences as valuable.

When we create from our own unique bodies, expressing ourselves in our authentic voices, using our own language.

When we dare to walk in the dark.

When our creative selves and daily selves are no longer kept separate.

When we dare to reach out beyond our comfort zones.

When we become dedicated explorers of the Mystery.

Then we bud and bloom.

Then we flourish.

Then magic happens.

Then transformation unfolds.

In our lives.

In the world.

Creativity is our way of channelling the magic through.

And our world needs all the magic we can give it right now.

Dare to offer the world the gift of you.

Don't keep it to yourself.

Keep diving into the flow.

Keep moving through the void.

Keep connecting.

Keep following your bliss.

This is The Creative Way,

And you, dear one,

Are a valued creatrix.

"

Creativity is the best answer.

Alice Walker

AFTERWORD

When I wrote my last book, *Medicine Woman*, I did not know if I would live to the end of it. Living was just too hard and my life force was spent.

Writing this book has brought me fully back to life. It has brought the magic back. *Creatrix* has brought me into a deeper understanding of my own creativity. It has deepened my love and respect for the journeys of the women whose voices appear in these pages and all of us who dare to travel this way. It has reiterated the vital need for creative community and collaboration. And it has helped reconnect me to the magic beyond my fear.

For all that, I am so very, very grateful.

I hope that it will do the same for you.

NOTES ON LANGUAGE

> To hear the feminine we have to dare to open our receptors to old words with new meanings.
>
> Marion Woodman

Every creatrix stands on the shoulders of others, weaving the threads from those who have come before with her own unique genius and perspective. My work is woven from the ideas of many others in so many disparate fields, to whose insight, research and hard work I am indebted.

For many of the terms below, I have developed my own separate understanding, which I explain in the book, but still I want to give credit to the people who coined these terms and the teachers who shared them with me, providing me the stepping stones I needed to build my understanding of this field.

I hope that you continue to explore the ideas that fascinate you, go direct to the source of them and bring them forward into your own life, as you further understand the depths of what it means to live creatively in this world.

Use of Capitalisation

When terms such as Creatrix and the Feminine are capitalised they refer to the archetypal understanding of a concept (following the style of my earlier books). When I refer to a human individual, the term is not capitalised, so a sculptor or dancer would be referred to as a creatrix.

The Work refers to the soul level aspect of our creative labours, work refers to the physical aspects of creating art and making a living.

Feminisation of language

You will notice that I have used female variants of terms that are traditionally masculine: *craftswomanship* (rather than craftsmanship), *misstery* (rather than mastery), *mistresspiece* rather than masterpiece, *his-story* and of course *creatrix*. This may inspire you or grate, but what it will do is to (re)awaken your knowing of how deeply woven masculine bias is in our culture. This change of perspective is at the root of transformation in rebalancing the masculine and feminine at the very roots of our culture: our language expresses our understanding of reality.

Glossary

ARCHETYPE

An archetype is a universal character or role, which, though it may differ subtly from culture to culture, is common to all human psychology. Common archetypes would be Mother, Teacher, Trickster or Queen. My understanding of archetypes is rooted in the work of the founder of analytical psychology, C.G. Jung, who first brought them to prominence in Western culture during the twentieth century.

For some it may help to imagine an archetype as real: a living, breathing, otherworldly inhabitant – a spirit or aspect of the divine expressed through us. For others it is an energetic force that can be tapped into and released into our world when we embody its qualities. For others it is merely a metaphor or idea that can inspire us and shape our thinking.

The focus of my work is on reclaiming lost archetypes of the Feminine – energies which have been forgotten, side-lined, ignored, silenced or buried during patriarchal times, but which hold great power for us in these transition times as we imagine new ways forward.

BODY OF WORK

The idea of a cohesive lifetime's work. Pam Slim brought this idea to life for me in her book of the same name. She writes within the mainstream, about business leaders and entrepreneurs. I like to take it further and consider the way that the work we do becomes part of our physical embodiment.

BODYMIND

The term bodymind is used throughout this book. Popularised by Ken Dychtwald in his book, *Bodymind*, it seeks to linguistically close the artificial schism between body and mind within Western culture and the English language, and instead approach the human being holistically. The literal reality of the bodymind is being confirmed by the most recent neurobiological research.

CREATRIX

From classical Latin, *creatrix* is the feminine form corresponding to the more common masculine term, creator. According to the *Oxford English Dictionary* it was first used in 1620.

I have seen this term used in passing in many places by many wise women over the years: Leonie Dawson, Marybeth Bonfiglio, Autumn Weaver and Baraka Elihu of *Birthing Ourselves into Being*, Max Dashu, and more recently as I was researching this book in a dedicated blogpost on the topic by Justine Musk. I am unaware of any extended study of the archetype.

DEEP TIME

Deep time is a concept of geological time spanning much wider timescales than those traditionally considered by human history. It was first used by Scottish geologist James Hutton in the eighteenth century.

DREAMLINES, THE DREAMING

Both terms are Aboriginal Australian in origin. They refer to the spiritual structures and mapping of deep time and place central to the sacred creation stories. They were brought to my attention in the writings David Tacey and Paul Theroux.

FEMININE

The feminine/Feminine is a term that many find challenging. We all have energies and drives within us which have traditionally, across many cultures, been referred to as 'masculine' and 'feminine'. Within patriarchal culture, "feminine" tends to be shorthand for: beautiful, gentle, slim, restrained, non-confrontational, carefully cultivated, domesticated, emotional, girlish and weak. It is often a term of disparagement. Most qualities deemed not masculine, or that are in any way pertaining to women, have been slighted, shamed or silenced within patriarchal culture.

Both genders in our culture have learned to suppress signs of the feminine in order to survive and be accepted. This has led to a deeply imbalanced and unhealthy hyper-masculinised culture of men…and women. As women in Western culture we have been taught to value more masculine traits and denigrate, disregard or trivialise more typically feminine ways of being.

My conception of the Feminine is one that includes the traditionally "female" characteristics of nurturance, fertility, intuition and a love of peace and beauty. It also includes concepts of strength, surrender and fierce elemental power that look very different to traditionally masculine expressions of these qualities. The Feminine is present in all people, regardless of gender, though is more commonly associated with women.

FLOW

Flow is a positive psychological state studied for over twenty-five years by Professor Mihaly Csikszentmihalyi at the University of Chicago. He described it as,

> *The state in which people are so involved with an activity that nothing else seems to matter; the experience itself is so enjoyable that people will do it even at great cost, for the sheer sake of doing it.*

GIFT ECONOMY

I first learned of the gift economy through the writings of Charles Eisenstein, and later in more detail from Mirror Living and Lewis Hyde. The gift economy is the most fundamental of human economies which pre-dates monetary compensation. In it, gifts are circulated through a community, rather than accumulated and hoarded, and individuals are socially obligated to pass on the gifts they have received to those in need.

INCOME STREAMS

Rather than thinking of our income as a set fee that we get in exchange for our labour at a job, the idea of income streams illustrates that we can receive income flowing towards us from many sources. I first discovered income streams in the paradigm-shifting books of Charles Handy and later, more practically, from Leonie Dawson's *Shining Business Academy*.

MULTI-PASSIONATE CREATIVE

These are creative folks who have many different interests, as explored by Barbara Sher in her book *Refuse to Choose*.

NEURODIVERSITY

An increasingly common term used to identify those whose brains deviate from the neurotypical (previously referred to as 'normal'). It includes autism, dyslexia, ADD/ADHD and many others. I first came across it in the powerful work of Jenara Nerenberg and the Neurodiversity Project.

PARADIGM

From the Greek for 'pattern', a paradigm is a map or model of reality. Paradigm shift, is a term coined by philosopher of science, Thomas Kuhn in the 1970s, and relates to a fundamental shift in our understanding of the way things are and underlying assumptions.

PATRIARCHY

We inhabit a system that has been constructed, ruled over and policed for millennia by men, one that has prioritised the needs, perspectives, bodies and minds of men. This System (often referred to as patriarchy in feminist thought) has forcibly separated humanity down gendered and sexed divides. It has violently enforced the primacy of what it recognises as the male and the masculine, whilst devaluing, destroying and suppressing that which it defines as female and feminine. We must, of course, be clear that the term patriarchy does not mean that men as individuals are innately bad, wrong or inherently guilty. After all, men suffer at the hands of patriarchy too. And many women claim to not even experience it.

PSYCHE/SOUL

The etymology of psyche is 'animating spirit,' from the Latin *psyche* and from Greek *psykhe* "the soul, mind, spirit; breath; life, one's life, the invisible animating principle or entity which occupies and directs the physical body." [lx] The way that soul is used in this book is as an acknowledgement of ourselves beyond the physical body. It is an attempt to express in a single word the innate beingness of each of us.

THE CREATIVE WAY

My terms The Rainbow Way and The Creative Way are of course nods to *The Artist's Way* by Julia Cameron, and also to the ancient Chinese philosophical text the Tao Te Ching, which states, "The way that can be seen is not The Way." The Rainbow Way was further influenced by the Creative Rainbow Mother archetype first put forward by Lynn V. Andrews, in her book *Jaguar Woman*.

THE HERO'S JOURNEY

The Hero's Journey was first articulated by Joseph Campbell in his 1949 book, *The Hero with a Thousand Faces*, as an archetypal journey arc, it was further explored in *The Writer's Journey* by Christopher Vogler.

THE HEROINE'S JOURNEY

The Heroine's Journey was shared by Maureen Murdock in her book of the same name, as a much-needed differentiation of the female experience. It is an inner-focused journey (unlike the outer focus of The Hero's Journey) that begins with separation from the feminine and finishes with integration of masculine and feminine.

THE HIGHLY CREATIVE PERSON

Scott Barry Kaufman and Carolyn Gregoire coined this term in their book *Wired to Create*.

THE HIGHLY SENSITIVE PERSON

Elaine M. Aron coined this term in her book of the same name. HSPs are easily overwhelmed by such things as bright lights, strong smells or loud noises. They tend to make it a high priority to arrange their life to avoid upsetting or overwhelming situations. They notice and enjoy delicate or fine scents, tastes, sounds, or works of art and have a rich and complex inner life.

Her extensive research suggests that between 15-20% of the population are Highly Sensitive. In the past, people with these traits have been called 'shy,' 'timid,' 'inhibited,' or 'introverted,' but these labels are often inaccurate, as around a third of Highly Sensitive people are actually extroverts.

THE WORK

This term is probably best known in the mainstream from the work of teacher and author, Byron Katie to refer to her popular system of enquiry. My own understanding of The Work is more aligned with the alchemical concept of The Great Work or *Magnum Opus,* and refers to the broader view of the process of transformation, the larger mission, if you will, that we are on.

ENDNOTES

i Justine Musk. "How to Heal the Feminine Wound". **justinemusk.com/2014/02/02/the-creatrix**

ii *Leaning into the Wind – Andy Goldsworthy*, a film by Thomas Riedelsheimer (2017).

iii *Chef's Table*, Season 1, Netflix.

iv Quoted in *Daily Rituals: Women at Work* by Mason Currey.

v J. K. Rowling. "On Writing". **jkrowling.com/opinions/on-writing**

vi Oliver Burkeman. "Danielle Steel works 20 hours a day, but is that to be envied?". The Guardian. **theguardian.com/money/oliver-burkeman-column/2019/may/31/danielle-steel-work-20-hour-day**

vii **agathachristie.com/about-christie**

viii Siri Hustvedt, "I'm writing for my life". The Guardian. **theguardian.com/books/2019/mar/03/siri-hustvedt-i-am-writing-for-my-life-memories-of-the-future-interview**

ix **etymonline.com/word/*magh-**

x **thefreedictionary.com/_/roots.aspx?type=Indo-European&root=magh-**

xi Fiona MacCarthy. "Morris, William (1834–1896), designer, author, and visionary socialist". Oxford Dictionary of National Biography.

xii Walter Crane. "Of The Revival of Design and Handicraft" in Arts and Crafts Essays, by Members of the Arts and Crafts Exhibition Society, 1893.

xiii Referencing the Guerilla Girls poster, 1989.

xiv "The Bechdel Test is a simple test which names the following three criteria: (1) it has to have at least two women in it, who (2) who talk to each other, about (3) something besides a man. The test was popularized by Alison Bechdel's comic Dykes to Watch Out For, in a 1985 strip called The Rule." **bechdeltest.com**

xv "Mark Wahlberg donates $1.5m reward for film reshoots to Time's Up fund". The Guardian. **theguardian.com/film/2018/jan/13/mark-wahlberg-all-the-money-in-the-world-michelle-williams**

xvi **bbc.com/news/entertainment-arts-48668652**

xvii Siri Hustvedt, "A Woman in the Men's Room". The Guardian. **theguardian.com/books/2019/mar/29/marcel-duchamp-fountain-women-art-history**

xviii Camille Gajewski. "A Brief History of Women in Art". Khan Academy. **khanacademy.org/humanities/art-history-basics/tools-understanding-art/a/a-brief-history-of-women-in-art**

xix Lanre Bakare. "Edit-a-thons aim to ensure craftswomen's legacy on internet". The Guardian. **theguardian.com/artanddesign/2019/may/30/edit-a-thons-aim-to-ensure-craftswomens-legacy-on-internet**

xx Hannah Ghorashi. "Inequality Endures: The Price of Being a Female Artist in 2015". **artnews.com/2015/12/30/women-art-status-in-2015**

xxi Hannah Ghorashi. "Inequality Endures: The Price of Being a Female Artist in 2015". **artnews.com/2015/12/30/women-art-status-in-2015**

xxii Mason Currey. *Daily Rituals: Women at Work.*

xxiii "All in the Mind: The psychology of motivation and procrastination". BBC Radio 4.

xxiv Lauren Laverne. Late Night Woman's Hour, "Aretha Franklin/ Imposter Syndrome" , 22 August 2018, BBC Radio 4, **bbc.co.uk/sounds/play/p06j46lx**

xxv First introduced to me in the work of Lynn V. Andrews, and later by Linda Schierse Leonard, in her fabulous book, *Meeting the Madwoman.*

xxvi E. C. White. *Kaironomia*

xxvii Sig Lonegren. "Labyrinths". Mid Atlantic Geomancy, **geomancy.org/index.php/12-labyrinths**

xxviii Desert Island Discs, BBC Radio 4

xxix A term I learnt from Flora Bowley in her *Brave Intuitive Painting* e-course.

xxx *Leaning into the Wind – Andy Goldsworthy*, a film by Thomas Riedelsheimer (2017).

xxxi **etymonline.com/word/psyche**

xxxii Wikipedia – Songline, **en.wikipedia.org/wiki/Songline**

xxxiii Amy Sophia Marashinsky. *The Goddess Oracle Deck.*

xxxiv Chris Zydel, a Facebook post, **creativejuicesarts.com**

xxxv Allyson Grey in *Women of Visionary Art* by David Jay Brown and Rebecca Ann Hill.

xxxvi Victoria Erikson, internet poet, in one of her many inspiring Facebook posts.

xxxvii David Tacey. *Edge of the Sacred.*

xxxviii For more on this see Robert MacFarlane's *Underland.*

xxxix *Leaning into the Wind – Andy Goldsworthy*, a film by Thomas Riedelsheimer (2017).

xl Siobhan Roberts. "Knitting Is Coding and Yarn Is Programmable in This Physics Lab". New York Times, **nytimes.com/2019/05/17/science/math-physics-knitting-matsumoto.html**

xli *Leaning into the Wind – Andy Goldsworthy*, a film by Thomas Riedelsheimer (2017).

xlii Judith Graham. "Children and Brain Development: What We Know About How Children Learn". University of Maine. **extension.umaine.edu/publications/4356e**

xliii "Synaptic Formation". BioNinja, **ib.bioninja.com.au/options/option-a-neurobiology-and/a1-neural-development/synaptic-formation.html**

xliv Brené Brown, quoted on **theofficeonline.com/2015/09/18/brene-brown-on-creativity**

xlv Clare Hunter. "The Calming Effects of Sewing Can Help People Express and Calm Themselves". The Guardian, **theguardian.com/lifeandstyle/2019/feb/23/the-calming-effects-of-sewing-can-help-people-express-and-calm-themselves**

xlvi Lorna Shaddick. "GPs to Prescribe Dance Lessons and Art Classes on the NHS". Sky News, **news.sky.com/story/gps-to-prescribe-dance-lessons-and-art-classes-on-the-nhs-for-modern-life-scourges-11619966**

xlvii Valarie Lee James. "Migrant women fleeing violence find beauty and healing in embroidery". American Magazine. **americamagazine.org/faith/2019/07/15/migrant-women-fleeing-violence-find-beauty-and-healing-embroidery**

xlviii Betsan Corkhill. *Knit for Health and Wellness.*

xlix Betsan Corkhill. *Knit for Health and Wellness.*

l BBC Radio 4. *Better World.*

li Eli Trier (ed). *Demystifying the Artist.*

lii Elizabeth Gilbert. **elizabethgilbert.com/magic-lessons**

liii Anna Lovind. *The Creative Doer.*

liv The Alchemist. "Glamour Magic – Definition and Use". **magicalrecipesonline.com/2018/09/glamour-magic-definition-and-use.html**

lv Kate Northrup, "How to Streamline Your To Do List". **katenorthrup.com/how-to-streamline-your-to-do-list**

lvi Alex Soojung-Kim Pang. "Work and Rest as Partners". *Ars Vitae*, (Volume 8).

lvii "Content Marketing 101". **copyblogger.com**

lviii Hillel Aron. "How Sia Saved Herself". Rolling Stone Magazine. **rollingstone.com/music/music-features/sia-face-songs-chandelier-maddie-ziegler-712691**

lix Daniel Lord Smail. *On Deep History and the Brain.*

lx **etymonline.com/word/psyche**

GRATITUDE

This book was inspired by so many creative women who were my initial guides to The Creative Way through their own books and teachings: Jennifer Louden, Leonie Dawson, Hali Karla, Oriah "Mountain Dreamer" House, Pat Allen, SARK, Flora Bowley, Shiloh Sophia, Pam England and Julia Cameron.

It is woven from many threads that I have developed over the years, as well as putting forward a large amount of new material. For those of you who have read my first book, *The Rainbow Way*, who have studied on my e-courses *Your Authentic Voice* and *WORD+image*, who have read my blogs and articles over the years or listened to my interviews, I am sure you will recognise many of the strands of these earlier works that I have revisited, rewoven and deepened here.

My deepest gratitude goes to the women who contributed to my first book, *The Rainbow Way* and to the folks that answered questions for this book when it was gestating. As well as to the couple of hundred women who have taken e-courses with me. I know I have learned as much from you, as you have from me.

My heartfelt thanks to the creatrixes who took time out of their packed schedules to share their wisdom for this book.

To my children and younger siblings, who are walking The Creative Way before my eyes. To my husband for his unending support and pep talks. My parents who raised me in a rich and nourishing creative environment.

And finally, to myself. Because I was brave, once again.

CONNECTIONS

My Creative Family

My mother and her parents are/were all highly creative, but are not included here as their work is not online.

My maternal grandmother, Lucy Crocker Pearce **blog.wellcomelibrary.org/2015/04/the-pioneer-health-centre-and-positive-health**

My father, Stephen Pearce **stephenpearce.com**

MY SIBLINGS

Oran Pearce **soundcloud.com/oranpeace**

Mirin Mooney **mirinmooney.com**

Tom Prior **imdb.com/name/nm4350114**

MY AUNTS AND UNCLES

Benedict Rubbra **benedictrubbra.co.uk**

Tessa Rubbra **azelledesign.co.uk/tessa-rubbra-pottery**

Camilla Gavin **camillagavin.co.uk**

Simon Pearce **simonpearce.com**

MY COUSINS

Andrew Pearce **andrewpearcebowls.com**

Kevin Pearce **en.wikipedia.org/wiki/Kevin_Pearce_(snowboarder)**

Adam Pearce **linkedin.com/in/adam-pearce-902138b**

Creatrixes

Mirin Mooney is a multi-faceted artist passionate about supporting and inspiring individuals and communities in coming into their fullest authentic expression of being. **mirinmooney.com**

Laura Whalen is a mother of five, living in West Cork, Ireland. She has been a doll maker for ten years, making dolls for all different kinds of people for all different kinds of reasons. Her real creative interest lies in making healing dolls: working with people to help them create a doll as part of their healing journey.
You can find her on Facebook as **Under Rainbows** or email **laura.whalen@yahoo.ie**

Lewis Barfoot is an Anglo-Irish singer songwriter, performer and co-founder of the Embodied Artists. She runs the Embodied Archetype workshop series and is current recording her debut album *Folkalism*. **lewisbarfoot.com**

Eli Trier is an artist, writer and community builder living in Copenhagen. She paints a lot of cats, reads a lot of books, and loves to help quiet revolutionaries connect. **elitriercommunities.com**

Lucy Pierce is a mother, artist, musician and wordsmith living in the Yarra Valley, Australia. Her work is born of dream and myth, vision and dance, survival and song, grief and quest. **lucypierce.com • etsy.com/ie/shop/lucypierce**

Rachael Crow lives with her two youngest children in the Wilds of West Wales where she's been on a pilgrimage journey alongside ancestors, crows and the land into peri-menopause and living with cancer.
rachaelcrow.co.uk • hellocervix.me.uk • moontimes.co.uk

Zoé Genet Berthoud walks the healing path of creativity seeking what is buried, vibrant, generous and intuitive through her art. Her diverse work reflects her aspiration to connect with the essential. **lunes.biz** • Instagram: **@l_u_n_e_s**

Jen Wallace is passionate about connecting with the wilder world, within and without. She creates workshops, paintings, drawings, poetry and prose. She can usually be found hanging out with plants. **jensart.heronsrest.ie**

Tracy (Tre) Breathnach PhD is a performance artist, writer, researcher and community activist. Past creations have included community arts festivals, performances, workshops, lectures, lessons, talks, films…She is currently working to establish her new company Silver Apples, which aims to support communities to have more agency in creating the changes they dream of. **www.silverapples.org**

Eleanor Brown is a songwriter and music maker who connects deeply with the natural world and the changing times, creating from both the descent and the rising. She lives in the UK. **eleanorbrownmusic.com • eleanorbrown.bandcamp.com**

Molly Remer, MSW, M.Div, D.Min writes about thealogy, nature, practical priestessing, and the goddess. Molly and her husband Mark co-create Story Goddesses, original goddess sculptures, ceremony kits, and mini goddesses at Brigid's Grove. Molly is the author of *Womanrunes, Earthprayer, She Lives Her Poems*, and *The Red Tent Resource Kit*. **brigidsgrove.com**

Erin Darcy is an artist raised by two creative parents – she expresses herself through creative writing, painting and photography. A mother of three, Erin is an activist for women's rights, creating and leading what became the largest grassroots campaign in Repealing the 8th Amendment in Ireland with 'In Her Shoes – Women of the Eighth'. She continues to marry her art and activism as one, generating conversations on taboo subjects. **edarcydesign.com**

Clare Jasmine Beloved carries art, poetry, hope, circle work, creativity and art to new audiences: from prisons to housing estates, government conferences to dole queues… reawakening lost dreams and inspiring a bigger vision of what is possible. A highly experienced facilitator, she has worked with thousands of people at workshops and retreats, as well as speaking at conferences around the world. **clarebeloved.com**

Dawn Conlan-Grant is a poet, doula and mother committed to shedding the layers of shame and untruth that surround the modern woman/Priestess and inviting others to do the same. **reclaimingbirth.co.uk**

Marsia Shuron Harris (aka Mother Turtle) is an abstract painter, singer, songwriter, photographer, and founder of 'Healing the Stories We Tell Ourselves', a unique interactive personal enrichment experience. **motherturtle.com**

RESOURCES

This is a collection of resources referred to in the text, and others which have inspired and supported me on my journey of creative discovery.

Join us on the Facebook Page **Creatrix: she who makes – tinyurl.com/CreatrixFB**

Listen to the Creatrix playlist on Spotify – **tinyurl.com/CreatrixSpotify**

Join me on the *WORD+image* e-course – see **lucyhpearce.com**

Books

Allen, Pat B. *Art is a Spiritual Path.*

Allen, Pat B. *Art is a Way of Knowing: A Guide to Self-Knowledge and Spiritual Fulfilment Through Creativity.*

Andrews, Lynn, V. *Jaguar Woman.*

Andrews, Lynn, V. *Medicine Woman.*

Andrews, Lynn, V. *Writing Spirit: Finding Your Creative Soul.*

ARAS. *The Book of Symbols.*

Aron, Elaine N. *The Highly Sensitive Person: How to Thrive When the World Overwhelms You.*

Beak, Sera. *Red, Hot and Holy.*

Bertrand, Seren and Azra. *Womb Awakening: Initiatory Wisdom from the Creatrix of All Life.*

Blackie, Sharon. *If Women Rose Rooted.*

Blackie, Sharon. *The Enchanted Life: Unlocking the Magic of Everyday.*

Bowley, Flora. *Brave Intuitive Painting – Let Go, Be Bold, Unfold!: Techniques for Uncovering Your Own Unique Painting Style.*

Brown, Brené. *Daring Greatly: How the Courage to Be Vulnerable Transforms the Way We Live, Love, Parent, and Lead.*

Brown, Brené. *I Thought It Was Just Me (But It Isn't): Telling the Truth About Perfectionism, Inadequacy and Power.*

Brown, David J. and Rebecca Ann Hill. *Women of Visionary Art.*

Buhner, Stephen Harrod. *Ensouling Language: On the Art of Non-fiction and the Writer's Life.*

Carrico, Eila Kundrie. *The Other Side of the River: Stories of Women, Water and the World.*

Cameron, Julia. *The Artist's Way: A Course in Discovering and Recovering Your Creative Self.*

Cameron, Julia. *Walking in this World.*

Campbell, Joseph. *The Hero with a Thousand Faces.*

Carroll, Lewis. *Alice's Adventures in Wonderland.*

Catto, Jamie. *Insanely Gifted: Turn Your Demons into Creative Rocket Fuel.*

Congdon, Lisa. *A Glorious Freedom: Older Women Leading Extraordinary Lives.*

Congdon, Lisa. *Art Inc: The Essential Guide for Building Your Career as an Artist.*

Corkhill, Betsan. *Knit for Health and Wellness: How to Knit a Flexible Mind and More.*

Csikszentmihalyi, Mihaly. *Creativity.*

Csikszentmihalyi, Mihaly. *Flow: The Psychology of Optimal Experience.*

Currey, Mason. *Daily Rituals: How Great Minds Make Time, Find Inspiration, and Get to Work.*

Currey, Mason. *Daily Rituals: Women at Work.*

Dawson, Leonie. *How to Be a Business Goddess.*

Dawson, Leonie. *How to Be a Creative Goddess.*

Dawson, Leonie. *My Shining Year – Life and Biz Planners.*

Dinwiddie, Melissa. *The Creative Sandbox Way: Your Path to a Full-Color Life.*

Donaldson, Danielle. *The Art of Creative Watercolor.*

Eisenstein, Charles. *Sacred Economics.*

Eisenstein, Charles. *The More Beautiful World Our Hearts Know is Possible.*

England, Pam and Rob Horowitz. *Birthing from Within: An Extra-Ordinary Guide to Childbirth Preparation.*

Farber, Seth. *The Spiritual Gift of Madness: The Failure of Psychiatry and The Rise of The Mad Pride Movement.*

Freeman Zachary, Rice. *Living the Creative Life: Ideas and Inspiration from Working Artists.*

Gaiman, Neil. *Art Matters: Because Your Imagination Can Change the World.*

Gilbert, Elizabeth. *Big Magic: Creative Living Beyond Fear.*

Godin, Seth. *The Icarus Deception.*

Godin, Seth. *Tribes: Why We Need You to Lead Us.*

Godin, Seth. *We Are All Weird: The Rise of Tribes and the End of Normal.*

Goldberg, Natalie. *Writing Down the Bones: Freeing the Writer Within.*

Haig, Matt. *Notes on a Nervous Planet.*

Handy, Charles. *The Invisible Raincoat.*

Handy, Charles. *The Age of Unreason.*

Havlir Cherry, Wendy. *The Mistress of Longing.*

Hayes, Shannon. *The Radical Homemaker.*

Heller, Sharon. *Too Loud, Too Bright, Too Fast, Too Tight.*

Hillman, James. *A Blue Fire.*

Hunter, Clare. *Threads of Life: A History of the World Through the Eye of a Needle.*

Hustvedt, Siri. *The Blazing World.*

Hustvedt, Siri. *The Shaking Woman: or A History of My Nerves.*

Hyde, Lewis. *The Gift: How the Creative Spirit Transforms the World.*

Jourard, Sidney. M. *The Transparent Self.*

Johnson, Jeremy. *Seeing Through the World: Jean Gebser and Integral Consciousness.*

Jung, C.G. *Memories, Dreams, Reflections.*

Jung, C.G. *The Archetypes and the Collective Unconscious.*

Jung, C.G. *The Red Book.*

Jung, C.G. *Word and Image.*

Kahlo, Frida. *The Diary of Frida Kahlo.*

Katie, Byron. *Loving What Is.*

Kaufman, Scott Barry and Carolyn Gregoire. *Wired to Create: Unravelling the Mysteries of the Creative Mind.*

Lammot, Anne. *Bird by Bird: Some Instructions on Writing and Life.*

Lee, Jennifer. *The Right-Brain Business Plan: A Creative, Visual Map for Success.*

Lord Smail, Daniel. *On Deep History and the Brain.*

Lorde, Audre. *Sister Outsider.*

MacFarlane, Robert. *Underland.*

Macy, Joanna. *Active Hope.*

Malachiodi, Cathy A. *The Art Therapy Sourcebook.*

Matthews, Rachael. *The Mindfulness in Knitting: Meditations on Craft and Calm.*

McNiff, Shaun. *Art as Medicine.*

Mason Miller, Christine. *Desire to Inspire: Using Creative Passion to Transform the World.*

Miller, Alice. *The Untouched Key.*

Mountain Dreamer, Oriah. *The Invitation.*

Mountain Dreamer, Oriah. *What We Ache For: Creativity and the Unfolding of Your Soul.*

Murdoch, Maureen. *The Heroine's Journey.*

Nordby, Jacob. *Blessed are the Weird: A Manifesto for Creatives.*

Palmer, Amanda. *The Art of Asking; or, How I Learned to Stop Worrying and Let People Help.*

Pearce, Lucy H. *Burning Woman.*

Pearce, Lucy H. *Full Circle Health: Integrated Health Charting for Women.*

Pearce, Lucy H. *Medicine Woman: Reclaiming the Soul of Healing.*

Pearce, Lucy H. *Moon Time: Harness the Ever-Changing Energy of Your Menstrual Cycle.*

Pearce, Lucy H. *The Rainbow Way: Cultivating Creativity in the Midst of Motherhood.*

Pressfield, Steven and Shawn Coyne. *The War of Art: Break Through the Blocks and Win Your Inner Creative Battles.*

SARK. *A Creative Companion: How to Free Your Creative Spirit.*

SARK. *Inspiration Sandwich: Stories to Inspire Our Creative Freedom.*

SARK. *Succulent Wild Woman: Dancing with Your Wonder-Full Self.*

Schierse Leonard, Linda. *Meeting the Madwoman: An Inner Challenge for Feminine Spirit Breaking Through Fear and Destructive Patterns to a Balanced and Creative Life.*

Schildkret, Day. *Morning Altars: A 7-Step Practice to Nourish Your Spirit through Nature, Art and Ritual.*

Sher, Barbara. *Refuse to Choose.*

Slim, Pam. *Body of Work.*

Smith, Keri. *Wreck this Journal.*

Solnit, Rebecca. *A Field Guide to Getting Lost.*

Solnit, Rebecca. *The Faraway Nearby.*

Solnit, Rebecca. *Wanderlust.*

Stanton, Philippa. *Conscious Creativity: Look, Connect, Create.*

Starhawk. *Dreaming the Dark.*

Tacey, David. *Edge of the Sacred: Jung, Psyche, Earth.*

Taylor, Cathy. *Pigments of Your Imagination.*

Trier, Eli (ed). *Demystifying the Artist.*

Trier, Eli (ed). *The Power of Ritual.*

Trier, Eli (ed.) *Naked Money.*

Tzu, Lao. *Tao Te Ching.*

Turner, Toko-Pa. *Belonging.*

Vogler, Christopher. *The Writer's Journey: Mythic Structure for Writers (3rd ed.)*

Woolf, Virginia. *A Room of One's Own.*

Audio

You will find a playlist on Spotify of the songs I listened to whilst writing this book, including songs by contributing creatrixes Eleanor Brown, Marsia Shuron Harris and Lewis Barfoot. **tinyurl.com/CreatrixSpotify**

Spirals – Eleanor Brown. (on Bandcamp.)

"We Will Not be Lost to these Times" – Eleanor Brown. (on Bandcamp.)

Only Artists – Grayson Perry. BBC Radio 4, (BBC iPlayer).

The Embodiment Conference – Jamie Catto.

Late Night Woman's Hour – "Aretha Franklin and Imposter Syndrome". BBC Radio 4, (BBC iPlayer).

All in the Mind. "The psychology of motivation and procrastination", BBC Radio 4, available as a podcast from (BBC iPlayer).

Desert Island Discs – Bruce Springsteen, Dustin Hoffman, Marion Keys, Ken Robinson, Dawn French, Russell Brand, Kate Atkinson. BBC Radio 4, available as a podcast from (BBC iPlayer).

Beginner's Guide to Dream Interpretation: Uncover the Hidden Riches of Your Dreams with Jungian Analyst – Clarissa Pinkola Estés, Amazon Audible.

Magic Lessons – Elizabeth Gilbert. **elizabethgilbert.com/magic-lessons**

Film

Lost in Living, Mary Trunk, Ma and Pa Films.

Sylvia, Christine Jeffs, Focus Features.

Frida, Julie Taymore, Miramax/VentanaRosa.

Pollock, Jackson Pollock Documentary, Netflix.

What Happened, Miss Simone? Nina Simone Documentary, Netflix.

Amy, Amy Winehouse documentary.

Rivers and Tides – Andy Goldsworthy documentary.

Leaning into the Wind – Andy Goldsworthy documentary.

The Creative Brain – Netflix.

The First Monday in May – Netflix.

Homecoming, Beyoncé Documentary, Netflix.

Finding Neverland.

Saving Mr Banks.

Underestimate the Girl, Kate Nash Documentary – BBC iPlayer.

Waking Life.

E-courses

Brave Intuitive Painting – Flora Bowley

Origins – Hali Karla

Mandala Magic – Julie Gibbons

Your Authentic Voice – Lucy H. Pearce

WORD+image – Lucy H. Pearce

Structuring with Soul – Lucy H. Pearce

How to be a Creative Goddess – Leonie Dawson

Shining Business Academy – Leonie Dawson

The Story between Stories – Charles Eisenstein

Several courses with Shiloh Sophia McCloud

Online Teachers for Creative Entrepreneurship

The work of these fabulous minds has shaped my own, and I highly recommend them.

Leonie Dawson – **leoniedawson.com**
(a massive library of e-courses and blog posts to support every aspect of The Creative Way.)

Marie Forleo – **marieforleo.com**
(creator of the well-known B-School, but also lots of fabulous free resources.)

Tara Gentile – **taragentile.com**
(jewellery maker and creative entrepreneurial coach and teacher.)

Seth Godin – **seths.blog** (visionary of the cybersphere and emerging trends in business.)

Tad Hargrave – **marketingforhippies.com** (great resources for the creative entrepreneur.)

Tara Prendergast – **thebiscuitfactory.ie** and Bite the Biscuit
(mentoring and courses in creative entrepreneurship + free Facebook community for Irish creatives.)

Mark Silver – **theheartofbusiness.com** (expert on integrating spirituality and business.)

Eli Trier – **elitriercommunities.com**
(communities and resources to support the creative entrepreneur.)

Online References

Aron, Hillel. "How Sia Saved Herself". Rolling Stone Magazine. **rollingstone.com/music/music-features/sia-facesongs-chandelier-maddie-ziegler-712691**

Art+Feminism **meta.wikimedia.org/wiki/Art%2BFeminism_User_Group**

Bakare, Lanre. "Edit-a-thons aim to ensure craftswomen's legacy on internet". The Guardian. **theguardian.com/artanddesign/2019/may/30/edit-a-thons-aim-to-ensure-craftswomens-legacy-on-internet**

Beak, Sera. "In All Trembling Fears and Trembling Boldness". **youtube.com/watch?v=pDmwLLqh7hk**

Brown, Brené "Brené Brown on Creativity". **theofficeonline.com/2015/09/18/brene-brown-on-creativity**

Brooks, Havi. "Chiaroscuro". The Fluent Self. **fluentself.com/blog/personal/chiaroscuro**

Brooks, Havi. "It's okay to clean before writing. Writers clear space. It's what we do". The Fluent Self. **fluentself.com/blog/habits/its-okay-to-clean-before-writing-writers-clear-space-its-what-we-do**

Burkeman, Oliver. "Danielle Steel works 20 hours a day, but is that to be envied?". The Guardian. **theguardian.com/money/oliver-burkeman-column/2019/may/31/danielle-steel-work-20-hour-day**

Esaak, Shelley. "Where Are All the Famous Women Artists? An Open Letter to Younger Sisters". About.com **arthistory.about.com/od/womenartists/a/where_are_women.htm**

Ferlic, K. "Sexuality and the creative process". Releasing Your Unlimited Creativity. **ryouc.info/creativesexuality/sex_creative_process.htm**

Franklin, Nicole. "The Hero's Journey vs. The Heroine's Journey: Rewriting Privilege". The Good Men Project. **goodmenproject.com/featured-content/heros-journey-vs-heroines-journey-rewriting-privilege**

Gaiman, Neil. "2012 commencement address to the University of the Arts". **uarts.edu/neil-gaiman-keynote-address**

Gajewski, Camille. "A Brief History of Women in Art". Khan Academy. **khanacademy.org/humanities/art-history-basics/tools-understanding-art/a/a-brief-history-of-women-in-art**

Godwin, Richard. "The G2 Interview: Kate Nash". The Guardian. **theguardian.com/music/2019/jul/15/kate-nash-artists-often-have-mental-health-issues-the-music-industry-needs-to-protect-them**

Graham, Judith. "Children and Brain Development: What We Know About How Children Learn". University of Maine. **extension.umaine.edu/publications/4356e**

Halliday, Lisa. "Louise Erdrich, The Art of Fiction No.208". The Paris Review. **theparisreview.org/interviews/6055/the-art-of-fiction-no-208-louise-erdrich**

Hunter, Clare. "The Calming Effects of Sewing Can Help People Express Themselves". The Guardian. **theguardian.com/lifeandstyle/2019/feb/23/the-calming-effects-of-sewing-can-help-people-express-and-calm-themselves**

Hustvedt, Siri. "I am Writing for my Life". The Guardian. **theguardian.com/books/2019/mar/03/siri-hustvedt-i-am-writing-for-my-life-memories-of-the-future-interview**

Hustvedt, Siri. "A woman in the men's room: when will the art world recognise the real artist behind Duchamp's Fountain?". The Guardian. **theguardian.com/books/2019/mar/29/marcel-duchamp-fountain-women-art-history**

James, Valarie Lee. "Migrant women fleeing violence find beauty and healing in embroidery". American Magazine. **americamagazine.org/faith/2019/07/15/migrant-women-fleeing-violence-find-beauty-and-healing-embroidery**

Jeffrey, Scott. "A Closer Look at Carl Jung's Individuation Process: A Map for Psychic Wholeness". **scottjeffrey.com/individuation-process**

Kaufman, Scott. "Consciousness and Flow". Huffington Post. **huffpost.com/entry/consciousness-and-flow_n_1108113**

Kelly, Kevin. "1,000 True Fans". **kk.org/thetechnium/1000-true-fans**

Kerr, Laura, K. "Capitalism Exploits the Body's Response to Traumatic Stress". **laurakkerr.com/2014/03/20/capitalism-traumatic-stress**

Leipzig, Adam. "Naomi Wolf: On Pleasure and Creativity". Cultural Weekly. **culturalweekly.com/naomi-wolf-on-pleasure-and-creativity.html**

Lonegren, Sig. "Labyrinths". Mid Atlantic Geomancy. **geomancy.org/index.php/12-labyrinths**

Lovind, Anna. "The Creative Life Interviews: Paul Jarvis". **annalovind.com/the-creative-life-interviews-paul-jarvis**

Lovind, Anna. "The Unexpected Gifts of Stepping Outside of Your Comfort Zone. **annalovind.com/the-unexpected-gifts-of-stepping-outside-of-your-comfort-zone**

Macfarlane, Robert. "What Lies Beneath". The Guardian. **theguardian.com/books/2019/apr/20/what-lies-beneath-robert-macfarlane**

Musk, Justine. "How to Heal the Feminine Wound". **justinemusk.com/2014/02/02/the-creatrix**

Nicholls, Christine Judith. "Dreamtime and the Dreaming". **theconversation.com/dreamtime-and-the-dreaming-who-dreamed-up-these-terms-20835**

Pearce, Lucy. "Overcoming Perfectionism in a Culture that Promotes it". TinyBuddha.com. **tinybuddha.com/blog/overcoming-perfectionism-in-a-culture-that-promotes-it**

Perry, Susan K, "Creating in Flow". Psychology Today. **psychologytoday.com/blog/creating-in-flow/201003/how-creative-flow-is-sex**

Pinkola Estés, Clarissa. Facebook Post. **facebook.com/29996683634/photos/a.391385543634/10153017179708635**

Plett, Heather. "Four Kinds of Fear". **upliftconnect.com/four-kinds-fear**

Prendergast, Tara. "The Creative Revolution" TEDex talk **youtube.com/watch?v=BOUqi4x6v3s**

Roberts, Siobhan "'Knitting Is Coding' and Yarn Is Programmable in This Physics Lab". **nytimes.com/2019/05/17/science/math-physics-knitting-matsumoto.html**

Rowling, J.K. "On Writing". **jkrowling.com/opinions/on-writing**

Schulte, Brigid. "A woman's greatest enemy? A lack of time to themselves". The Guardian. **theguardian.com/commentisfree/2019/jul/21/woman-greatest-enemy-lack-of-time-themselves?**

Solnit, Rebecca. "Every Protest Shifts the World's Balance". The Guardian. **theguardian.com/books/2019/jun/01/rebecca-solnit-protest-politics-world-pcterloo-massacre**

Spillman, Robert. "Louise Erdrich: The Creative Instinct". Salon. **salon.com/1996/05/06/interview_16**

Tacey, David. "The subtle threads that bind us to nature: ecopsychology and the spirituality of place". 2008 'Sustainable Future' Culture and Knowledge Workshop at University House, ANU, Canberra. **planning.act.gov.au/__data/assets/pdf_file/0009/891639/Paper_-_David_Tacey.pdf**

Wendig, Chuck. "25 Reasons to Keep Making Stuff". TerribleMinds.com. **terribleminds.com/ramble/2018/11/14/25-reasons-to-keep-making-stuff**

Zydel, Chris. **CreativeJuicesArts.com**

Wikipedia

Goodreads.com/quotes

INDEX

ABOUT THE AUTHOR

Lucy H. Pearce is the author of numerous life-changing non-fiction books for women and a vibrant artist of lost archetypes of the Feminine.

Several of her books have been Amazon #1 bestsellers around the world, including Nautilus Silver award-winning *Medicine Woman: reclaiming the soul of healing* and *Burning Woman*, an incendiary exploration of women and power written for every woman who burns with passion, has been burned with shame, and in another time or place would be burned at the stake; *The Rainbow Way: cultivating creativity in the midst of motherhood* and *Moon Time: harness the ever-changing energy of your menstrual cycle.*

Lucy's work is dedicated to supporting empowered, embodied expression through her writing, teaching and art.

A mother of three, she lives in East Cork, Ireland, where she runs Womancraft Publishing, creating life-changing, paradigm-shifting books by women, for women. She blogs on creativity at: LUCYHPEARCE.COM

Social Media

dreamingaloudnt (Facebook)

lucyhpearce (Instagram)

dreamingaloudnt (Twitter)

dreamingaloudnt (Pinterest)

Artist Statement

Spirals weave their way through my books and my art. I love pattern finding and making, and the spiral is the pattern I am drawn back to again and again. So many of my paintings have this snail trail of spiralling white dots over the surface, for me it is a way of making visible the magic, the creative matrix that underlies all of existence. I am a colour lover, and the majority of my artwork includes a vivid full spectrum of rainbow hues, seeking to include all colours within a careful visual balance.

ABOUT WOMANCRAFT

Womancraft Publishing was founded in 2014 on the revolutionary vision that women and words can change the world. We act as midwife to transformational women's words that have the power to challenge, inspire, heal and speak to the silenced aspects of ourselves.

The Womancraft community is growing internationally year on year, seeding red tents, book groups, women's circles, ceremonies and classes that honour the Feminine.

We are the change we want to see in this world.

Join the mailing list for samples of all our new titles, plus exclusive pre-order offers, discounts and Womancraft news.

WOMANCRAFTPUBLISHING.COM

And join the community on social media…

womancraftpublishing

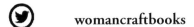

womancraftbooks

womancraft_publishing

Use of Womancraft Work

Often women contact us asking if and how they may use our work.

We love seeing our work out in the world. We love you sharing our words further. And we ask that you respect our hard work by acknowledging the source of the words.

We are delighted for short quotes from our books – up to 200 words – to be shared as memes or in your own articles or books, provided they are clearly accompanied by the author's name and the book's title.

We are also very happy for the materials in our books to be shared amongst women's communities: to be studied by book groups, discussed in classes, read from in ceremony, quoted on social media...with the following provisos:

- If content from the book is shared in written or spoken form, the book's author and title must be referenced clearly.

- The only person fully qualified to teach the material from any of our titles is the author of the book itself. There are no accredited teachers of this work. Please do not make claims of this sort.

- If you are creating a course devoted to the content of one of our books, its title and author must be clearly acknowledged on all promotional material (posters, websites, social media posts).

- The book's cover may be used in promotional materials or social media posts. The cover art is copyright of the artist and has been licensed exclusively for this book. Any element of the book's cover or font may not be used in branding your own marketing materials when teaching the content of the book, or content very similar to the original book.

- No more than two double page spreads, or four single pages of any book may be photocopied as teaching materials.

We are delighted to offer a 20% discount of over five copies going to one address. You can order these on our webshop, or email us.

If you require further clarification, email us at info@womancraftpublishing.com

OTHER BOOKS BY WOMANCRAFT

Medicine Woman: reclaiming the soul of healing

Lucy H. Pearce

NAUTILUS SILVER AWARD 2018

This audacious questioning of the current medical system's ability to deal with the modern epidemic of chronic illness, combines a raw personal memoir of sickness and healing, woven through with voices of dozens of other long-term sick women of the world and a feminine cultural critique that digs deep into the roots of patriarchal medicine. Pearce takes us from its ancient Greek roots, through the influences of the Enlightenment and Christianity, the wholesale destruction of the wise woman tradition and Western colonial destruction of native medicines to the current technocratic, capitalist model of medicine.

Medicine Woman voices a deep yearning for a broader vision of what it means to be human than our current paradigm allows for, calling on an ancient archetype of healing, Medicine Woman, to re-vision how we can navigate sickness and harness its transformational powers in order to heal.

Packed with dozens of healing arts exercises and hundreds of medicine questions to help integrate body and mind in the healing process. Like *Burning Woman*, this book promises initiation by transmission, reconnecting us directly with the soul of healing.

Burning Woman

Lucy H. Pearce

NAUTILUS SILVER AWARD 2017

A breath-taking and controversial woman's journey through history – personal and cultural – on a quest to find and free her own power.

Uncompromising and all-encompassing, Pearce uncovers the archetype of the Burning Women of days gone by – Joan of Arc and the witch trials, through to the way women are burned today in cyber bullying, acid attacks, shaming and burnout, fearlessly examining the roots of Feminine power – what it is, how it has been controlled, and why it needs to be unleashed on the world in our modern Burning Times.

A must-read for all women! A life-changing book that fills the reader with a burning passion and desire for change.

Glennie Kindred, author of *Earth Wisdom*

The Mistress of Longing

Wendy Havlir Cherry

An invitation to listen and trust the deep feminine that longs to be heard.

A love letter from, and for, devotion.

A prescription for a passionate and creative life.

A sacred reclamation.

A liberation of desire.

A hymn to kindness.

The voice of a modern mystic.

The Mistress of Longing is like the fragrance and softness of rose petals offered to our collective hearts. Wendy speaks directly to the Soul and whispers to our fear and hesitation, beckoning us to live the fullness of ourselves. She not only inspires but also offers concrete, potent exercises to help guide our journey. Don't miss this bounty.

Heidi Rose Robbins, The Radiance Project podcast

The Other Side of the River: Stories of Women, Water and the World

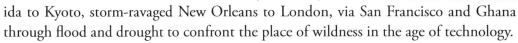

Eila Kundrie Carrico

Rooted in rivers, inspired by wetlands, sources and tributaries, this book weaves between the banks of memory and story, from Florida to Kyoto, storm-ravaged New Orleans to London, via San Francisco and Ghana through flood and drought to confront the place of wildness in the age of technology.

Part memoir, part manifesto, part travelogue and part love letter to myth and ecology, *The Other Side of the River* is an intricately woven tale of finding your flow...and your roots.

An instant classic for the new paradigm.

Lucia Chiavola Birnbaum, award-winning author and Professor Emeritus

Full Circle Health: integrated health charting for women

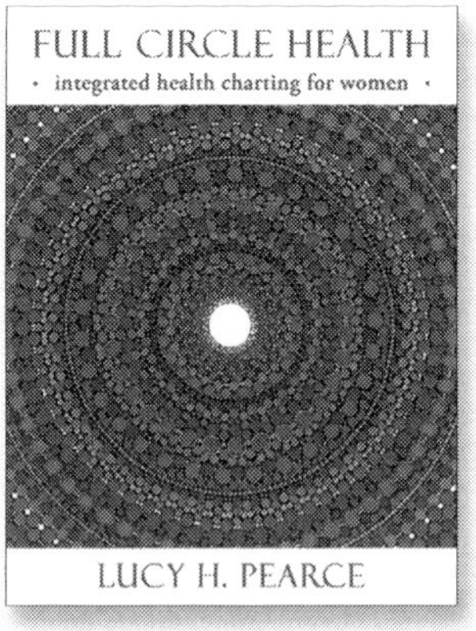

Lucy H. Pearce

A creative approach to holistic health for all who love planners, trackers and bullet journals to guide and support you in a greater understanding of your physical, mental and emotional health.

Whether menstruating or not, pregnant or post-partum, *Full Circle Health* provides a highly flexible, deeply supportive way of tracking your health, whatever your current health conditions.

With 35 daily charting spreads, a monthly habit tracker, planner, and charting grid, this integrated tool will help you to track symptoms, medication, self-care, energy levels, build positive health habits and mindful awareness.

Printed in Great Britain
by Amazon

22099016R10207